# CASTLES

## THEIR HISTORY AND EVOLUTION
## IN MEDIEVAL BRITAIN

# MARC MORRIS

PEGASUS BOOKS
NEW YORK  LONDON

*To my parents*

*who took me to a lot of castles*

—w—

CASTLES

Pegasus Books Ltd.
148 W 37th Street, 13th Floor
New York, NY 10018

Copyright © 2017 Marc Morris

First Pegasus Books cloth edition April 2017

Interior design by Maria Fernandez

Library of Congress Cataloging-in-Publication Data is available.

ISBN: 978-1-68177-359-9

10 9 8 7 6 5 4 3 2 1

Printed in the United States of America
Distributed by W. W. Norton & Company

# CONTENTS

# INTRODUCTION

—◦◦◦—

The county of Kent has more than its fair share of castles, and my parents and schoolteachers conspired to ensure that I was familiar with most of them from a young age. Not, you understand, that I needed much encouragement—trips to castles were always my favorite. Around every corner, through every doorway, there was the promise of fresh excitement. An over-imaginative little boy could easily picture knights in shining armor, damsels in distress, sieges, feasts and tournaments. Whether ruinous or restored, castles were magical places.

Or at least, most of them were. Some of them, I'm sorry to say, I found a bit boring. Certain castles, I noticed, had lots of cannon, but nowhere for the king to eat his dinner. Others, by contrast, had plenty of fancy bedrooms, but nowhere for the soldiers to sleep. Either way, one or two of the castles I visited as a child seemed to lack certain important things, and I would return home a little disappointed, though for reasons I couldn't quite fathom. Clearly these buildings didn't measure up to my idea of what a castle should be.

So what is a castle? Is there a good definition? The *Oxford English Dictionary* helpfully tells us that the word itself derives from the medieval Latin word *castellum*, and ultimately from the classical Latin word *castrum*, meaning "camp." A castle, it goes on to say, is "a large building, or set of buildings, fortified for defense against an enemy; a fortress, stronghold." Many people, I think, would find nothing to disagree with in this statement. The word "castle" tends to conjure up images of boiling oil, bows and arrows, catapults and battering rams.

But is that all there is to it? Are castles just about fighting, or even self-defense? Haven't the dictionary compilers missed an important point? On the outside of a castle, we expect to see drawbridges and battlements, portcullises and arrow-loops; but what about on the inside? There, surely, we expect to see evidence of luxury and creature comforts. There are great halls for banqueting, and huge kitchens to prepare lavish feasts; bedrooms, chambers, and chapels, all once sumptuously decorated; stables, granaries, bakeries, breweries—everything, in short, that was necessary to make them perfect residences for their owners.

So a castle might be a fortress, but it is also, crucially, a home. This was the definition famously offered by Professor R. Allen Brown in his groundbreaking book, *English Castles*. From the moment it was first published in 1954, the book established itself as the most influential work on castles, and it is still required reading today for anyone even remotely interested in the subject. A castle, to quote Professor Brown, is basically "a fortified residence, or a residential fortress." Castles were not simply buildings into which people retreated when the going got tough; they were places where people spent time willingly. When I read the book for the first time, I realized why certain castles had bored me as a boy; the less interesting ones had been either entirely military in purpose, or else they had no defensive capability at all. These so-called castles, it turned out, were really nothing more than forts, and mere stately homes. According to Brown's definition, a real castle was a fortress and a stately home rolled into one.

For many medieval historians—myself included—this textbook definition of a castle seemed to fit the picture perfectly. It also explained why we love castles so much. For how can a building be warlike and homely at the same time? Luxury demands more space, thinner walls, bigger windows. Security, on the other hand, says keep everything crammed inside thick walls, and make the windows small. For castle designers, the major challenge was reconciling these two apparently contradictory imperatives. For castle enthusiasts, the ingenious ways in which they did so is part of what makes castles so endlessly fascinating.

Recently, however, castle experts have begun to question this definition. The problem with deciding that a castle is a fortress and a home, they say, is that this excludes a lot of castles from the club. Take, for example, the subject of Chapter Four—the gorgeous Bodiam Castle in Sussex. There is no doubt at all that this was once a classy home for a rich aristocrat. But did its owner ever intend to use it as a fortress? Most of the exterior features (as we shall see) seem to be just stuck on for effect. The moat, the battlements, and the portcullises, all of which might suggest we are dealing with a formidable stronghold, are in actual fact all highly suspect. If Bodiam had ever ended up in a really serious fight, chances are it would have been quickly clobbered into submission.

So does this mean that Bodiam, and other similarly weedy castles, are not really castles at all? The answer must surely be no. We can call Bodiam a castle because . . . well, because it plainly looks like a castle. And, more importantly, the people who were around when Bodiam was built also called it a castle: it would be very arrogant of us in the twenty-first century to disqualify Bodiam on the grounds that we knew better than they did. Clearly it is not Bodiam Castle that is the problem—it is our definition. None of the castles I've visited recently seem to be having an identity crisis, but some of the experts I've encountered have grave doubts. Professor Matthew Johnson has just concluded his new book by confessing that he is "less certain than ever about what castles 'really are.'"

And yet, in spite of the uncertainty among historians, there still seems to be a general consensus about which buildings are castles, and which ones are not. What we no longer have is an easy, no-nonsense, one-size-fits-all definition. This, of course, makes it tough if you find yourself writing a book on castles, because, as R. Allen Brown rightly said, "Any book about castles should begin by saying what they are."

So, with this advice in mind, here's what I think. A castle was first and foremost a home to its aristocratic owner and his or her household. That, I believe, must be our starting point. Down to the end of the thirteenth century in England, and slightly later in Wales and Scotland, these noble residences were also strong, defensible buildings that we can reasonably describe as "fortresses." Some of the castles in this book were—indeed, are—tremendously tough buildings, designed to withstand the most deadly assault weapons of the Middle Ages. From 1300 onward, they could afford to be less effective at keeping people out, even to the point of not being defensible at all. But, as with Bodiam, what made a castle was not how tough it was, but whether or not it looked like one. In order to be considered a castle, a building had to have at least some of the physical attributes that contemporaries associated with castles, such as battlements, portcullises, arrow-loops, and drawbridges. Whether they actually worked or not was irrelevant. They were still essential, because they had come to symbolize something—that the people inside were important, that they had a right to rule others, and that they expected deference, obedience, and respect.

Of course, it is the portcullises and the drawbridges that we all love, especially as children, and I was no exception. The older I get, however, it is the thought that castles were homes that really provides the attraction. As residences, they possess a richness of historical association that mere fortresses can't even begin to offer. Naturally, as great strongholds, some castles were absolutely decisive in determining the course of British history. But other castles, perhaps less strong and warlike, were decisive in other, subtler ways. As the homes to kings, queens, and nobles, they were the places where plots were hatched, marriages were consummated, and murders were committed. As places of work, they were important to scores of others: clerks, cooks, farriers, stable lads, traveling players, and troubadour poets. And even for those who lived outside their walls, castles were a central part of their lives. It was to the castle that people would come to pay their taxes, or to stand trial in their lord's court. Whether royal or noble, castles were the administrative hubs of the Middle Ages, and were important to every rank of society.

What follows is not a guide to castles, nor a comprehensive gazetteer. It is certainly not the final word on the subject, which is currently attracting more scholarly interest than ever before. It is simply my version of the castle story, and an invitation to readers to think further about these magnificent buildings. I hope it will encourage people to reflect on the motives of the men who built them, the experiences of the families who lived in them, and the pain of the people who died defending them. Most of all, I hope it will incite people to visit the castles themselves. To stand on top of the battlements of Rochester in the middle of winter, whipped by the wind and the rain, is enough to make you sympathize with those knights who were trapped inside during King John's great siege of October and November 1215. To gaze on the massive walls of Caernarfon, one can only wonder what on earth drove Edward I to construct such an undeniably impressive, but colossally expensive and ultimately unsustainable demonstration of power. To walk around the moat at Bodiam in the early morning sunshine, and see the reflection of the castle shimmering on the water, is a sufficient reminder, if any reminder is necessary, of just how splendid and beautiful these buildings can be.

# CHAPTER ONE

# HUMBLE ORIGINS

—〰—

The story begins almost a thousand years ago. A monk was sitting in Canterbury, writing his chronicle of the year's events. It was the year 1051—and what a year it had been! A great struggle had taken place in the kingdom between two powerful factions. On the one side stood the king, Edward the Confessor, with his friends and allies. On the other stood Earl Godwine and his sons, the most powerful noble family in England. The question they were debating, with armies and swords at the ready, was of the highest importance. Who was going to be king after Edward died?

The monk set down these events in detail. At one point, however, he departed from his main account to report an incident that had taken place in distant Herefordshire. Some members of the king's party—Frenchmen, if you don't mind—had been given lands in that county, and had been getting up to some outrageous things.

"The foreigners," wrote the monk, "committed all kinds of insults and oppressions on the men in that region." But that wasn't the worst of it. What really surprised the monk was the thing that these foreigners had built.

It was a great mound of earth, topped with a large wooden tower, surrounded by an enclosure of wooden palisades. It was so new and so different that the monk didn't even have a word of his own to describe it. In the end he settled for the word the foreigners themselves used, and called it a castle.

We know all this, of course, because the monk's chronicle has survived. It's one version of the famous *Anglo-Saxon Chronicle*, now kept in the Bodleian Library in Oxford. Sadly, this manuscript doesn't tell us anything about the monk—not even his name—other than the fact he lived in Canterbury. But it is the first surviving document, written in English, to use the word "castle," and the earth-and-timber structure that the monk was describing was the first castle to be built in England.

No one is exactly sure where this castle was. Most historians think that the monk was talking about the mound of earth at Ewyas Harold on Herefordshire's border with Wales. Two other castles were built in the county at the same time, in Hereford itself and at Richard's Castle, while a third was constructed at Clavering in Essex. None of them is much to look at today. They are overgrown with trees and bushes, and their wooden towers and walls have long since vanished. If you didn't know what you were looking for, you'd probably never guess they were there at all. Yet these few mounds of earth are the earliest castles in England. None of them were built by Englishmen—they were all built by the French friends of Edward the Confessor.

Although he came from a long line of English kings, Edward had grown up a stranger to England. When he was about ten, in the year 1013, the country was invaded and conquered by the king of Denmark. Edward's father, King Æthelred the Unready, gathered up his family and fled across the English Channel to France, where he sought refuge at the court of his brother-in-law, the duke of Normandy. It was in Normandy, living the life of an exile, that Edward grew to manhood.

For a long time, it looked as though he would remain in France forever. His father and elder brothers made several attempts to win back the kingdom they had lost, but to no avail; one by one, they all died trying. But disaster overtook the Danish royal house just as quickly as it had engulfed Edward's family. In 1035, the Danish king, Cnut, died. By 1042, his two sons had followed him to the grave. The way was suddenly clear for Edward to reclaim his inheritance. In 1043, with the consent and support of the English aristocracy, Edward found himself back in England, being crowned king.

His fortunes had improved no end, but after his accession Edward still had one major problem. In his bid for the throne he had been supported by Earl Godwine, an Englishman who had collaborated with the Danes and was now the greatest aristocrat in England. After Edward's coronation, the two men cemented their alliance when the king married Godwine's daughter, Edith. But Edward had grave doubts about his new father-in-law, and one very good reason to dislike him—the earl, it was rumored, had been involved in the murder of the king's brother. After a few years, therefore, of ruling with Godwine by his side, Edward decided it was time to take action. He invited to England some of his old friends from France, and began appointing them to positions of power. In 1050, he made his nephew, Ralph of Mantes, earl of the East Midlands; shortly afterward he appointed his Norman friend Robert of Jumièges as archbishop of Canterbury. The king's intention, it seems, was to create a counterweight to Godwine. By 1051, surrounded by his Continental supporters, Edward seems to have felt that he was powerful enough to take on the earl and his family.

That year, a major row erupted between the two men. The official cause of the dispute was petty—some local trouble in Godwine's town of Dover. The more likely cause for disagreement, however, was the question of the succession. Despite seven years of marriage, Edward and Edith had produced no children. Godwine couldn't be certain—and neither, of course, can we—but it seemed that his son-in-law was deliberately resisting his daughter's charms, and spitefully frustrating any chance that there would one day be a little Godwine sitting on the English throne.

In 1051, Godwine's worst suspicions were confirmed. In the summer of that year—or so it was later claimed—Edward promised the throne of England to his cousin, an energetic young man called Duke William of Normandy. This, it seems, was the real trigger for Godwine's defiance. It was now absolutely clear to the earl that he and his family were being cheated of their inheritance. In September, the row boiled over and threatened to come to blows. Robert of Jumièges, the archbishop, accused Godwine of plotting Edward's death. The king's other French friends started building their castle at Ewyas Harold in anticipation of the coming storm. Both sides were squaring up ready for a fight, amassing hundreds of troops in their own territories. It looked, to everyone's despair, as though England was about to be plunged into a civil war.

But then, at the last minute, Godwine and his sons sensed it was a struggle that they could not win, and fled the country. Edward, finally, was free—master in his own kingdom after years of ruling in the earl's shadow. He set the seal on his victory by confiscating the lands of the Godwine family and giving them to his French allies. Tellingly, he banished his queen to a nunnery, and later that autumn William of Normandy paid a visit to the English court.

Edward's victory, however, was short-lived. The following year, the Godwines returned, invading the country and demanding the restitution of their lands. Confronted with superior numbers, the king had no choice but to give in. His French friends, realizing that this time their defeat was inevitable, chose to run. Some of them went west, to the castle at Ewyas Harold. The archbishop headed east, and set sail for the Continent. Our Canterbury monk, who clearly despised the Frenchmen, reported their departure with undisguised glee, and laid all the blame for the dispute at their door.

"Archbishop Robert was declared an outlaw unconditionally, together with all Frenchmen," he wrote, "for they had been mainly responsible for the discord which had arisen between Earl Godwine and the king."

So by 1052, everything was back to normal. The Godwines had been restored to power. Edward had taken back his queen. No one, if they were wise, was saying anything more about Duke William of Normandy. It was as if the events of 1051 had never happened. There were no more arguments, no more Frenchmen, and no more of their new-fangled fortifications—these so-called "castles." Everything in England was back as it should be.

And so it might have remained, had not Edward made his famous promise in 1051. It was a promise that meant that when the king died fifteen years later, the French would be back. No one could have guessed it at the time, but that castle in Herefordshire was the first drop of rain before the deluge. Within a generation of its construction, England would be filled with hundreds and hundreds of castles, from sea to sea.

But let's not race too far ahead. Instead, let's dwell for a moment on the events of 1051, and what they tell us about castles. One thing emerges very clearly: the French definitely had them, and the English definitely didn't. The Canterbury monk was quite outraged to discover that there were people building a castle in his backyard. Castles were a French invention and, as far as people in England were concerned, the French could keep them. By the same token, Edward the Confessor's Continental friends had shown themselves to be enthusiastic and experienced castle-builders. At the first sign of trouble, they had quickly constructed a castle, and they must have built the other early castles in England at around the same time. Had this been France, where people had been building castles for generations, no one would have blinked an eyelid. Constructing a huge mound of earth was simply what you did in such circumstances. In France, when the going got tough, the tough built castles.

This difference in attitudes might seem, on the face of it, quite strange. After all, here were two societies, both governed by warrior aristocracies, both at roughly the same level of economic development, and separated from each other by only a narrow strip of water. Yet their feelings and opinions about fortification were apparently quite divergent. So how had this divide come about?

The simple answer is: because of the Vikings. The Vikings, we used to believe, were the bad boys of medieval Europe, looting and pillaging with fire and sword long after everyone else on the Continent had calmed down a bit and taken up farming. Nowadays, of course, we are taught to see them differently. Economic migrants rather than shameless pirates, traders as much as raiders: the Vikings, it turns out, were not such a bad bunch after all. But whether the indigenous peoples who lived in northern England at the close of the eighth century saw the Vikings in such a rosy light remains open to question. The monks on the island of Lindisfarne, who in 793 encountered the first batch of new arrivals, might well have disagreed. In the century that followed, the Norsemen swept all before them. One by one, the several kingdoms that made up ninth-century England collapsed in the face of the Viking onslaught. The ancient kingdoms of Northumbria and East Anglia, and even the mighty Midland kingdom of Mercia, all eventually succumbed. By the 870s, only one Anglo-Saxon kingdom, the kingdom of Wessex, remained.

Wessex, however, fought back. The resistance was led by King Alfred (871–99), who for this reason, as well as for his legendary lack of culinary skills, became an English national hero. The king and his descendants protected their people by instituting a sophisticated program of defenses, which they called *burhs*, or boroughs. These were nothing less than planned towns, strongly fortified so as to protect large communities within their walls. In many towns in southern England, the outline of a *burh* can be still be identified, and in each case the total area enclosed is very similar, suggesting that *burhs* were built to something approaching a standard model. By building them, Alfred and his successors were able to push forward their frontier with astonishing speed and success. By 927, they had all but reversed the effect of the invasions; that year the Viking capital of York fell, and the power of the Viking leaders was

broken. Many Scandinavian settlers, of course, remained in the northern and eastern parts of the country, but they were now ruled by the kings of Wessex—or, as they had begun to style themselves, the kings of England.

Indeed, by driving the Vikings back, the kings of Wessex created a country that, in territorial terms, was recognizably similar to modern England. Where formerly there had been a handful of competing English tribes, there was now a single, united English state. As states went in the Middle Ages, it was a mighty one. The kings of England enjoyed powers on a scale unrivalled by any other European rulers at the time. They issued one type of coin throughout their realm, and manipulated the currency for their own profit. Their laws and their government likewise extended to all parts of their kingdom. Most importantly, they restricted the building of fortifications. *Burhs* were public defenses, maintained and owned by the king. Building a private fortification—like a castle—was not permitted. When Alfred's descendant Athelstan took the city of York in 927, his first action was to destroy the stronghold that the Viking leader had built there. If you were a reasonably prosperous landowner in tenth- or early eleventh-century England, the most you could get away with was a small fortified homestead, confusingly also known as a *burh*, but sometimes called a *burhgeat*. Archaeological excavation suggests that these amounted to a collection of domestic buildings surrounded by an earthwork and a wooden stockade. In England, serious fortification was the business of the king, and the king alone.

On the other side of the Channel, however, it was a different story. Here, too, the Vikings attacked in the ninth century, sailing their longboats up the Seine in 854 and burning Paris. But whereas in England the Viking attacks ultimately brought unity, in France the end result was political fragmentation. The formerly strong kingdom created in the late eighth century by the famous Charlemagne crumbled away during the rule of his heirs. In France there was no national epic in the making, no hero in the mold of

Alfred to lead resistance against the invaders. Instead of building communal fortifications under the direction of the king, powerful men began to take the matter of defense into their own hands—to protect themselves, their families, and their households. In 864, the then king of France, Charles the Bald, watching his kingdom disintegrate before his very eyes, attempted to reverse the process with a royal proclamation.

"We will and expressly command," he said, "that whoever at this time has made castles and fortifications and enclosures without our permission shall have them demolished."

This is the first recorded use of the word "castle" in French—almost two hundred years before it occurs in English. It is also an indication that the spread of private fortification in France had reached the extent where it was irreversible; the French king might as well have ordered back the sea.

Of course, the Vikings weren't the only cause for castle-building. Castles might be necessary for defense, but they were also very useful for enforcing one's right to rule over others. As royal authority began to disintegrate in France, all aspects of government—law-making and law-enforcement, tax-collecting and control of the coinage—began to fall into private hands. French society, in a word, was becoming feudalized, and the symbol of a lord's feudal authority was his castle.

Next comes an elegant twist in the tale. The Vikings who raided France, like the ones who raided England, decided to stay for good. However, whereas in England the power of Norsemen was eventually broken, in France they just kept getting stronger. In 911, the French king recognized the authority of the Viking ruler Rollo, who had colonized a large chunk of territory in the northwest of his kingdom. The region became known as the land of the Norsemen, or Normans. The province of Normandy had been born.

The remarkable thing about the Normans was how quickly they shook off their Viking past, and how readily they adopted the ways of their more sophisticated French neighbors. Within a couple of

generations they had started speaking French, and had embraced the Christian religion. Their leaders started experimenting with French titles, like "count," and later, "duke." They also adopted French ideas about fortification and defense—the very ideas that their not-too-distant Viking ancestors had inspired as a result of their initial raids. By the eleventh century at the very latest, the Normans were following the fashion of French lords, and building castles.

What did these early French and Norman castles look like? Unfortunately, in the case of the very early ones—the kind against which Charles the Bald tried to legislate in the ninth century—we have no idea. The earliest surviving castles date from over a hundred years later, and are to be found along the River Loire. In the small town of Langeais, for example, not far from the city of Tours, are the remains of a stone tower, built around the year 1000. Stone castles, however, were highly exceptional at such an early date. It was far, far more common in the tenth and eleventh centuries for castles to be built from earth and timber. Like the stone castles of later periods, these castles came in all shapes and sizes, depending on the needs and resources of the owner. At the simplest end of the spectrum, they might consist of timber buildings encircled by a ditch and an earthen rampart. However, while there was no single design, by the eleventh century something approaching a standard procedure had evolved. Looking back from the early twelfth century, a French clergyman remembered:

> The richest and noblest men . . . have a practice, in order to protect themselves from their enemies, and . . . to subdue those weaker, of raising . . . an earthen mound of the greatest possible height, cutting a wide ditch around it, fortifying its upper edge with square timbers tied together as in a wall, creating towers around it and building inside a house or citadel that dominates the whole structure.

It was these huge mounds of earth that ultimately distinguished the strongly fortified, private defenses of French lords from the comparatively weakly defended homes of their Anglo-Saxon counterparts. Contemporary authors, writing in Latin, described these great mounds as *aggeres*, but the popular thing to call them was "mottes"—which is curious, because the word "motte" itself seems to be Celtic in origin. Mottes were almost always accompanied by a much larger enclosure, known as a bailey, created by digging a ditch and making an earthen rampart. The two elements, taken together, produce the common or garden early castle—the classic "motte and bailey" design.

Today, of course, all the timber parts of such castles have long since rotted away, leaving only the earthworks, and even these have been considerably diminished by erosion over the centuries. Working out what these buildings looked like when they were first constructed therefore requires considerable detective work. In the absence of surviving timbers, we have to look for other evidence. Of course, we have some descriptions of castles, like the one above. We also have one or two bits of pictorial evidence, of which the Bayeux Tapestry is by far the best. The famous Tapestry, commissioned shortly after 1066, not only describes the Norman Conquest of England; it also deals with events in France leading up to the invasion. In the first section of the story, we find some of the earliest and most detailed images of wooden castles.

Altogether, there are four French castles on the Bayeux Tapestry—three in Brittany (at Dol, Rennes, and Dinan) and one in Normandy (Bayeux itself). As you can see, when the artist who directed the work thought of a castle, he clearly pictured a motte in his head. Castle experts have pored over these images for many long hours, trying to work out what the artist's highly stylized depictions actually represent. All the mottes are clearly covered in buildings, and the appearance of two crafty Norman knights at Dinan, attempting to set fire to the castle with burning torches, strongly suggests that these buildings are made of wood. In the case of three of the castles (Dol, Dinan and Bayeux), access to the top of the motte from the ground is made possible by a "flying bridge," which has a shallower angle than the steep side of the motte itself. At Rennes, visitors seem

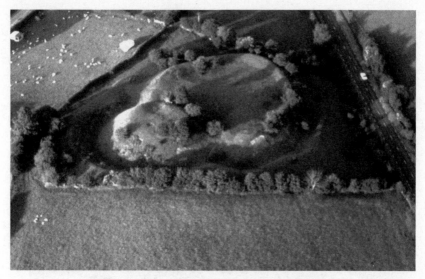

*The earthworks of a motte-and-bailey castle*
*(Tomen y Rhodwydd in Wales).*

to have made their way to the top of the motte using steps cut into the side—taking care, of course, to avoid the animals grazing on the slope. It also appears that we might be looking at gatehouses, both at the top of a flying bridge (Dol) and also at the bottom (Dinan).

It is, however, the towers on top of the mottes that have generated the most interest and speculation. Are they one, two, or more stories tall? All of them certainly look very different. The one at Dol is particularly difficult to interpret—what are the curvy things hanging off the left-hand side of the tower? Are they shields belonging to the defenders, or flames licking the side of the building? Nobody can say for sure. The picture of Dinan, which has the most activity, shows a garrison of half a dozen knights defending the castle during a siege. It seems clear enough that the top of the motte is protected by a wooden fence or palisade around its edge, but what about the tower at the center? Is it a solid building, or is it raised up on stilts to make it even higher? One of the knights on the motte, readying himself to throw his javelin, seems to pass his arm behind a post supporting the building above. Is that the main entrance to the

*The Bayeux Tapestry—castles at Dol, Rennes, and Dinan (top to bottom).*

tower, shrunk out of all proportion, squeezed in against the top border of the Tapestry? And what are we to make of the fancy tower on top of the motte at Bayeux, complete with what appears to be a domed roof, stepped gables, and round-arched windows, as well as an elaborate entrance, decorated with a carved animal head? Are these depictions realistic, or just something the tapestry artist invented? Had he actually visited the castle at Bayeux, or had he just heard secondhand that it was a very impressive building? As you can see, the Bayeux Tapestry, wonderfully rich source that it is, raises as many questions as it answers.

Another problem with the Tapestry is that it offers us no information about the baileys of the castles it depicts. A bailey was a large area that housed all the buildings necessary for a medieval household—not just the lord and his immediate family, but also their domestic servants and a number of soldiers. There had to be accommodation enough for all these people, as well as a chapel to cater for their religious needs, and buildings for the storage of grain and tools. Most importantly, the bailey had to have a hall, so that the lord could sit down with his whole household and dine in public, and so that he could receive and entertain guests in style.

*The Bayeux Tapestry—the castle at Bayeux.*

So the bailey is quite straightforward—it is simply an enclosure for all the buildings needed by a small private community. But what was the purpose of the motte, with its wooden tower on top? From some contemporary descriptions of mottes, it is clear that their towers could provide additional accommodation for the lord. A famous description exists of the twelfth-century wooden tower at the now vanished castle of Ardres in northern France. The chronicler, one Lambert of Ardres, describes at great length a magnificent three-story building, with storerooms and chambers piled on top of one another. It contained just about everything the lord of Ardres could wish for—not just a great chamber for him and his lady, but private rooms for their servants, as well as a chapel, a kitchen, and numerous cellars, larders, and smaller rooms. In many cases, however, the surviving earthworks are too small to have accommodated such a huge structure, and must have supported something rather more humble.

Part of the reason for building a motte, of course, was defense. By raising a tower well above the ground, the castle-owner gained an obvious advantage over any attacker. There is also, however, an element of showing off. According to that twelfth-century description, French lords built mottes not just to protect themselves, but also "to subdue those weaker." By building a great earthen mound, and topping it with a big wooden tower, you were making a statement. It was not so much, "I'm a bit concerned about my own safety," as "I'm in charge here, and don't you forget it."

We can also begin to understand why mottes were a popular option. Most obviously, they were cheap to build, and the building materials—earth and clay—were at hand and plentiful. It took some time of course, and you needed to persuade a lot of peasants with strong backs to do the digging, but it wasn't nearly as demanding or expensive as building in stone. When stone is hard to come by and peasants are ten a penny, building a motte makes good sense.

All of this, however, is fairly obvious, and none of it gets us any closer to the heart of the question. Why France, and why the eleventh century? We can look at a motte and understand the motives that prompted a person to build it, but at the same time, the reasons seem to be universal and timeless—the desire to protect oneself and one's family, while simultaneously lording it over everybody else. There's no apparent reason why the Normans should have built mottes, but not the Romans, the Celts, or the Vikings. Clearly someone somewhere in northern France must have had a brainwave one day around the turn of the first millennium, and the idea caught on fast.

One reason for the sudden adoption of motte-building might have been the advances that the French aristocracy were making in mounted warfare at the time. The turn of the first millennium was the period when we see the emergence of a class of men who would dominate European society for the next five centuries—knights. If strong-armed men in mail shirts were starting to charge around the place on horseback, a big mound of earth could be interpreted as a counter-cavalry measure.

Certainly, there is an important relationship between cavalry and castles. Castles, it has been observed, work a bit like aircraft carriers; they might be big and impressive, but without their moving parts—the aircraft, or the horses—they are not much use. Setting out at dawn, the cavalry garrison could ride out on daily patrols, making their presence felt and striking at their enemies, before returning to the safety of the castle in the evening. For the same reason, I tend to think of early castles as being like old-fashioned US cavalry forts. Surrounded by timber stockades, overlooked by watchtowers, and home to cavalry garrisons, such forts have much in common with motte-and-bailey castles.

Their use of cavalry was one of the great differences between the way the French and the English made war in the eleventh century. The English, of course, had horses, but they did not ride them into battle, preferring to dismount and fight on foot. The French aristocracy, on the other hand, galloped into battle, armed with swords and javelins, and were perhaps starting to experiment with lances. The cross-Channel difference in opinion was made very clear to

Ralph of Mantes, one of Edward the Confessor's castle-building chums. When he tried to train Englishmen from his earldom in the French art of cavalry warfare, and led them against the Welsh at Hereford, the result was a military disaster. "Before a spear was thrown," sighed the author of the *Anglo-Saxon Chronicle*, "the English fled, because they had been made to fight on horseback."

Castles and cavalry, then, were the two major differences between the English and French approaches to warfare in the middle of the eleventh century. The gulf, however, may have opened quite quickly and recently, especially in the case of the Normans and the English. The Normans, after all, had been Viking settlers at the start of the tenth century, and as such they were originally accustomed to travelling by longship and fighting on foot. Only in the course of the tenth century can they have adapted to fighting on horseback. In the case of castles, the gap between the two peoples had appeared even more recently. It used to be thought that every self-respecting Norman lord had a little castle of his own to call home, but recent research has shown this was far from the being the case. It is, in fact, very difficult to find rock-solid evidence that the Normans were building castles to a motte-and-bailey design before 1066. When it comes to establishing dates, archaeology relies on identifying disturbances in the soil; this becomes difficult when the thing you are excavating (in this case, a motte) is made up entirely of soil that has been disturbed. Fortunately, however, the reputation of the Normans as castle-builders appears to be safe. At several mottes that have been excavated, pottery and other small finds have suggested a construction date somewhere in the first half of the eleventh century.

Archaeology, therefore, has emphasized the fact that the majority of Norman castles are likely to date from a period only a generation or so before 1066. This discovery tallies well with what we know of the history of Normandy around this time. From its creation in 911 down to the early years of the eleventh century, the story of Normandy had been one of unmitigated success. From 1026, however, the duchy experienced twenty years of almost perpetual crisis. In that year, the old duke of Normandy, Richard II, died after a long and successful rule of thirty years, leaving behind two sons by his first wife. The elder of the two sons, Richard, succeeded his father as duke, but only one year elapsed before he also dropped dead—murdered, some would later claim, by his younger brother and successor, Robert. Whether or not Robert was indeed guilty of his brother's death, his rule was an unsuccessful one, which saw the leading nobles of Normandy appropriating local offices and powers that properly belonged to the duke himself. In 1035, things went from bad to worse when Robert set off on a pilgrimage to the Holy Land and never returned. When news reached Normandy that he had died on the way back home, many must have despaired—their new duke was Robert's only son, a boy of eight years old, and a bastard. His name was William.

Little William, as we all know well, would grow up to become the most famous of all Norman dukes. In 1035, however, few would have put money on him living past his ninth birthday. Normandy was soon plunged into a state of civil war, and all the evidence suggests that it was in this period, and during the rule of William's father, that the number of motte-and-bailey castles in the duchy began to shoot up. Until this time, castles had only been built by the duke and his most powerful supporters. Now they were being built by anyone who could lay their hands on enough materials and manpower to do so.

Tackling these new castles was the principal challenge for Duke William. His career as a young man reads as the story of one siege after another. Controlling the duchy became a matter of destroying the castles of his enemies, and building new ones of his own. After a successful battle against his greatest opponents in 1047, a Norman chronicler observed that the balance of power had been tipped in William's favor.

"All those magnates who had renounced their fealty to the duke," wrote the chronicler, "now bent their stiff necks to him as their lord. And so, with castles everywhere destroyed, none afterwards dared to show a rebellious heart against him."

From that point on, William went from strength to strength. By the time he was in his late thirties, he could reflect with a great deal of satisfaction on his success. The dark days of his boyhood were far behind him; he was now respected and feared not just in Normandy, but throughout all of northern France. At the same time, however, he had not taken his eyes off a far bigger prize—the one that had been held out to him in 1051, only to be immediately snatched away. In 1065, the throne of England was once again uppermost in William's thoughts.

On the other side of the Channel, things had been reasonably quiet since the dramatic events of 1051–52. After their triumphant return to England, the Godwine family had maneuvered themselves into positions of power. Old Earl Godwine himself had died in 1053, but he left several healthy sons to succeed him. The eldest, Harold, had inherited his father's position as earl of Wessex, and his younger brothers had become earls of Northumbria, East Anglia, and Kent. By 1065, the Godwine boys were easily the most powerful force in English politics.

However, the sad contrast between the Godwine clan and the royal family was plain for all to see. King Edward the Confessor, now in his sixties, was clearly not going to produce a son to succeed him, and his brothers, of course, had died decades ago. Attempts to find a suitable candidate for the English throne were becoming increasingly desperate. A few years beforehand, the great men of England had sent messengers to find the king's long-lost nephew, Edward the Exile, who for half a century had lived in Hungary. They managed to find him and ship him home; but he died the moment he set foot on English soil, leaving only a young son, Edgar, in his place.

With a lack of obvious strong candidates, the wolves were beginning to growl and snarl around England, sensing easy prey. The king of Denmark was known to be interested. So, too, was the king of Norway. Most worryingly, the duke of Normandy had apparently not forgotten King Edward's rash promise of 1051.

Back then, no one had been very concerned about this. Duke William was a young man, with a few easy victories behind him, but a ruler barely able to control his own territories, nevermind seriously threaten England. Now, though, in 1065, the duke looked considerably more menacing. He was undisputed master of northern France, and an experienced general with a reputation for brutality and success.

In the event, however, when Edward finally gave up the ghost in January 1066, it was Harold Godwineson, the man on the spot, who unexpectedly seized the moment. How long he had been plotting this move we don't know. Certainly, his nomination by the dying Edward the Confessor can't have come as a surprise—it was simply a useful piece of last-minute propaganda. For many years now Harold had been the power behind the throne, and he seems to have decided he might as well just sit on it himself and deal with the consequences. Of course, this meant that he had to push young Edgar out of the way first, but no one of any importance seemed particularly bothered about that. The choice was between a strong, powerful, and experienced man with a weak claim, and an inexperienced child with a better one. With England threatened by other, much less appealing overseas contenders, ready to wage war in pursuit of their ambitions, most people probably thought that backing Harold was the wise choice.

And so it proved, for most of 1066. Throughout the summer, Harold showed what a capable leader he was, summoning and holding together a great army in readiness for the invasions that everybody now expected. When the king of Norway landed in September, Harold marched straight up to Yorkshire and won a famous victory. The Norwegians had arrived in three hundred ships, but they sailed home in just twenty-four. The more poetical English soldiers were probably already composing songs to their new king's greatness when messengers arrived from the south, bringing the news that William of Normandy had landed with an army of seven thousand men.

Landing his ships at Pevensey on the morning of September 29, William's first concern was to establish a beachhead, and he did this by building a castle. Pevensey was the site of an old Roman fort, and William and the Normans proved adept at customizing such ancient sites. There is also the intriguing possibility, suggested by a twelfth-century chronicler, that the Normans brought this castle with them. The fact that this is only mentioned in a later source casts some doubt upon its veracity, but there is nothing inherently implausible in the idea of a flat-pack fortress. The Bayeux Tapestry shows the elaborate lengths to which the Normans went in preparing their invasion fleet—transporting barrels of wine, armor, weapons, and the like. Landing in hostile territory, they didn't necessarily want to go scurrying around looking for suitable timber, and waste time cutting it to shape. We have at least one example in later centuries of an invading army taking a wooden castle with them ready to assemble when they landed. It seems quite possible, therefore, that the first castle built in England by William the Conqueror was a prefab.

The castle at Pevensey, and the second castle that the duke began further along the coast at Hastings, can be used to explain in part why Harold rushed headlong into battle with William. The new English king, as recent events had shown, was by no means a bad general, yet he plunged his exhausted army straight into battle at Hastings without pausing for breath. Why was he so hasty and intemperate? Historians have tended to conclude that Harold was responding to William's provocation. For his part, William knew that his only hope of success was to draw his opponent into battle as quickly as possible; above all, he needed a decisive victory. Landing in Sussex made this somewhat easier—the county was part of Harold's own earldom. William was deploying a tried-and-tested technique of medieval warfare: Attack your enemy in his own back yard. Terrorize his tenants, burn his crops, slaughter his sheep and cattle. To act in this brutal way exposes the weakness of your opponent's lordship, and underlines his inability to protect his own people. Castle-building, of course, fits perfectly into this catalogue of terror. One need only recall the words of the Canterbury monk, for whom the construction of a castle was associated with "insults, injuries and oppressions." Forcing Harold's tenants to build castles and burning them alive in their houses (activities which are shown side by side on the Bayeux Tapestry) were all part of the same process of humiliating the king and provoking him to fight. And it was a tactic that proved highly effective.

The Battle of Hastings, as contemporaries recognized, was a strange affair. One side—the English—just stood stock still, trusting to the ancient tactic of presenting a solid wall of shields to the enemy. The Normans, for their part, had little option but to try and break this wall, using archers to rain down arrows on to their enemies' heads, and charging up the hill on horseback, throwing their spears at the English line. It went on all day, which shows that it was a very close-run thing, with both sides equally matched. Two mistakes, however, eventually cost Harold the battle, the crown, and his life. First, the English line failed when some of the less-experienced recruits, seeing the Normans retreating, and thinking the day was theirs, broke ranks and charged down the hill in pursuit. It was, it turned out, a cunning Norman ruse. No sooner had the line broken than the Normans wheeled around and attacked their pursuers. The second mistake, as everyone knows, was Harold's own. Late in the day, at precisely the wrong moment, he looked up.

Few battles ended as decisively as Hastings. Not only was Harold killed; two of his brothers and a large number of major English landowners also perished. And yet, in spite of this catastrophic defeat, the remaining English leaders in London showed themselves in no rush to submit to William. Instead, they persuaded young Prince Edgar to wear the crown. William was obliged to continue pressing his candidacy with violence. After a short rest at Hastings, he headed east along the coast, burning and sacking the towns of Romney and Dover. The town of Dover was protected by an ancient fort on the top of the cliffs, which quickly submitted. At this point, one of our main sources for the duke's career, his chaplain, William of Poitiers, says that, having taken possession of this fortress, William "spent eight days adding the fortifications that it lacked." This has long been taken by some historians as an indication that, when the chips were down, it was possible to build a motte-and-bailey castle really quickly. You will notice, however, that the chaplain's words are not very specific, and it takes a considerable leap of imagination to believe that what Dover "lacked" was a motte—especially since there is no trace of one at the castle today. Nevertheless, the figure of eight days has in the past been eagerly seized upon, and seems to be supported by the comments of another chronicler on the building of a castle at York, which did have a motte.

The figure of eight days can be tested, to some extent, by measuring the size of an "average" motte, and the amount of soil one man could shift in a day. A recent geophysical survey of the motte at Hamstead Marshal in Berkshire has revealed its volume to be 10,000 cubic meters—a weight of 22,000 tons. How much earth a man could move in a day is more speculative, but some idea can be gleaned from nineteenth-century military manuals. The regulations of the Victorian Army suggest that one soldier could dig fifteen cubic feet in an hour, or eighty cubic feet in a day (they evidently allowed for tiredness as the day wore on). By using these figures, therefore, we can say that to build an average-sized motte in eight days, we would need about five hundred men.

While this might at first seem a feasible recruitment target— especially if you had Normans with swords and whips to round up the diggers—it is doubtful whether such a large workforce could be effectively deployed on such a small site without the whole operation descending into chaos. Building a motte was not simply a matter of making a big pile of soil. If that were the case, the Normans' earthworks would have been washed away by the first shower of rain, and would certainly not have made suitable foundations for the buildings that we know went on top. Where mottes have been excavated, archaeologists have found that they were constructed by using alternating layers of different material: a band of soil would be followed by a band of stone or shingle, followed by another band of soil, and so on. This is also reflected by the picture of the motte being built at Hastings on the Bayeux Tapestry, which shows several men raising a mound with different colored bands. What we might first imagine to be an artist's impression of height or depth turns out to be another very literal rendering of reality by the tapestry artist, who clearly understood the fundamentals of motte construction.

To build a motte in eight days, therefore, would seem to be pushing it. It would take several weeks, probably running into months, if you didn't want the whole thing to subside under the weight of the tower. A week might be enough to lay out and establish the site, but a full-scale motte-and-bailey castle would take a lot longer.

It seems, then, that Duke William probably only had time to carry out a few improvements to the existing defenses of the *burh* at Dover before heading off with his army eight days later. They marched through Kent, and set about laying waste to the land south of London in an effort to induce the remaining English leaders to submit. William crossed the Thames at Wallingford, where several leading Englishmen surrendered, and eventually stopped his army at Berkhamsted, where the final capitulation of the Londoners took

*The Bayeux Tapestry—men building a motte at Hastings.*

place. If he stayed in Berkhamsted for any length of time (and it seems quite likely that he did), then the very large motte-and-bailey castle standing in the town today might have been begun by his men.

The next significant date in William's diary was, as far as we know, Christmas. On Christmas Day, 1066, in the new abbey church which Edward the Confessor had built at Westminster, the duke of Normandy was crowned king of England.

After his coronation, William was faced with the dilemma common to many conquerors: how to rule his new subjects with fairness, and at the same time reward his victorious comrades-in-arms. Having claimed to be the legitimate successor of King Edward, he wanted to prove to the English that he would be a good king, willing and able to uphold the laws and customs of his predecessor. At the same time, however, he had an army of seven thousand men at his back, all recruited by the promise of rich pickings, and all now hungry for payment. In the early days of his reign, we see William trying to balance these contradictory expectations and demands. Certainly, many Normans grew rich at the expense of Englishmen. Plunder and booty—which the Continental chroniclers called "gifts"—were shipped back to Normandy in large quantities.

Yet even as churches and monasteries were being pillaged, William was being lenient and generous in his dealings with the governing class of England. Of course, a lot of aristocrats, including Harold and his brothers, had perished at Hastings, but there was little anyone could do about that. To those who survived, however, William was quite charitable, allowing them (once they had sworn allegiance, naturally) to remain in possession of their existing lands and titles. When it came to governing his new subjects, the king exhibited the same sensitive streak. Letters drafted by his ministers continued to be written in English, and William was so keen to make a good impression that he even started learning the language himself. He seems to have believed that, given enough time, the English and the Normans could settle down and live happily side by side.

But William's lenient approach did not endear him to the English. On the contrary, treating them with kid gloves actually provoked the opposite reaction. In the first five years of his reign, William faced a series of rebellions up and down the country. His response was to deal with them in much the same way as he had dealt with his opponents in Normandy. At the first sign of trouble, he marched his army into the affected region, put down the insurrection, and began to build a major new castle. These new royal foundations were, almost without exception, constructed in the larger towns and cities of England, where the population and the resistance were most concentrated. The king had already enforced his authority in London in the weeks immediately after his coronation, building a castle in the southeast corner of the city. When, early in 1068, the first rebellion broke out in the West Country, William wasted no time marching his troops down to Exeter and repeating the exercise. Likewise, when in the summer the two English earls who controlled the Midlands and the north cast off their allegiance, William pushed his way northward, establishing castles at Warwick and Nottingham. When he reached York, he began the construction of the giant motte that still stands in the city center (Clifford's Tower). Returning south, the king planted three more new castles at Lincoln, Cambridge, and Huntingdon, mopping up pockets of resistance as he went.

None of this, of course, was especially good for Anglo-Norman relations. When building these new castles, the king and his engineers showed little concern for the English inhabitants of the town or city in question. Nothing was allowed to stand in the way once the optimum site had been selected. At Cambridge, twenty-seven houses were razed to the ground to clear a space for the works to begin. In Lincoln, the number of dwellings destroyed was 166. But while William showed few or no scruples about building castles over people's homes, he could at least claim to be acting out of strategic necessity. Outside the towns and cities, the king was still reluctant to indulge in any wide-scale disinheritance of Anglo-Saxon landowners.

A handful of his leading men had been rewarded with grants of land at this time, and they were busy asserting their own authority in similar fashion. In Sussex, for example, a number of Continental-style lordships, each organized around a castle, were created immediately after 1066. But how far castle-building extended in general is not known. Writing just one year after the Norman invasion, a monk at Worcester said that, when the king was away in Normandy, his regents "built castles far and wide throughout the land, oppressing the unhappy people." How much this statement reflects the general situation, however, is open to question. One of the regents, William Fitz Osbern, had been made earl of Hereford, and constructed several castles in the Severn valley region before 1070; our Worcester monk may have heard more horror stories about castles going up than most people. We should also perhaps allow for the fact he was clearly very depressed about the Conquest in general.

"Things went ever from bad to worse," he said in his next sentence. "When God wills, may the end be good."

What did transform the situation, however, was the great rebellion of 1069. It was a response, in part, to William's castle-building program of the previous year. The king's new foundations were seen as a provocation—an invitation, even, for the English to rise up and smash them. When the men of Northumbria and Yorkshire rose early in the year, the lightly defended motte and bailey at York was an obvious and tempting target. William soon retook the castle and ordered the construction of another, but the city still fell for a second time in the summer. On this occasion the northerners came in greater numbers, aided in their rebellion by the arrival of a Danish army.

"Forming an immense host, riding and marching in high spirits, they all resolutely advanced on York and stormed and destroyed the castle, seizing innumerable treasures therein, and slaying many hundreds of Frenchmen."

For the third time in eighteen months, William was obliged to move his army into Yorkshire and retake its principal city. On this, his final attempt, defeating the rebels took considerable effort, and the Danes had to be paid to withdraw. By the time he rode triumphant through the smoldering ruins of York, the king himself was fuming.

Dealing with the rebellion of 1069 appears to have caused something inside William to snap. He had, after all, tried to be nice to the English, letting many of them keep their lands and promising to uphold their ancient laws and customs. Yet all they had done in return was repay his generosity with contempt, and force him to spend time, money, and energy in putting down their insolence. What's more, even now, after three years, they showed no signs whatsoever of giving up. So, since the softly-softly approach had evidently failed, William now allowed the more brutal side of his character to take over. After a somber Christmas in York, he divided his army into small contingents and sent them out into the countryside of Yorkshire and Northumbria. Their mission was to burn crops, homes, and livestock, in order to render the entire region incapable of supporting human life. Modern historians have dubbed this the "Harrying of the North," but only a contemporary author can fully capture the horrific consequences of the king's decision. One northern chronicler described it thus:

> So great a famine prevailed that men, compelled by hunger, devoured human flesh, [and also] that of horses, dogs, and cats . . . [Some] sold themselves to perpetual slavery, so that they might in that way preserve their wretched existence; others, while about to go into exile from their country, fell down in the middle of their journey and gave up the ghost. It was horrific to behold human corpses decaying in the houses, the streets, and on the roads, swarming with worms while they were consuming in corruption with an abominable stench . . . There was no village inhabited between York and Durham; they became lurking places to wild beasts and robbers, and were a great dread to travelers.

In retrospect, the Harrying was seen as the most savage and merciless act of William's whole career. At the time, however, the king regarded it as just the beginning of a new direction in royal policy. If the English did not want him as their king, and were never going to give him their love or loyalty, why should he worry about respecting their laws or customs? This cold logic soon translated itself into action. Not only did William abandon his English lessons, and start spending much less time in England; he also decided there was no point in upholding the rights of Englishmen when there were loyal Normans who needed rewarding. In the year 1070, therefore, he deposed many native bishops and abbots, including the archbishop of Canterbury, and replaced them with Continental newcomers. In the same year, the king permitted English monasteries to be plundered for cash.

The biggest change, however, was not felt in church cloisters, but in the countryside at large. In the wake of the English rebellions, William created huge new blocks of power for his most trusted followers, and charged them with holding down their new territories by whatever means they chose. Above all else, this meant building many hundreds of castles.

One of the main beneficiaries of William's change of heart in 1070 was Roger of Montgomery. Roger was one of William's oldest and closest friends: we first spot the pair of them together when William was in his late teens, and their friendship may have stretched back even earlier. Two major things underline the degree of trust between the two men. First, when William set sail for England in 1066, Roger was the man he left in charge of Normandy during his absence. Second, when Roger joined William in England shortly after the invasion, the king rewarded him with large grants of land. Roger was one of the individuals who profited from the early redistribution of property in Sussex, and in 1070 he received an even bigger prize. In the carve up following the Harrying of the North, William made Roger earl of Shrewsbury (or Shropshire).

This was a very large gift, and it catapulted Roger right to the top of English society. In the list of the top ten Normans in England after 1066, Roger ranks number three—below William himself and his half-brother, Odo, but above the king's other half-brother, Robert. With great power, however, came great responsibility. As earl, Roger was expected to keep order in the region, and also to defend the English border with Wales. Shropshire, like Yorkshire, was one of the remotest and wildest parts of William's new kingdom. In order to carry out the task appointed to him, Roger built several new castles. One of the most important of these, to judge from its name, was the one he called "Montgomery," after his own home town of Montgommeri in Normandy. This castle, a perfect little motte and bailey, still survives, but for centuries it has been known by its Welsh name, simply meaning "the old mound." It is called Hen Domen.

Hen Domen provides an interesting contrast with castles built by William the Conqueror at around the same time. Rather than being constructed in the middle of a town or city, Roger of Montgomery's new castle was built in the open countryside. Despite its isolation, however, it was of crucial importance for Roger in controlling his earldom. He picked the site in order to command an ancient crossroads, and also to control the traffic across a major ford on the River Severn. Today the castle is no less lonely than it was nine centuries ago. It squats between two farmers' fields, is overgrown by trees and bushes, and looks for all the world like nothing more than a woodland copse. But despite its apparent obscurity, Hen Domen has once again become very important. In fact, it is one of the most talked-about castle sites in Europe.

For a period of almost forty years, Hen Domen was the site of a massive archaeological dig. Every summer, from the early sixties to the late nineties, archaeologists gathered at the castle for weeks on end to try to uncover its secrets. With a total of over two years spent digging, this was the biggest and most sustained archaeological investigation of its kind ever undertaken. Thanks to the work done at Hen Domen, a great deal has been learned, not only about the nature of early castles, but about what life was like within their vanished wooden walls.

In itself, Hen Domen has good reason to be considered special. Although it is only a small- to medium-sized motte and bailey, the strength of the castle's defenses reflect both the high status of its builder and the dangerousness of its position on the border. As at the royal castle at Berkhamsted, built by either William or his half-brother Robert, we find multiple lines of defense. Three earthen ramparts ring the whole site, forming two deep ditches around the castle. Anyone approaching with hostile intent would have had to cross the first ditch, climb over a wooden fence with a fighting platform behind it, and then negotiate another, deeper ditch—all this before they reached the castle's main walls, which stood twelve to fourteen feet high.

Of course, it is impossible to say exactly what stood above the ground by digging underneath it. Nevertheless, the excavations at Hen Domen permitted some reasonable estimates. They revealed two rows of post-holes, one set behind the other, which indicated that the walls must have been backed by a fighting platform, raised off the ground by the posts. In order to allow a man to pass underneath it, the platform must have been raised to a height of at least six or seven feet. Similarly, a man standing on top of the platform would need to be protected from attack, so we must assume that the wall rose at least another six or seven feet in front of him, bringing the total height of the wall up to the suggested height of twelve to fourteen feet.

In a similar fashion, the archaeologists were able to estimate the size of bailey buildings at Hen Domen. Certain post-holes were evidently home to very large timbers, and from the scale of these foundations the overall shape of the buildings can be guessed. At the foot of the motte, for example, the archaeologists uncovered the remains of a very large building. In all probability, this was the castle's great hall. Judging by the massive size of its foundation ditch, the hall stood two stories high, providing space downstairs for storage, and a main first-floor room where Roger and his household would have sat and dined. Behind the hall the team discovered evidence of a flying bridge of exactly the kind depicted on the

*This artist's impression of Hen Domen, based on the archaeologists' findings, shows how the castle might have appeared in the twelfth century.*

Bayeux Tapestry. Again, it was the size of this structure that was striking. The foundations (and also, remarkably, a surviving timber that was found preserved in the ditch) indicate that the bridge must have been twelve feet wide; large enough to ride a horse up, if necessary. Finally, on the top of the motte, the diggers uncovered evidence for a great tower—or rather, several great towers, for it seems that the buildings on the motte were replaced several times over the years. Again, the scale of the foundations suggest that the greatest of these towers was at least two stories tall.

How were these buildings actually constructed? The trees, as you might expect, were felled using axes and dragged to the site by animals in order for construction to begin. The trunks, however, were not cut to shape using saws, but by the more efficient process of splitting. Starting with a large oak tree, wooden or metal wedges were driven into the trunk along its length, using a wooden mallet or hammer. Eventually a crack would open and, with a little encouragement from crowbars, the tree would split in half. After this, the process could be repeated several times—the half could be split into quarters, the quarters split into eighths, and so on. In fact, if you had a good-sized oak tree, it was possible to get over a thousand square feet of planking from a single trunk. Once you had produced enough timber in this manner, you could start building with them right away—provided your boss wasn't too concerned about the rough quality of the finish. If, however, he demanded smoother surfaces on his castle walls, these could be produced by working the split wood with an axe, and then dressing it with a smaller, subtler tool called a T-axe.

Other materials besides timber went into constructing an early castle. The walls of buildings could be built or reinforced with clay, as well as the well-known "wattle and daub." When it came to roofing, slate tiles may have been used in some cases, but no such slates were ever uncovered at Hen Domen. Thatched roofs may also have existed, but using thatch obviously meant that there was a much greater danger from fire. Bearing both these things in mind, the archaeologists assumed that the roofs at Hen Domen would also have been made of timber, built either from planking or by using shingles. There was nothing low-status about any of these materials—especially wood. Roger of Montgomery was a very powerful man, and wood was his material of choice. Likewise, the castles built by William the Conqueror and his brothers were constructed in almost every case from earth and timber. The diggers at Hen Domen were slightly disappointed that none of the buildings there seem to have been very ornate—no carved timbers were uncovered. Roger's castle, it seems, was not a fancy example like the one at Bayeux on the Bayeux Tapestry, with its dragon's head over the doorway. Nevertheless, the size and number of the buildings was in itself revealing. It gradually became clear to the archaeologists at Hen Domen that they were not uncovering a small huddle of shabby-looking structures, but a site that was thickly planted with buildings, built on a scale that matched the fabulous descriptions of the chroniclers.

The only genuine disappointment for the archaeologists at Hen Domen was the limited number of "small finds" they uncovered, and the fact that none of these items suggested a truly aristocratic lifestyle. There were no brooches or jewelry to compare with the finds at Threave (see Chapter Five); the most exciting find was half a wooden bucket. Of course, we can make certain allowances for the lack of luxury items. This was a castle, not a town or a battle-field; people were not necessarily dropping and losing things all the time. They must have had rubbish pits in which to throw away their unwanted or broken items, but these were never found: despite digging for forty years, the archaeologists only had time to excavate half the bailey. Who knows what treasures—or rubbish—might be concealed in the other half? Hen Domen has by no means given up all its secrets.

But even with all these excuses, the inescapable conclusion was that life at Hen Domen was not exactly luxurious. It was not a place where Roger of Montgomery turned up with his precious things: certainly no gold or jewels, and probably not even much money—only one coin was found on the site. In its early days at least, it was a garrison castle, manned entirely by knights and soldiers, whose standard of living was basic, not to say Spartan. Only two of the bailey buildings showed signs of being heated by fires and, to judge from the animal bones that were found, the diet of the occupants was quite simple. They typically ate beef, mutton, and pork, and from time to time they got to dine on deer—a slightly classier dish. All this food, however, could be sourced locally; there was no indi-cation that fancier foodstuffs ever found their way to the castle.

But this would not have been unusual. In the eleventh century, knighthood was still a long way from the fine living and pageantry of the late Middle Ages (see Chapter Four). In Roger of Montgom-ery's day, it was not such an exclusive club; knights were numbered in thousands, not hundreds, and the poorer ones were not much better off than peasants who had done well for themselves. The men whom Roger sent to Hen Domen to guard the fringes of his earldom no doubt cursed the cold and criticized the cooking. But their experience was probably little different from that shared by Norman knights all over England.

Hen Domen was just one of Roger of Montgomery's castles in his new lordship of Shropshire. He built several others, including the one that used to stand in Shrewsbury itself. But the region he had been given to govern was too big for one man to manage. So, just as William the Conqueror relied on Roger, the earl likewise delegated lands and authority to his supporters, and they in turn built castles of their own. The mottes at Clun, Maesbury, and Kinnerley were all built by such men. One of the earl's most powerful followers, Roger Corbet, decided to follow his boss's example in an even more direct fashion. Caus Castle commemorates the region known as the Pays de Caux in Normandy—another example of a Norman knight, a long way from home, choosing to commemorate the old country when he came to name his castle. The effect of all this building by Roger and his tenants was that Shropshire was soon thickly planted with new fortresses. Today there are eighty-five surviving castle earthworks in the county, and an additional thirty-six in the former county of Montgomeryshire. The vast majority of these were established in the early years after the Conquest by Roger and his allies. Between them, they transformed the region into the most thickly castellated area of England.

It was, however, only in terms of overall numbers that Shropshire was exceptional. The pattern of castle-building in the border region was replicated all over the country, with the greater Norman lords establishing castles, and their minions soon following suit. There was little about this process that was systematic, and very little supervision between one layer of authority and the next. William the Conqueror, for example, personally directed the business of building castles in the major towns and cities of England, but he had little control over what went on in Roger of Montgomery's

earldom of Shropshire. Having decided on a policy of total conquest, he had to place a lot of power in the hands of others. This
meant, of course, that the way these men exercised that power
was largely up to them—the king had no way of monitoring and
supervising their activities. As a means of establishing Norman
control over the English, William's decision was remarkably successful. After 1075, there were no more rebellions in England;
the last one took place in East Anglia that year, and the *Anglo-
Saxon Chronicle* put its failure down to the fact that the castles in
the region were too strong. However, at the same time, a policy of
handing large amounts of power to individuals was a double-edged
sword. The king knew that, left unchecked, a *laissez-faire* approach
to conquest and castle-building might one day make matters worse.
He had, after all, spent most of his youth fighting his enemies in
Normandy to deprive them of their castles.

So it was that twenty years after he had landed at Pevensey beach,
William made another momentous decision. The king decided it
was time to take stock of his accomplishment, to draw a line under
the process of conquest, and to remind everyone—Norman and
Anglo-Saxon alike—exactly who was in charge. At Christmas 1085,
he launched a great inquiry—a survey of his kingdom so expansive
in its scope and so intrusive in its nature that men compared it to
the last reckoning of God. They called it Domesday.

After the Conquest itself, the Domesday Book is William's most
famous achievement. As one of the most important documents in
English history, it has attracted a lot of controversy over the years.
Was it really a one-off original, or had the Anglo-Saxons been carrying out similar surveys for years? More importantly, what was the
Domesday Book actually for? It has been suggested several times
that it was a tax inquiry, but the arguments never quite convince.
The best explanation, to my mind, is that Domesday was created
for two reasons. In the first place, it was intended to serve as a refer-
ence work for William's ministers; in order to conduct the business
of government effectively, they needed an accurate record of who

owned what. Domesday, however, was intended to do much more than this. The point of the exercise was that it was a legally binding document, like a charter or title deed. England had seen twenty years of chaotic land acquisition, but the survey set a seal on this process. It was no longer going to be possible, in theory at least, to grab land from someone else and claim it was yours by right of conquest. The Domesday Book set everything in stone. Like God's last judgment, the book's verdict was final.

All this means that the Domesday Book is very useful for historians, since it provides rock-solid documentary proof for lots of things—including the early existence of castles. If a castle is mentioned in Domesday, we know that it must have been built before the survey was carried out in 1086. For example, if we turn to the county of Shropshire in Domesday, the first major landowner we find is (surprise, surprise) Roger of Montgomery. At the bottom of his entry, we find the Latin sentence *Ipse comes construxit castrum Muntgumeri vocatum* (The earl himself built the castle called Montgomery). Hen Domen, in other words, was built between 1070, when Roger was made earl, and 1086, when the Domesday scribe wrote that sentence.

When it comes to working out exactly how many castles the Normans built, however, Domesday is a bit of a letdown. Although it mentions castles from time to time, the book is a long way from being comprehensive. The king's surveyors were much more interested in recording the number of manors, plow teams, and peasants than they were in noting down where all the castles were. Certain castles, which we know from other evidence had been built before 1086 (such as Dover), are not mentioned in Domesday. Altogether, William's great survey provides us with evidence of only fifty castles.

How, then, can we go about coming up with a total number? One option is to go looking for mentions of castles in all the other written evidence that survives from the eleventh century. Doing this pushes the total number up to just under one hundred. It is quite clear, however, from surviving numbers of earthworks, that there must have been considerably more than this. For castle scholars, therefore, the only solution has been to go out and count the sites on the ground—not as easy as it sounds, as some have been concealed or destroyed by later rebuilding. In recent decades, however, historians and archaeologists have between them come up with a total figure of around a thousand sites in England and Wales. Probably at least half of these castles were built before the year 1100, with the majority of them being built in the years immediately after the Conquest. This means that, even if we err strongly on the side of caution in our calculations, we have to conclude that around five hundred castles were built by the Normans in England during the reign of William the Conqueror.

When you arrive at a figure as big as this, it really makes you think about the scale of William's achievement, and the invaluable role that castles played in the Norman Conquest. By 1086, the king's policy of building castles himself and entrusting his great men with castle-building had proved spectacularly successful. Using five hundred castles, a force of seven thousand men had conquered and held down a country of almost two million people. Not since the days of Julius Caesar, a thousand years before, had such a feat been achieved; never again in the history of the British Isles would it be repeated.

Of course, William's success was not due entirely to the fact that he and his followers built castles. We could also point to the king's outstanding ability as a general, and remind ourselves that men like Roger of Montgomery were also zealous and experienced military leaders. Similarly, we should not forget that William and the Normans had more than their fair share of luck. The Battle of Hastings, after all, was almost too close to call—things would have been very different had it been William and not Harold who died that day. Perhaps most importantly, the country William invaded, for all that it had been buffeted by misfortunes in the eleventh century, was still the strong, centralized kingdom of England created by Alfred and his heirs. Taking over such a well-organized state was far easier than conquering a land where government was weak—as later generations of Normans in Wales and Ireland found to their cost.

Bearing all these qualifications in mind, have we been exaggerating the importance of castles? Recently, historians have begun to suggest as much, even to the extent of denying that castles were important at all. The technological differences between the Normans and the English, we are now informed, actually counted for very little in practice: knocking out the Anglo-Saxons in battle was the most important thing. Building huge mounds of earth was all very well but when it came down to it, they were really symbols of lordship and not weapons of conquest. Personally, however, I wonder if we can really push castles out of the picture to this extent, or redefine them in such terms. Historians have, of course, the enviable advantage of hindsight. From a safe distance across the centuries, and using every available source, we imagine we can see the general picture better than contemporary chroniclers. Men who lived through such traumas are not only likely to be biased; their opinions are also fatally compromised by their provincial perspectives. I have already questioned the credentials of the Worcestershire monk who reported the events of 1067 earlier in this chapter.

But not all chroniclers were so confused and befuddled, or wrote with such enormous axes to grind. Our principal authority for the Norman Conquest is a monk called Orderic Vitalis. He too wrote with hindsight, composing his chronicle fifty years after the invasion, from the safety of his monastery at St. Evroul in Normandy. Orderic himself, however, was only half-Norman. His father was a servant in the household of Roger of Montgomery, who traveled to England after 1066, and married an English girl. Originally, this Continental monk was a Shropshire lad; as he tells us in his history, he arrived in Normandy unable to speak French. Unlike his other contemporaries, therefore, Orderic was able to see things from both sides. He still, like all of us, had his prejudices and his bugbears, but his is the least biased contemporary opinion we have on the Norman Conquest. And for him there was absolutely no doubt as to why the Conquest was successful:

> *The fortifications which the Normans called castles were scarcely known in the English provinces, and so the English, in spite of their courage and love of fighting, could put up only a weak show of resistance.*

For Orderic at least, the castle was the instrument with which the Normans had riveted their power into place.

When the Domesday Book was compiled, William the Conqueror was aged sixty or thereabouts. He had lived to grow old, and he had grown to be fat. Neither age nor girth, however, could persuade him to slacken the pace of his lifestyle, or to desist from the brutal kind of warfare that he had made his specialty. In 1087, he was at war with the king of France, and had recently captured and burned the French town of Mantes. As he rode through its smoking ruins, however, his victory was suddenly undone. His horse started and reared up in fright, driving the pommel of its saddle into the king's ample stomach. It was a fatal injury. In great pain, William returned to his ducal capital at Rouen, to the priory at Saint-Gervais. It was there, at dawn on September 9, that he died.

The news of William's death sent shock waves throughout Normandy and England. When it reached Canterbury, where our story began, the author of the *Anglo-Saxon Chronicle* interrupted his record of the year's events to record a detailed and impassioned obituary. "What can I say?" he began. "If anyone desires to know what kind of man he was, or in what honor he was held . . . then we shall write of him as we have known him, who have ourselves seen him, and at one time dwelt in his court."

The chronicler went on to describe the king in a balanced way, setting down both his good and evil deeds. William, he wrote, "was a man of great wisdom and power. Though stern beyond measure to those who opposed his will, he was kind to good men who loved

God. We must not forget the good order he kept in the land, so that a man of substance could travel unmolested throughout the country with his bosom full of gold. No man dared slay another, no matter what evil the other might have done him."

Among his blacker deeds, however, castle-building topped the list. "Assuredly in his time men suffered grievous oppression and manifold injuries," wrote the chronicler. "He caused castles to be built, which were a sore burden to the poor."

So ends William's story. But the story of earth-and-timber castles, which started well before William's day, had a long way to go once the king was gone. Some motte and baileys, particularly those built along the Welsh border, continued to be inhabited and improved right down to the end of the thirteenth century. Hen Domen, for example, was not abandoned until the 1280s. When civil war erupted in the middle of the twelfth century, many new earth-and-timber castles were built from scratch, and hundreds of older ones were quickly repaired and refortified. Likewise, when the Normans later carried war into Ireland and Scotland, motte and baileys were still the weapon of choice.

However, in England after the Conquest, the trend was toward peace rather than war. Men who had built castles to secure their acquisitions in the years immediately after 1066 soon found there was no need to keep all of them in constant readiness and good repair. In many cases, they followed the example of Orderic Vitalis's father, and settled down to marry a nice English girl. Later generations of Norman knights found there was little point in investing time, energy, and money in repairing and renovating all the castles that their fathers and grandfathers had built. From the start of the twelfth century, the number of occupied sites began to fall. Abandoned and left to decay, in time their baileys grassed over, and their timbers rotted away.

With castles no longer needed as instruments of conquest and oppression, those which survived this process of thinning down were the ones that could adapt to play new peacetime roles. Many royal castles, for example, survived because they were necessary as prisons, as residences for sheriffs, and as treasuries for the king's gold and silver. In most cases, however, the castles that survived were simply the ones their owners liked best, either because they were conveniently situated at the heart of their estates, or because they were well-placed for hunting, trade, and travel. As they let some of their earlier castles fade into the landscape and began to invest more and more of their resources in one or two favorite residences, later generations of Normans found they were able to invest in something a little more spectacular than earth and wood.

It was William the Conqueror, once again, who had led the way. In the weeks and months after his coronation, he had built a timber castle in the southeast corner of London. By the middle of the 1070s, however, the king had decided that his new capital required a more permanent and more grandiose royal residence—a building made of stone. It was a castle that took almost thirty years to build, and which William never lived to see completed. Its importance to future generations of castle-builders was correspondingly colossal. As the great stone building slowly inched its way skyward, it became known simply as the Tower. This, without question, was the shape of things to come.

# CHAPTER TWO

# TOWERS OF STONE

—⚬〰⚬—

The city of Rochester lies on the north coast of Kent, at the mouth of the River Medway. Like most modern cities, it has its fair share of tall buildings, from elegant Victorian mansion blocks to ugly sixties high-rises. The building that dominates this city's skyline, however, was built not in the modern age, but almost nine centuries ago. The great tower of Rochester Castle still dwarfs everything for miles around, including the Norman cathedral that stands in its shadow. Even a modern visitor who is used to tall buildings, and familiar with stone castles, cannot help but be impressed; in terms of sheer size alone, Rochester bowls you over.

It becomes almost impossible, therefore, to imagine the impact this building must have had on people when it first appeared. Back in the early twelfth century, when construction work began, what emerged was not just a brand new castle, but a brand new type of building. By this time, the citizens of Rochester must have thought they knew all about castles. An earth-and-timber affair had been foisted upon them shortly after the Conquest, and a few years later some of its wooden walls had been replaced with stone ones. But these earlier structures, whether wood or stone, paled into insignificance in comparison with the monster that now began to rise against the city's skyline. No one in Rochester, or anywhere else for that matter, had ever seen anything like it.

To begin with, Rochester's size is truly superlative. Measuring 125 feet from its base to the top of its turrets, it takes the prize for being the tallest great tower in the country. Built from 1127, it is also one of the earliest examples of its type, and was the property of the archbishop of Canterbury—then one of the most powerful lords in the kingdom.

The castle's greatest claim to fame, however, is not its early origins or its distinguished ownership, but the sequence of events that later engulfed it. In 1215, Rochester had the misfortune to be visited by one of England's worst kings, and subjected to the biggest and most spectacular siege that the country had ever seen. For two months in the autumn of that year, the struggle for Rochester Castle decided the fate of King John—and whether his kingdom would stand or fall.

This chapter focuses on great towers like Rochester, and attempts to ask all kinds of questions about them: how they were built, what they were for, how they were attacked, and how they were defended. But it is important to remember that such towers, or "keeps" as they are often called, were not intended to stand alone. Like the wooden tower on a motte, a great tower needed to be supported by a whole range of other buildings, grouped together in a bailey. Even though many keeps seem isolated today, we should not forget that they were once surrounded by (and to some extent dependent on) a host of smaller buildings that were huddled around their feet.

It is also important to stress that there is no sense in which the great tower "evolved" from the wooden tower on top of a motte. Stone castles were, of course, bigger, stronger, and taller, nicer to live in and much more expensive to build. But, as we saw in the previous chapter, they originated in France at exactly the same time as wooden ones. Likewise, timber castles continued to be built in England and France well into the thirteenth century. It is not a case of a "Wood Age" being followed by a "Stone Age." The switch to the building of keeps cannot be represented as a technological advance; one type of castle did not "develop" out of the other. Nevertheless, stone castles themselves did develop, and by the time Rochester was constructed, building a keep was the norm—for the tiny minority of castle-owners rich enough to afford one. The twelfth century was the golden age of the great tower.

Although Rochester is an early example of this type of building, it is by no means the earliest. In England, the tradition of building towers began with the most famous of them all—the Tower of London. Today, when people talk of "the Tower," they mean the entire complex of royal buildings that occupies the southeastern corner of the city. They also tend to think of it in terms of its later history as a Tudor prison—a place of ravens, Beefeaters, and beheadings. Yet all the important buildings on the site were erected long before Henry VIII, Mary, and Elizabeth I gave them their bloody reputation. The Tower was built not as a prison, but as a castle—arguably the most important castle in England. Most of the outer walls, towers, and chambers are the work of England's thirteenth-century kings. The building at the heart of the complex, however, which has given its name to the whole, was constructed earlier still. The White Tower was the work of William the Conqueror, and it was the first keep in England.

If motte-and-bailey castles came as a shock to the Anglo-Saxons, then the new castle that William started to build beside the Thames in the 1070s must have knocked them for six. The Anglo-Saxons had seen stone buildings before (many churches were built in stone), but they were not internationally renowned for their masonry skills. Before the Norman Conquest, the kings of England were accustomed to living in wooden halls, much as their distant Germanic ancestors had done. In fact, when the Anglo-Saxons talked about "building," they used the word *timbrian*; if an Englishman told you he was going to build something, you took it for granted he was talking about woodwork.

In France, of course, building a stone residence would not have raised nearly as many eyebrows. But even the most sophisticated French mason would have been surprised and impressed by the scale of the building project that William had embarked upon in London. Nothing on the Continent could compare in size and grandeur with the Tower. It has recently been suggested that the smaller tower of Ivry-la-Bataille in Normandy, now in ruins, might have provided the inspiration for the basic shape, but the scale of William's new building was entirely novel.

So what prompted William the Conqueror and his engineers to build on such a scale, and to build in stone? Even today, the Tower is a hugely impressive building, and impressing people was without a doubt one of William's intentions: this was a building project which said that the Normans were here to stay.

Monumental pride, however, might be only half the story. The other way of understanding the Tower is to imagine how nervous and edgy the Normans were in the 1070s—it was, after all, still only a few years after the Conquest, and the English continued to be obstinate and rebellious. In more peaceful circumstances, if a king wanted a palace complex, he might have preferred to distribute the buildings—the hall, the chapel, the bedrooms—over a wider area. Instead, what William and his architect decided to do was to stack all these rooms one on top of the other, and encase the whole structure in immensely thick stone walls. A great tower like this might be first and foremost a monument to vanity, but it also betrays a crucial element of fear.

Whatever the actual inspiration, the final result was an astounding building. Measuring 107 by 118 feet at its base, and standing 90 feet high, William and his sons created a giant among castles. Construction on this scale had not been witnessed in Britain since the time of the Romans. The Normans were well aware of this, and seem to have been deliberately styling themselves as new

Romans, come a-conquering in imperial style. William of Poitiers, the Conqueror's sycophantic biographer, regularly compares his royal master to Julius Caesar (William was better, naturally), and suggests that the king's leading men were equivalent in wisdom and power to the Roman senate. It is possible to see this attitude reflected wherever William built in stone. At the Tower of London, parts of the old Roman city wall were incorporated into the wall of the castle's bailey. At Colchester, the former Roman capital, William built another great tower, very similar in design to the Tower of London and probably created by the same architect. Although it now stands only two stories high (and, thanks to misguided restoration in the eighteenth century, looks faintly ridiculous), it was once even bigger than its London counterpart. The new building was constructed on the ruins of the old Roman Temple of Claudius. This, of course, gave the Normans a convenient head start, but importantly it also emphasized their authority as rulers. Finally, at Chepstow in Wales, the castle's original two-storey stone hall still stands on the clifftop high above the River Wye. Once thought to be a creation of William's close friend, William Fitz Osbern, it has recently been reinterpreted as an audience chamber built for the king himself, perhaps in order to receive tribute from his Welsh subjects. Again, it is a building with Roman resonances. It was built with materials taken from the nearby Roman town of Caerwent, and decorated throughout in an imperial style.

So William the Conqueror's great towers in London and Colchester, and the hall-keep at Chepstow, are our prototype English keeps. Few other stone towers can be dated with certainty to the period before 1100. Taken together, these buildings provided inspiration for the next generation of castle-builders, and supplied them with a model for the next hundred years. By the time building work began at Rochester Castle, some fifty years later, the prototype had settled down into something approaching an archetype.

Despite its monumental size, Rochester is in many ways a "typical" building of its time. On the one hand, it shares many features with the stone castles that William constructed. Like the

Tower of London, Rochester was built to be strong and defensible. At its base, its walls are twelve feet thick, and only slightly thinner at the top, where they narrow to ten and a half feet. The windows on the lower floors are small, only becoming larger toward the top of the building.

But while there are superficial similarities between William's buildings and castles of later decades, there are also important differences. Whereas both the Tower of London and Colchester Castle are quite squat in appearance (Colchester, even at its full height, was broader than it was tall), Rochester is a slender, soaring building, four stories in height compared to the Tower's three. While William's architect was apparently inspired by a Continental original at Ivry in Normandy, the mason who built Rochester seems to have based his design on the giant castle at Loches in France.

However, the biggest difference between Rochester and earlier towers in England is in the nature of its entrance. William's towers were entered via a first-floor doorway, reached by means of an external wooden stair. At Rochester, the entrance was much more elaborate: the front of the building was covered by an additional wing, known as the forebuilding. This became a fairly typical feature of towers in the twelfth century: an entrance block contrived to frustrate attackers and impress visitors. To get into Rochester Castle, friend or foe had to mount a stone staircase that snaked around the base of the tower, creating a passageway that could be blocked with portcullises and barred with a drawbridge. Clearly, this was a building whose owner, if he wanted to, could keep you out. At the same time, however, it was equally important for a castle-owner to impress his guests. At Rochester, once visitors had negotiated the grand sweep of the outer stairway, they were admitted to the entrance level of the forebuilding. This room, of course, would shield the castle's main doorway from a direct assault. But it is also a very large and impressive chamber, with high ceilings and beautiful rounded archways, decorated with the chevron or zigzag pattern that the Normans liked so much. As at other castles, it was probably intended as a waiting room, where visitors would be deliberately delayed, giving them time to admire the building, and putting them in a mood of suitable reverence prior to meeting the owner.

The slender stone tower, with a forebuilding over its entrance, was the commonest design for keeps in the twelfth century. But while these buildings share certain basic characteristics, it is important to stress the enormous overall variety in their design. In one way or another, each one is different from its peers, and there are many examples that are far removed from the simple stone box. In Suffolk, for example, the little stone keep at Orford is a particularly ingenious and intentionally whimsical creation, with circular rooms and three large buttressing towers. More imposing and hardly less original, the tall, almost windowless keep at Conisbrough is a similarly rounded and buttressed affair. At Norwich, the great keep, much-restored in the nineteenth century, is thought to belong to the early decades of the twelfth century and has no close parallels in England, except nearby Castle Rising, which was clearly inspired by its bigger neighbor. But whatever shape he settled on, the twelfth-century lord who wanted to dazzle his neighbors was going to be building a great tower. From the start of the century, new keeps were constructed up and down the country, from Newcastle in the north to Portchester in the south; altogether, more than fifty had been erected by the century's end. Dover in Kent, one of the last to be built, was also one of the greatest—a final hurrah for the keep, and a worthy descendant of the Tower of London.

To build on this scale, of course, took enormous resources, and for this reason many of the more important keeps were built by kings. In twelfth-century England, there were four of them: Henry I (1100–35), Stephen (1135–54), Henry II (1154–89), and Richard I (1189–99). From the point of view of castle building, Stephen and Richard were not very important. Stephen was too busy fighting his cousin Matilda for control of the country throughout his troubled reign, and had neither the time nor the money to invest in large-scale building projects. Richard I does enjoy a reputation as a castle-builder, but it derives from his magnificent new fortress

(Château Gaillard) at Les Andelys in Normandy, rather than the improvements that he carried out to his English castles. Our great castle-building kings in the twelfth century are the two Henrys. Henry I, youngest son of William the Conqueror, was a famously unpleasant individual, but nevertheless a noted builder of stone castles. Usually credited with the huge keep at Norwich, he is also thought to have built new towers at Canterbury, Gloucester, and Corfe. He ruled England successfully, through a combination of administrative genius and calculated brutality (unlike Edward I, who only does it in a Hollywood film, Henry really did throw one of his enemies out of a castle window). As duke of Normandy, however, Henry had a much harder time, and therefore invested most of his castle-building budget in his troubled dukedom. The king was responsible for the keeps at Caen, Domfront, and Arques, as well and repairs and rebuildings at other Norman castles.

The prize for building keeps in England, however, must go to Henry II. Always remembered for his ill-timed rhetorical question, "Who will rid me of this turbulent priest," Henry II also deserves lasting fame as England's preeminent builder of great towers. At the start of his reign, young Henry's position was the opposite to that of his namesake and grandfather, Henry I. With strong support from his Norman barons, the new king's grip on his Continental inheritance had long been secure. In England, however, he was a newcomer, and found at his accession that the power of the Crown had been much diminished during the reign of his predecessor, King Stephen. Henry therefore set about re-establishing the Crown's authority, and he did this in the most visible way possible—by building castles. The king was responsible for brand new keeps at Scarborough, Newcastle, Orford, and Dover, as well as the small keep at the Peak in Derbyshire, and perhaps a now-vanished tower at Nottingham.

But, as with motte and baileys, the building of stone towers was not exclusively a royal affair. Great barons of the twelfth century also adopted the stone tower design, and built some of the most distinguished and important examples. Rochester, of course, was built by the archbishop of Canterbury, while Conisbrough was built by Henry II's half-brother, Hamelin. The giant square keep at Kenilworth was built by the sheriff of Warwick, and the vanished keep at Bungay by the earl of Norfolk. Several of these baronial towers were constructed during the reign of King Stephen, who, along with his rival, Matilda, embarked upon a policy of creating new earls in order to win support. Building a keep was an excellent way of proclaiming one's newfound importance, and there is good reason to think that it was recent ennoblement that inspired the building of towers at Hedingham and Castle Rising.

When it comes to working out how much these castles cost, however, we have to rely on royal examples, because Crown records always survive much better than their aristocratic equivalents. For our detailed knowledge of costs in the twelfth century, we have to thank Henry I. Henry, when he wasn't indulging his enormous sexual appetite (he had a string of mistresses before and after his marriage, and fathered at least twenty bastard children), was busy inventing new ways to govern the country. He is credited not only with the introduction of a new breed of administrative sheriff to manage his affairs in the English counties, but also with the creation of a new financial court to check on their activities. Twice a year, his sheriffs were obliged to come before the officers of this court and account for all the money they had received from rents, fines, and taxes. The process was made easier with the help of a large visual and mathematical aid—a kind of abacus, with counters placed on a checkered cloth. Almost at once, people began to refer to the court as the Exchequer. When a sheriff was summoned before it, he either had to produce the money he owed, or give a good reason for its absence. One such good reason might be the building of a royal castle in the county at the king's orders. Provided the sheriff could account for the money he had spent on building (produce receipts, if you like), the corresponding amount would be deducted from what he owed.

Amazingly, the records of the Exchequer have survived. The clerks wrote up their accounts on huge parchment rolls, known as "pipe rolls" (for the simple reason that, when rolled up, they looked like pipes). Using these ancient documents, we can find out rough costs for royal castles, and also gauge the length of time it took to build them.

The sad thing is that although Henry I invented the whole accounting system, only one roll survives from his reign. As a result, we are not very well informed about the king's castle-building activities. In fact, early twelfth-century towers—whether royal ones like Norwich, or baronial ones like Rochester—belong to a mysterious Dark Age, almost entirely unilluminated by written records. Fortunately, in Rochester's case, we know from a copy of a royal charter that building began in 1127, and a Kentish chronicler noted in passing that the archbishop of Canterbury began to construct "a noble tower" at this time. But as to how long it took to build the mighty keep, and how much it cost, we can only make intelligent guesses by comparing it with examples from later in the century.

From the start of Henry II's reign, the pipe rolls survive in an almost unbroken series, and we can calculate the cost of some of the king's keeps. The great tower at Dover, for example, which is shorter than Rochester but bigger at the base, cost around £4,000 and took ten years to build (1180–90). The much smaller keep that Henry built at Orford cost about £1,500 and took just six years to build (1166–72). With these figures in mind, and allowing for a small amount of inflation, the keep at Rochester must have cost at least £3,000, and taken between eight and ten years to construct.

To the modern reader, of course, these sound like castles at knock-down prices. When you look at the contemporary pay packets, however, you begin to realize that would-be castle-owners had to start saving early. In the twelfth century, an unskilled laborer earned a penny a day, while a skilled laborer might take home tuppence. A fully armed knight, risking life and limb and providing his own kit, would expect to receive a shilling (twelve pence) in return for a day's military service. Only at the top of the scale did things start to improve. The king's annual income—which was also the government's annual budget—was somewhere between

£10,000 and £20,000 a year. Even for the king, therefore, building a tower like Dover or Rochester would absorb between a quarter and a third of his money for a year, or 3 to 4 percent of his annual budget spread over a decade. In the twelfth century, then, there were only a handful of people who could afford to build a great tower.

What our records cannot tell us is how these towers were actually built. We have to wait until the thirteenth century before we get really detailed building accounts for castles (see Chapter Three). Occasionally, the pipe rolls will record the name of the architect or mason working on a particular building. Henry II's favorite builder, responsible for the keeps at Dover and Newcastle, was one Maurice the Engineer. In almost every other case, however, the names of the geniuses who designed and erected these wonderful buildings are lost to us.

The towers themselves, however, provide us with some clues as to how they were built. Rochester, for example, was constructed with two types of stone. Most of it is Kentish ragstone, very probably quarried near Maidstone, and shipped from there up the River Medway to Rochester. The fine details, however—the fireplaces, the window arches, and the cornerstones—are fashioned from a softer stone, more suitable for carving. This is Caen stone, which (as the name suggests) had to be transported from Caen in Normandy, a journey of over a hundred miles. Tons and tons of stone, quarried in northern France, ferried hundreds of miles by scores of ships over dozens of voyages—this is the scale of the enterprise we have to imagine to explain how Rochester Castle came to be built.

From the enormous cost of their construction and the many years they took to build, it is evident that keeps like Rochester were not simply thrown up without design or purpose. They are complex structures, built to serve the needs of a great lord and his household. Each room in a tower was built with a specific purpose in mind.

For this reason, there's a certain sense of disappointment when you step inside the main part of the keep at Rochester, because the interior is open to the sky. At some point after the

Middle Ages (it is not known exactly when), a ferocious fire ripped through the tower, destroying the wooden floors and melting the lead roof. If you look closely, you can see the scars left by this inferno on the interior walls. The keep's present condition, however, does offer certain compensations. In the first place, it allows you once again to appreciate the building's huge size. The first reaction is to gaze upward to the roof, but it soon strikes you that you are only observing half the interior space—the tower is divided in two by a cross-wall, which gives the whole structure greater solidity.

The other advantage of this perspective is that it enables you to see all four floors at once, and appreciate their common architectural features. Each principal chamber has a large ornately decorated fireplace, with a chimney flue that curves

*The great cross-wall that divides Rochester's keep. At the level of the hall, the wall breaks into columns, allowing passage between the two halves of the tower.*

into the thickness of the wall. Similarly, there are garderobes (toilets) on every floor, and the well that runs up through the center of the cross-wall is also accessible at every level. In other words, we have a building with mod cons and creature comforts throughout—central heating, lavatories, and water "on tap." As in the forebuilding, the quality of the stonework is an indication that the living here was luxurious. The beautiful rounded Norman arches, with their zigzagged chevrons, tell us that this was once a residence of the first rank.

It does, however, take a considerable feat of imagination to picture the castle in its heyday. In spite of the evidence of quality, the interior of Rochester today has a grim, dark, and industrial feel, like an abandoned Victorian factory. What must it have been like to wander around these rooms, to walk between the giant pillars, and to stand beside a roaring fireplace? We can get some idea by comparing Rochester to other, better-preserved twelfth-century keeps. Take Hedingham Castle, for example, which stands near the banks of the River Colne in Essex, where the great tower was built at almost exactly the same time as Rochester. Hedingham was begun by Aubrey de Vere, probably after he was promoted to the rank of earl of Oxford in 1141, and shares many architectural features with its Kentish cousin. From the outside it is slightly less imposing, as it is somewhat smaller and has lost its forebuilding; but it is quite a lot smarter, being finished with expensive blocks of cut stone. The arrangement of the interior is also slightly different, but it nevertheless gives us a very strong sense of what life was like in a twelfth-century tower.

Stepping inside Hedingham's keep is like stepping back eight hundred and fifty years in time. As at Rochester, the key word is luxury, which is evident everywhere. The difference at Hedingham is that the masonry is in almost perfect condition. Although the castle has lost its roof and floors on several occasions over the centuries (most recently at the start of the previous century, when soldiers stationed on the roof started a fire to keep warm—and got more than they bargained for), the castle's owners have always replaced them. Consequently, the interior is almost perfectly preserved. At Rochester, all the soft stone used to make windows, archways, and fireplaces has been worn away by the wind and the rain, or stolen for use in other buildings. At Hedingham, however, these details look as though they were carved yesterday. Despite the fire, original medieval plaster still clings to the walls, and if we peer closer we can still see traces of paint. What's more, by looking closely at the whole building, we can begin to understand the actual purpose of twelfth-century keeps.

Curiously, one of the most important things to understand about castles like Rochester and Hedingham is how little time their owners actually spent in them. The kings and nobles of the twelfth century were constantly on the move. One of Henry II's courtiers, Peter of Blois, described how the king's movements were a constant burden to his household:

> If the king has said he will remain in a place for a day—and particularly if he has announced his intention publicly by the mouth of a herald—he is sure to upset all the arrangements by departing early in the morning. And you then see men dashing around as if they were mad, beating packhorses, running carts into one another—in short, giving a lively imitation of Hell. If, on the other hand, the king orders an early start, he is sure to change his mind, and you can take it for granted that he will sleep until midday. Then you will see packhorses loaded and waiting, the carts prepared, the courtiers dozing, traders fretting, and everyone grumbling.

Henry's constant traveling, however, was not exceptional—it's just that it would have been nice if he'd made his mind up. ("I hardly dare say it," said Peter, "but I believe that in truth he took delight in seeing what a fix he put us in.") Every medieval king traveled around the country from place to place. So too did their great nobles: earls, bishops, and barons. Like the king, these men owned estates that were widely scattered across the country and, like the king, they wanted to visit all of them on a regular basis.

They did this for two reasons. In the first place, as landlords, they wanted to see that their officials were managing their estates properly, and also to remind their tenants who was in charge. Secondly, the economic needs of their households compelled the aristocracy to keep moving around. The household of a medieval magnate was large—it included not just the lord and his immediate family, nor just their domestic servants, but a whole host of others. A handful of knights, usually quite young and boisterous, would have been part of the household, and would have accompanied their lord when he was out riding and hunting. A number of clerks were also in constant attendance, in order to perform divine services, and also to write letters and keep records (most aristocrats could read, but they didn't dirty their hands with quill and ink). In addition, there were cooks and carters, huntsmen and falconers, stable-lads and skivvies. All told, a lord in the twelfth or thirteenth centuries might move around the country with up to fifty people in tow. All these people required food and drink, and also ran up other expenses for things such as fuel, candle wax, and clothing. In a medieval economy, without many big market towns, it was impossible to feed this many people (and, of course, their horses) if they stayed in one place for very long: they would quickly consume all the available food. The simplest solution was to keep the household moving around, gobbling up reserves of food as it went, then moving on to the next place when the cupboard was bare. So twelfth-century lords rarely stayed in one place for more than a few weeks, and would sometimes move on after just a few nights.

Of course, they would not have had a castle at each of their manors. The greatest lord—the king—had many castles dotted around the country, as well as palaces and hunting lodges. Great earls and the greatest barons may have had two or three castles among their many properties. But most noblemen only had the resources to invest in one major castle, and would have contented themselves with timbered lodgings—still luxurious, naturally—on their other manors. So for most of the time, a castle such as Hedingham or Rochester remained almost empty while its owner and his household were away touring the other parts of his estate. In their absence, a skeleton staff would remain attached to the castle, in order to supervise the lands around it, and to guard it in the unlikely event of an attack.

The most important member of this permanent staff was the constable, who was responsible for the building itself. Also important was the lord's estate steward, who would reside in the castle and use it as an administrative center. His job was to manage his master's lands, and this meant holding court to discipline tenants, as well as collecting monies and rents from them. The first floor of a keep may have been used for such purposes, and may also have been used as accommodation for the steward and the constable. At Hedingham and Rochester the first-floor chambers are comfortable and well appointed, with en suite toilets and large fireplaces. At the same time, they are grand enough for an official like the steward to hold court there when occasion demanded.

All such humdrum business was forgotten when news reached the castle that the lord was on his way. If the constable was lucky, and his master didn't behave like Henry II, this wouldn't take him completely by surprise. Either the visit was prearranged, or outriders from the lord's household arrived a few days in advance to warn the constable to put the castle in a state of readiness. First things first—was there enough food? The cellars had to be checked. Certain types of food and drink could be stockpiled; salted meat, cheeses, and barrels of wine would keep for weeks or months. But they had to be quickly supplemented with plenty of fresh food. Fresh meat, especially deer, was either hunted in the parks, or walked into the kitchens in the bailey. Perishables like fish and eggs had to be sourced rapidly, and ale—which also went bad quickly—had to be brewed. Typically, the lord would send his baker in advance of his arrival to ensure that the household had plenty of bread for the duration of its stay.

It wasn't just food the constable had to worry about. Fresh reeds had to be cut as bedding for those sleeping in the castle, and fresh oats and hay were gathered for the many horses that would need stabling. All these preparations, as well as any repairs to the castle, had to be carried out quickly, and the whole place had to be cleaned from top to bottom before the lord arrived.

On arrival, the focus of the lord and his household would have been the castle's great hall. The hall was celebrated in medieval literature as the place of light, warmth, and good cheer. The household would have dined here with the lord, his lady, and their noble guests seated at one end at the high table, and the remainder of the household at tables to either side. During dinner they might have been entertained by musicians or storytellers. The twelfth century was a golden age for troubadour poets, and they often wrote for aristocratic patrons, especially rich women. Like a hall in a school or college, the hall could be used for solemn ceremonies as well as elaborate feasts. Then, when the feasting was over, the hall served as a bedchamber for all but the most important members of the household. The hall, in short, was all-important.

But where was it? In old guidebooks to castles, it is often assumed that the hall was part of the keep. In many ways, this is a natural assumption, given the grandeur of certain chambers in towers like Dover and Orford. The chambers on the second floor of the keeps at Rochester and Hedingham are in each case the grandest rooms of all, stretching to twice the height of the other rooms, and both surrounded by a gallery built into the thickness of the outer wall. Without question, these rooms are "halls" of some kind. But is either of them the main hall, where the household dined and slept? A close study of both buildings suggests perhaps not. For one thing, most great towers don't have integral kitchens (though there are exceptions—Castle Rising in Norfolk, for example, has one). Any food cooked at Rochester or Hedingham must have been prepared in a separate kitchen, which stood in the bailey. If, therefore, a feast was held at either castle, the kitchen staff would have had a long

walk across the open courtyard of the bailey and up two different
sets of stairs before they even reached the entrance to the second
floor. It seems far more likely that the feasting took place in a separate hall in the bailey, positioned next to the kitchen so that the
food could be brought in with ease. Few such bailey halls survive
today, but we have already seen that Roger of Montgomery had a
great hall in the bailey of Hen Domen. Rare examples of stone halls
in the bailey survive at Richmond Castle in Yorkshire, and also at
Great Oakham in Rutland.

Dormitory floor, or *solar*

Hall with mural gallery

First floor (entrance level)

Basement
(for storage)

*An eighteenth-century cross-section of Hedingham.*

So if they were not for dining, what was the purpose of the halls in the towers at Rochester and Hedingham? Clearly they were not private chambers, because in both cases they are overlooked by galleries. They were, it has been suggested, purely ceremonial spaces. We might call them presence chambers: grand rooms where their owners could sit in state, receive important guests, and hold court. This, of course, did not necessarily prevent them from being used for dining if the owner thought it appropriate—feasting was also a matter of ceremony. Of course, it would have meant that the kitchen staff had to work much harder; but then there is no evidence to suggest that medieval magnates ever worried unduly about making life hard for other people.

Most great towers, like their wooden counterparts, provided additional accommodation for their owners. At Rochester, the top floor of the castle is thought to have contained private sleeping chambers for the archbishop of Canterbury, as well as a very large and ornate private chapel for his personal use. Similar sleeping quarters existed at Dover and the Tower of London. At Hedingham, however, there was originally no such private space for the lord to rest his head. Although from outside, the keep appeared to have four floors (like Rochester), the top floor was in fact a "dummy"—the walls, despite their windows, merely concealed a countersunk roof. The present third floor is actually a late medieval addition—a very early example of loft conversion. Such "dummy" floors were not, in fact, uncommon—the keeps at both Richmond and Scarborough were similarly constructed. The point in each case was that the tower should look big and impressive, so that everyone could see it for miles around; a useful reminder that keeps were constructed for their ceremonial and symbolic value as much as their residential and defensive potential.

The interior of castles like Rochester and Hedingham, therefore, can tell us a great deal about the needs and pretensions of their owners, and the kinds of activities that they considered important. It is appropriate to dwell on these peacetime functions, because castles are too often regarded in exclusively military terms. One of the great myths about the nobility of the Middle Ages is that they loved nothing better than to wage war against the king or, failing that, each other. Nothing could be further from the truth. Of course, medieval aristocrats relished the practice of arms, and used their prowess to justify their high position in society: it would be disingenuous to call them peace-loving, or even peaceable individuals. But they were not marauding idiots (in most cases, at least), and were well aware that peace brought material advantages. In order to build castles, stuff them with nice things, and put enough venison and pheasant on the table, kings and barons alike depended on a steady flow of cash. They needed their tenants to pay rent and their bailiffs to sell off agriculture surpluses. Put crudely, great magnates were landlords and farmers, and as such they sought to safeguard their income by protecting their tenants rather than terrorizing them. Nothing is more damaging to the economy than war, and for that reason most right-thinking individuals did their best to avoid it.

However, then, as now, politics and principles could on rare occasions force men—even men who were normally peaceable—to take up arms. When they did so, castles became all-important, and warfare was all about the struggle to control them.

On October 11, 1215, a crack troop of a hundred knights arrived at the gates of Rochester Castle and demanded to be admitted. The constable of the castle, Sir Reginald de Cornhill, did not hesitate, for he had been expecting them. The drawbridge was lowered, the doors swung open, and the horsemen swept inside.

These men were rebels, come into Kent on a highly dangerous mission. Earlier in the year, along with scores of other noblemen, they had seized control of London in defiance of their king. In recent days, however, they had started to sense that the tide was turning against them, and had therefore decided to take action. Selected by their fellows as the bravest and most skilled in arms, they had ridden southeast to open up a second front. If London was to hold out, they knew they had to distract the king, and draw his fire away from the capital.

Their plan, in this respect, was brilliantly successful. Two days later, a royal army drew up outside the walls of Rochester. King John had arrived.

John was the youngest son of Henry II, and the runt of his father's litter. He is familiar to all of us as the bad guy from the Robin Hood stories—the sniveling villain who betrayed his elder brother, "Good" King Richard the Lionheart, and made a grab for the English throne. It will hardly surprise most people to learn that this picture of John is a caricature—the Robin Hood legends originated long after the king was dead. Nevertheless, even if we scrape off all the mud that has been flung at John over the centuries, he still emerges as a highly unpleasant individual, and a man unsuited to the business of ruling. Contemporaries might not have recognized the hideous, depraved monster of legend, but they would have acknowledged the basic truth of the matter—John was a bad king.

To find out what people really thought about King John, we have to leave the stories of Robin Hood, and turn instead to another piece of writing, very different but no less famous. In 1215, shortly before they set off to seize Rochester Castle, John's enemies compiled a list of complaints about him, and presented it to the king in the hope of persuading him to behave better in the future. The list was drawn up in the form of a charter and, because it was so long, the charter itself was very big. People soon started referring to it simply as the Big Charter; or, in Latin, Magna Carta.

So, by looking at Magna Carta, we can work out why people were annoyed with King John. What aggravated them most, it seems, was the way in which he constantly helped himself to their cash; the first clauses of the Charter are all concerned with limiting the king's ability to extort money. In 1204, five years into his reign, John had suffered a major military and political disaster when he lost Normandy, Anjou, and Poitou to the king of France. These provinces had formed the heart of John's empire, and trying to get them back had kept him busy for the past ten years. Ultimately, however, by plotting his recovery, John was paving the way to his own downfall. The cost of building an alliance to strike back against the French king was enormous, especially because it was John's misfortune to rule at a time when inflation was causing prices (of mercenaries, for example) to soar. With increasing frequency, John passed the costs on to his English subjects, imposing ever greater and more frequent taxes, fining them large sums of money for trivial offenses, and demanding huge amounts of cash in return for nothing more than his grace and favor. Very quickly, John managed to create a situation where the people who didn't want him in charge outnumbered those who did—a dangerous scenario for any political leader.

In some respects, however, the rebellion that the king faced in 1215 was not entirely his own fault. Both his father and his brother had governed England in much the same fashion, expanding their power at the expense of the power of their barons. One very visible way of measuring their success is by looking at their castles. At the start of Henry II's reign in 1154, only around 20 percent of all castles in the country were royal. The two decades before Henry's accession had seen a proliferation of private castles (mostly motte and baileys) built without the king's consent. One of Henry's first actions as king was to order (and, where necessary, to compel) the destruction of such fortifications. Moreover, Henry and his sons, as we have seen, built new castles—big, impressive stone towers like Newcastle, Scarborough, Orford, and Odiham. By the time of John's death, the ratio of royal castles to baronial ones had altered drastically; almost half the castles in England were in royal hands. Castles, therefore, provide a good index of the king's power against the power of his barons.

It is evident that the rebels brought long-term grievances such as this to the negotiating table in 1215, because John tried to address them in Magna Carta.

"If anyone has been dispossessed without legal judgment from his lands or his castles by us," the king said, "we will immediately restore them to him."

But John went on to add that his subjects should make allowances for anyone who had been similarly dispossessed "by King Henry our father, or King Richard our brother." Such hair-splitting, however, ignored the basic truth of the matter, which was that Henry and Richard were simply better kings than John. They were skilled warriors, while he was condemned for his cowardice. Although he proved a capable administrator (John could be dynamic and efficient when it came to collecting taxes), he was a bad manager, unfit to command the loyalties of his leading subjects, unable to check or channel their ambitions, and uneven in his distribution of rewards. Most of all, John was just an unpleasant guy. He sniggered when people talked to him. He didn't keep his word. He was tight-fisted and untrusting. He even seduced the wives and daughters of some of his barons. Henry and Richard might have acted unfairly from time to time, but overall people liked them; almost nobody liked John.

It was John's personality, in the end, that doomed Magna Carta to failure. There was little point in persuading John to make such an elaborate promise, because he was bound to try and wriggle out of it. Sure enough, no sooner had negotiations ended than the king was writing to the pope, explaining how the Charter had been forced out of him, and asking for it to be condemned. By the time the pope wrote back, however, John's opponents had already worked out for themselves that Magna Carta was not worth the parchment it was written on. The king would never keep his promises, and they had no way of compelling him to do so. They too abandoned the Charter as a solution, in favor of the much simpler plan of offering John's crown to someone else. By the autumn of that year, both the king and the rebels were openly preparing for war.

This war was eventually fought right across the country. The southeast of England, however, and especially Kent, was the most important arena of conflict, because both parties were seeking assistance from the Continent. The rebels, for their part, had decided to offer the crown of England to Prince Louis, eldest son of the king of France. They had already made overtures to him in the course of the summer, and were hoping he would soon arrive and stake his claim in person, bringing with him much-needed reinforcements. John, meanwhile, was also looking across the Channel for help, but in his case from Flemish mercenaries. The king had recently dispatched his recruiting agents overseas, and was hovering anxiously on the south coast, trying to secure the loyalty of the Channel ports, and waiting for his soldiers of fortune to arrive.

In such circumstances, control of Rochester Castle, which stood at the point where the main road to London crossed the River Medway, became all-important. John understood this as well as anyone, and for this reason had been trying to get his hands on the castle since the start of May, when the rebellion against him had first raised its head. The king had already written to the archbishop of Canterbury twice, asking, in the nicest possible way, if he would mind instructing his constable to surrender the great tower into the hands of royal representatives. Both times, however, the request fell on deaf ears. The archbishop was one of John's leading critics and, realizing only too well what the king's intentions were, had promptly done nothing. Likewise, there was no love lost between the king and Rochester's constable, Sir Reginald de Cornhill. He was one of the hundreds who were heavily in debt to the Crown, and John had recently deprived him of his job as sheriff of Kent. Cornhill's response was probably more decisive; the likelihood is that he got a message through to the rebels in London, pledging his support, and expressing his willingness to help them.

When they realized that Rochester was theirs for the taking, the rebels in London formulated their plan. A detachment of knights would be sent to occupy the castle and hold it against John, and the man to lead it would be Sir William de Albini. Sir William is quite a dark horse: we don't have a great deal of information about him. Of course, the fact that he was chosen (or volunteered) to lead the mission indicates that he must have been a skilled and respected warrior. One contemporary writer calls him "a man with strong spirit, and an expert in matters of war." More puzzling is the fact that he does not seem to have had any of the personal grudges harbored by John's other opponents. On the one hand, he was clearly one of the leaders of the rebellion: back in the summer he had been named as one of the twenty-five men who were to enforce Magna Carta. On the other hand, Albini only joined the other rebels a week before the Charter was drafted. Whatever his own motivation for taking up arms against his king, in the weeks that followed there was no doubt about the strength of his commitment to the rebel cause.

Albini and his companions arrived at Rochester on a Sunday. On entering the castle, they found to their alarm that the storerooms were badly provisioned. Not only were they short on weapons and ammunition; there was, more worryingly, an almost total lack of food. They quickly set about remedying the situation, plundering the city of Rochester for supplies. In the event, however, their foraging operation only lasted forty-eight hours. By Tuesday, John and his army were outside the castle gates.

In such circumstances, we might not necessarily expect there to have been much of a fight. Just because one side in a dispute occupies a castle, and the other side turns up outside with an army, it does not automatically follow that a siege must take place. The defenders inside a castle might peer over their battlements at a colossal army, rapidly calculate the odds, and conclude that surrender is in their own best interests. Likewise, in many cases the prospective besieger will roll up with his army, assess the defenses to be far too strong to break, and move on to take easier, softer targets. In this dispute, however, with each side playing for the highest stakes, and Rochester being so crucial to their respective plans, the king and his enemies exhibited an uncommon degree of determination. The rebels in the castle, in spite of their poor provisions, decided they were going to tighten their belts and stick it out. King John, pitching his camp outside the castle, looked up at the mighty walls of Rochester, and vowed he was going to break them. The scene was set for a monumental siege.

It is a wonderful siege to investigate, not only because it turned out to be one the biggest sieges of the Middle Ages, but also because the evidence we have for it is so good. For English history up until the end of the twelfth century, we are for the most part at the mercy of monastic chroniclers for our knowledge of what went on. These men were the journalists of their age and, like modern journalists, their quality is remarkably varied; some are highly accurate, but others are partisan, ill informed, and over-imaginative. Fortunately, we have several good, sober, and reliable chroniclers to guide us through the siege of Rochester, who supply us with all kinds of accurate information about the way the struggle progressed. For example, one of our informants, Ralph of Coggeshall, provides us with an account of the preliminary encounter between John and the rebels. The king's aim on arriving in Rochester was to destroy the bridge over the Medway, in order to cut off his enemies from their confederates in London. On the first attempt he failed; his men moved up the river in boats, setting fire to the bridge from underneath, but a force of sixty rebels beat them back and extinguished the flames. On their second attempt, however, the king's men had the best of the struggle. The bridge was destroyed, and the rebels fell back to the castle.

This kind of reporting is invaluable, and some of the additional details that Ralph provides are no less compelling (he tells us, for instance, in the shocked tones that only an outraged monk can muster, how John's men stabled their horses in Rochester Cathedral).

For the first time in English history, however, we do not have to rely entirely on writers like Ralph. From the start of John's reign, we have another (and in some respects even better) source of information. When John came to the throne in 1199, the kings of England had long been in the habit of sending out dozens of written orders to their deputies on a daily basis. But John made an important innovation: he instructed his clerks to keep copies. Every letter the king composed was dutifully transcribed by his chancery staff on to large parchment rolls, and these rolls are still with us today, preserved in the National Archives. The beauty of this is that every letter is dated and located. Even if John's orders were humdrum, we can still use them to track the king wherever and whenever he traveled. We know, for example, that on October 11 the king was at Ospringe, and that by October 12 he had reached Gillingham. His first order at Rochester was given on October 13, and on the following day, he wrote to the men of Canterbury.

"We order you," he said, "just as you love us, and as soon as you see this letter, to make by day and night all the pickaxes that you can. Every blacksmith in your city should stop all other work in order to make [them] . . . and you should send them to us at Rochester with all speed."

From the outset, it seems, John was planning on breaking into Rochester Castle by force.

In the early thirteenth century, siege warfare was a fine art with a long history, and a wide range of options were available to an attacker. Certain avenues, however, were closed to John, because the tower at Rochester had been deliberately designed to foil them. The fact that the entrance was situated on the first floor, and protected by its forebuilding, ruled out the possibility of using a battering ram. Equally, the tower's enormous height precluded any thoughts of scaling the walls with ladders, or the wheeled wooden towers known as belfries. Built of stone and roofed in lead, the building was going to be all but impervious to fire. Faced with such an obstacle, many commanders would have settled down and waited for the defenders to run out of food. John, however, had neither the time nor the temperament for such a leisurely approach, and embarked on the more dangerous option of trying to smash his way in. But simply getting close enough to land a blow on the castle was going to be enormously risky. We know for a fact that the men inside had crossbows.

Crossbows had been around since at least the middle of the eleventh century, and were probably introduced to England (along with cavalry and castles) at the time of the Norman Conquest. In some respects, they were less efficient killing machines than conventional bows, in that their rate of "fire" was considerably slower. To use a longbow (the simplest kind of bow imaginable), an archer had only to draw back the bowstring to his ear with one hand before releasing it; with a crossbow, the same procedure was more complicated. The weapon was primed by pointing it nose to the ground, placing a foot in the stirrup and drawing back the bow with both hands—a practice known as "spanning." When the bowstring was fully drawn, it engaged with a nut which held it in position. The weapon was then loaded by dropping a bolt or "quarrel" into the groove on top, and perhaps securing it in place with a dab of beeswax.

Such an involved readying routine meant that crossbows were not suited to every type of warfare—in the thick of battle, for example, they were of limited use. For men under siege, however, with ample time to span, load, aim, and release, the crossbow was the weapon of choice. What the crossbow lost in speed, it more than made up for in range and penetrative power. Spanning created far greater tension in the bar across the top of the bow (the prod) than the equivalent action with a longbow. By John's day, moreover, the crossbow had become even more deadly, because prods were being constructed using a new technique. Earlier versions were made from a simple strip of wood—typically yew or ash. From the end of the twelfth century, however, crossbow-makers were producing laminated or "composite" prods, made not only from wood but also from strips of whalebone and animal sinew, glued together and wrapped in parchment (dried sheepskin). These new composite prods created a weapon with an enormous range—anything up to 900 feet was attainable. In terms of penetrative power, they were lethal. A knight dressed in a mail shirt and carrying a wooden shield might have stood some chance against conventional archery (unless, like poor old King Harold, he got hit in the eye). Against a well-aimed crossbow bolt, however, he had no hope: the bolt would shatter his shield and pierce right through his mail. All of a sudden, survival in warfare was much more of a lottery, even for those rich enough to afford the most expensive armor. Small wonder that the pope

*A diabolical weapon. This twelfth-century carved capital
shows devils using crossbows.*

condemned crossbows, and that people claimed they were invented
by the Devil.

According to Matthew Paris (a monk of St. Albans, and one of
the more tabloid chroniclers of the thirteenth century), King John
came closer than he knew to being killed by a crossbow during the
siege of Rochester. From inside the tower, the king was spotted by a
rebel crossbowman, who promptly drew a bead on his royal target,
and made ready to shoot. Before he pulled the trigger, however,
he asked William de Albini for permission, and the rebel leader
refused. As mere men, said Albini, it was not for them to end the
life of kings—only God could decide how to deal with John. The
story shows every sign of being made up; the monk wrote it down
almost twenty years after the siege, and immediately followed it
up by pointing out a biblical parallel. But even if we can't take the
tale at face value, it shows at least that contemporaries were aware
of the huge potential of the crossbow—even a lowly foot soldier,

armed with such a weapon, could contemplate killing a king. John of all people would have been well aware of this. In 1199, the seemingly invincible Richard the Lionheart had been felled by a single crossbow bolt to the shoulder, and the festering wound had later ended his life. As well as his own legendary cowardice, the memory of his big brother's untimely death probably persuaded John to stay well out of crossbow range in 1215.

But if John was kept on his guard by his opponents, he was not content merely to cower behind his own defenses. On the contrary, the king had also come equipped with the latest in siege technology, and his new toys were far bigger. Another very reliable and well-informed chronicler, the anonymous Barnwell Annalist, tells us that the king came to Rochester with "five throwing machines." Without doubt, these machines were the heaviest artillery of the age: trebuchets.

Trebuchets were giant slingshot or catapults, deliberately designed and built to smash down castle walls. The idea of creating such a weapon was not new; machines that hurled missiles at masonry had been around for hundreds of years. Trebuchets, however, were a new twist on this old idea, a product of a revolutionary piece of thinking in the late twelfth century.

Throwing machines worked on one of two basic principles. Either they were powered by torsion, or they worked like a see-saw. Torsion machines had been in use since Roman times; the mangonel, for example, was a simple sprung throwing arm attached to a heavy wooden base, winched back, loaded, and released. Similarly, the ballista or springald, a kind of giant crossbow, was another weapon used by the Romans that was still being deployed by both defenders and attackers in the Middle Ages. By contrast, machines which used the see-saw principle were a more recent development, but nevertheless were still well established by King John's day. In the tenth century, the Chinese invented a simple device that became known in the West as a perrier. A triangular frame supported a long throwing arm, rather like a see-saw, but with the pivot very close to one end of the beam. To operate it, men would heave on a set of

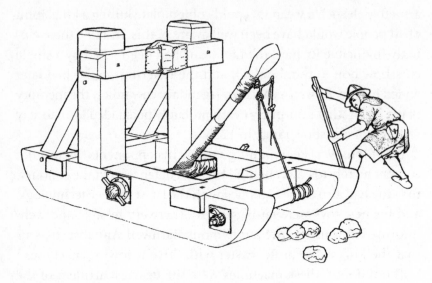

*A man readies a mangonel.*

ropes that hung from the short end of the arm, sending the long end up into the air, hurling its missile skyward.

The trebuchet was a more sophisticated version of the perrier, devised by the Arabs in the course of the twelfth century. Rather than having its throwing arm flipped by men pulling on ropes, it relied on a large counterweight to perform the same function.

There are no surviving originals from the Middle Ages, but we do have pictures and diagrams of trebuchets in medieval manuscripts. Using this information, a team of historians and engineers has built a replica at Caerphilly Castle in Wales. Like a crossbow, the trebuchet is a machine which works on the principle of stored energy. The first part of the process involves heaving the counterweight—a wooden box filled with around two tons of earth and rocks—up and into place. A team of four or five men pulling on ropes can do this in about five minutes. Once the weight is raised and secured in place, the machine can be loaded. The missile—here a ball of cast concrete, but originally made of stone or lead—is then placed in the end of a sling attached to the long end of the throwing arm. When all is ready, a sharp pull on the trigger causes the counterweight to drop, pulling the short end of the arm downward with tremendous force, hurling the long end upward, and pulling the rope-sling after it.

The whole motion, difficult to describe, is extremely elegant to watch; it looks like a cricket ball being bowled over-arm. The surprising thing is the noise—or rather, the lack of it. Instead of the explosive charge of a cannon, and the whistling of the missile, there is just a scrape as the ball moves from under the frame, a shudder as the arm is stopped in its spin, and then—nothing. The ball moves through the air in total silence. It's like watching a film with the sound turned off. The effect is utterly captivating: the motion of the machine and the arc that the missile describes are both exceedingly graceful.

The Caerphilly trebuchet, it must be said, is an impressive beast. With a twenty foot-long throwing arm, it is a "full-sized" replica, and its twenty-five-pound missiles would cause serious damage

*A perrier.*

*The replica trebuchet at Caerphilly. The counterweight (within the frame) is raised by pulling the arm at one end and winching at the other.*

if directed against buildings (at Caerphilly, they splash down into the moat). It would have been quite possible, however, for medieval engineers to build much larger trebuchets—monster machines more than twice the size, with throwing arms up to fifty feet long. Very little could stand in the way of such huge weapons. Wooden buildings in a castle's bailey would be smashed to smithereens. Lead roofs would offer no resistance. The only thing that might withstand a direct hit was masonry. Whether or not it did so would depend on a number of factors—how close the attacker dared to bring his engines, how large the machines were, and how heavy the missiles. It would also depend on the skill of the engineer and the precision of his catapult, since to bring down solid stonework would in most cases require several hits in the same place. Above all, it would depend on one question: How thick and well built were the walls?

The men inside Rochester Castle were now asking themselves much the same thing: Would the walls of the tower, twelve feet thick, hold out against King John's trebuchets? The Barnwell Annalist says that the bombardment of the keep did not cease by day or night. There is no suggestion, either from Barnwell or from any of the chroniclers, that the defenders were subjected to the kind of psychological and biological horrors we often hear about in other sieges. Sometimes rotting animal carcasses or the heads of fallen comrades were hurled over the walls of a besieged city or castle, in an attempt to spread plague and terror. John may not have resorted to such tactics (though one would hardly put it past him), but he knew, in any case, that the relentless barrage was piling psychological pressure on his enemies. As the stones rained down on them, as their food ran short, and as the winter cold began to set in, surely they could not hold out much longer?

And yet they did. Part of the reason for the rebels' dogged determination was an earnest belief that the cavalry would arrive—either in the shape of Prince Louis, or in the more likely form of their London associates. According to one chronicler, the knights who remained in the capital had sworn to Albini and his colleagues that, should Rochester be besieged, they would ride to their aid. Up to a point, they kept their promise. Two weeks into the siege, a force of seven hundred horsemen left London and headed toward Rochester. Halfway there, however, their nerve failed; at Dartford, they turned and headed back. Why they did this is unclear, but it is possible that their scouts had returned with news of the size of the John's army. We don't know how large the king's force was, but we can get some idea from the fact that seven hundred fully armed knights turned in fear and fled.

John would have learned soon enough that his other enemies had retreated back into their hole, and the news must have gladdened him somewhat. It was only a small consolation, however, because the fact remained that Rochester Castle and its defenders were still holding out, despite everything his expensive siege engines could throw at them. With every day that passed, it was becoming increasingly, maddeningly clear that the trebuchets were not going to work. The king, therefore, placed all his faith in his last remaining option: to drive a mine under the great tower, in the hope of bringing it crashing to the ground.

The technique of undermining was not a new one; the Romans and the Vikings are known to have used mines when laying siege to cities. The aim was to drive one or more tunnels under the foundations of the walls, supporting the ground above with timber props, which were then burnt away to create a collapse. But this wasn't always possible. If the defenses were built on solid rock, tunneling underneath them was virtually impossible. Water defenses, or even just soft or waterlogged ground, also meant that mining was out of the question. And even if the conditions for mining were ideal, conditions for miners themselves were anything but. The environment in which such men worked was dark, damp, and dangerous: the process could easily end in disaster if the soil above them suddenly subsided.

Digging a mine in peaceful circumstances was difficult enough, but doing so during a siege was doubly dangerous, since the besieged would do everything in their power to frustrate the miners' progress. Just getting close enough to begin digging would involve dodging a shower of arrows and crossbow bolts, so miners took care to approach under the cover of a "tortoise" or "cat"—a wooden canopy, moved on wheels, and covered in damp animal hides to prevent it being set on fire. Even once they were underground, the miners were still in danger of attack. Roman writers speak of defenders flooding enemy mines and drowning their assailants. A more common approach was for the defenders to dig a counter-mine, either in the hope of causing a collapse, or simply with the intention of meeting their opponents head on, and engaging them in subterranean hand-to-hand combat.

Luckily for John, his engineers reported that the ground around Rochester was suitable for mining. Even so, it was far from being an easy task. Despite having at their disposal all the picks that the men of Canterbury could manufacture, the operation was set to take weeks. At one point, progress ground to a halt when the miners came up against solid stone foundations—not those of the keep or the bailey walls, but the old Roman walls of Rochester. Only by making a detour could they continue with their tunneling.

For the defenders trapped inside the keep, it was an agonizing waiting game. There is no indication that they tried any of the advanced techniques of counter-attack above, beyond of course trying to pick off miners with crossbows when they emerged from tunneling. As with the trebuchets, they could only pin their hopes on the solidity of the tower and its foundations. These, we know, were profound; excavations in the late nineteenth century failed to find the bottom of the walls. Getting right underneath the keep must have been a hellish task.

Finally, however, John's miners managed it. By November 25, the mine was ready. Hundreds of tons of masonry were now supported only by wooden pit props. On the same day, John sent a letter to his trusted servant, Sir Hubert de Burgh. "We order you," he said, "to send us forty bacon pigs." This was not, however, the makings of a thank-you dinner for the hardworking miners—even a glutton like John would have struggled to finish that many ham sandwiches. The kind of pigs the king wanted, he went on to specify, were "the fattest and least good for eating." It was not food that John was after, but fuel. The unfortunate animals were needed "to set fire to the stuff which we have put under the tower at Rochester."

Once the mine was finished, it would have been stuffed with brushwood, straw, and kindling to feed a great fire. How the pig fat was introduced is a matter of debate. An older generation of more imaginative historians envisaged the forty-strong herd being driven into the tunnels while still alive, burning torches tied to their tails. Sadly, modern military experts now think this unlikely; the idea of live pigs running around with firebrands attached is just too farcical, even for King John. It is now believed that the pigs were slaughtered and rendered down for their fat, which was subsequently poured into barrels and rolled into the mine.

With or without an accompaniment of squealing pigs, the scene that followed must have been both horrifying and spectacular. Torches were introduced to the tunnels. Deep underground, the kindling caught and the pig fat crackled. Flames started to lick the fatty wooden props and, as the fire grew to a roar, the props started to snap. Suddenly, the ground above the mine fell away. The great keep shuddered and split. With a final deafening roar, a quarter of the building came crashing to the ground.

The dust had hardly settled before John's men were pouring into the keep through the gaping hole. Amazingly, in spite of the terror and confusion that the collapse must have caused, the men inside fought on. The southeast corner of the keep had been reduced to rubble, but its great cross-wall remained standing; using this, the rebels mounted a last, desperate line of defense. It was successful: try as they might, the king's men were still unable to force their way in.

At the start of the siege, John had openly derided his opponents' stamina.

"I know them too well," he allegedly spat. "They are nothing to be accounted of, or feared."

Having now spent seven weeks besieging them the king must have felt like eating his words.

In the end, despite all John's military ingenuity, it was starvation that finally forced the rebels to surrender. By this stage the men in the keep were totally out of supplies, and had been reduced to living on the flesh of their own expensive war-horses. This, says the Barnwell Annalist, "was a hard diet for those who were normally used to fine food." At first the defenders tried to cut their losses by sending out "those who seemed the least warlike": perhaps those too exhausted to fight, or possibly non-military personnel, such as clerics or blacksmiths. John, however, was in no mood for such half-measures. When these men emerged he had them mutilated, lopping off their hands and feet in an effort to persuade those still inside to surrender. Eventually, lacking the strength to fight on any longer, the remaining rebels gave themselves up. By curious coincidence, it was November 30—the feast of St. Andrew, Rochester's patron saint. The struggle for the city's castle had lasted for the best part of two months.

"Living memory does not recall," concluded the Barnwell Annalist, "a siege so fiercely pressed, and so staunchly resisted."

After such a long, costly and bitter struggle, John was apparently in no mind to be merciful. According to one of the chroniclers, the king intended to celebrate his victory by having every member of the rebel garrison hanged. This would not have been entirely out of character—the king was famous for gloating when he had the upper hand. However, according to the same writer, one of John's foreign captains persuaded him to show clemency in the name of self-interest. The war, he argued, was not yet over. What if John or his allies were themselves captured at some later stage? Better the king should imprison his enemies, rather than start a round of tit-for-tat killing that might end up with his own neck in a noose.

It is doubtful that John really needed to have the logic of this argument explained to him by one of his own men. Showing mercy toward a defeated opponent was perfectly normal behavior in the early thirteenth century. Ever since 1066, warfare in England had been regulated by the code of chivalry. In John's day, this had nothing to do with later perversions like laying your cloak over a puddle, or letting your enemy strike the first blow. It meant, in essence, that political killing was taboo. Naturally, this did not apply to the non-noble members of society. John had already demonstrated as much when he ordered the mutilation of the "less-than-warlike" members of Rochester's garrison during the final stages of the siege. After the surrender, he proved the point a second time by hanging one of the rebel crossbowmen (apparently punished for his treachery—the lowborn bowman had been raised in John's household). Chivalry was not about a high regard for human life in general; it was a code that condemned killing among the upper classes, based on exactly the kind of enlightened self-interest advocated by John's foreign captain.

Chivalric self-interest, moreover, extended beyond insuring against future reprisals. The man who spared his noble opponents stood to make a significant profit in the form of ransoms.

Prisoners were valuable assets, as John fully appreciated. When the rebels were being clapped into chains, the king personally confiscated the most important ones for himself. For example, William de Albini was dispatched to the king's castle at Corfe, and ended up with a price on his head of £4,000. Having appropriated the choicest prisoners in this manner, John generously distributed the less important individuals among his cronies as gifts.

For the rebels themselves, the defeat at Rochester was a massive blow to their cause, and it left the remaining barons in London feeling totally discouraged. The Barnwell Annalist, concluding his section on the siege of Rochester, commented that "there were few who would put their trust in castles," and he was absolutely right. When John moved into East Anglia at the start of 1216, the castles of Colchester, Framlingham, and Hedingham fell in quick succession. All three were mighty stone castles, and before Rochester, men might have hoped to defend them. After the great siege of that autumn, there was no longer the will to do so.

John, however, despite scoring these new successes, never managed to pluck up the courage to risk a decisive assault on London. His delay cost him dearly. In May 1216, a full year after the rebellion had flared up, Prince Louis landed in Kent and quickly gained control of southeastern England. All the castles that had fallen to John were suddenly back in the hands of his enemies. Only those fortresses which the king had placed in the hands of his closest servants held out for him. Hubert de Burgh—the man who came through with the pigs—successfully defended the great castle at Dover against the French assault.

By the autumn of 1216, the war was deadlocked. John held sway in the Midlands, but the south and east remained in the hands of his opponents. Ultimately, the situation was resolved by the king's overexertion and overindulgence. In early October, after a really good dinner with the burgesses of King's Lynn, John fell sick with dysentery. He struggled on for a few days, time enough to reach the castle at Newark. By the time he got there, however, it was plain to everyone that he was dying. In the small hours of the morning on October 18, as a gale howled around the castle walls, the king finally gave up the ghost.

Since the cause of the war had been John himself—his bad governance, his untrusting personality, and his broken promises—the king's death removed most of the reasons for fighting. It was much more difficult for the die-hard rebels to justify their opposition to John's blameless nine-year-old son, now crowned as King Henry III. Moreover, the new king's governors encouraged a cease-fire by recognizing the legitimacy of many of the rebels' grievances. They issued a new version of Magna Carta, and indicated that in future the king would respect its terms. The only person who stood to lose out now was Prince Louis; it took a decisive battle at Lincoln and a large payment of cash to persuade him to go home.

By 1217, the war was over; John was dead and peace had been restored. Rochester Castle, however, remained shattered and broken—a pale reflection of its former glorious self. It was not until

*The rebuilt corner of Rochester's keep.*

ten years later that builders arrived to make good the damage. The work they carried out was not a reconstruction, but a repair job. Inside the castle, the new archways look shabby in comparison with the elegant originals. Outside, the contrast is even more striking. The collapsed corner of the keep was rebuilt, not with a square tower as before, but with a round one. This had nothing to do with aesthetics; the repairs make a real mess of what was previously a very handsome building. But the king's masons weren't interested in making the castle look pretty, or putting it back together piece by piece. The recent siege had demonstrated, in the most dramatic way imaginable, that great towers—even the greatest towers—were vulnerable. Masons, however, had already thought of ways to make castles stronger.

CHAPTER THREE

# BUILDING AN EMPIRE

—◦◦◦—

C aernarfon is one of my favorite castles in the UK. It sits
right beside the sea on the coast of north Wales, opposite
the island of Anglesey, surrounded by swans and besieged
by seagulls. Despite its remote location, the castle is familiar to
millions of people because of the spectacular ceremony that took
place there in 1969—the investiture of Prince Charles as prince
of Wales.

It was, for many reasons, the perfect place for such an occasion,
not least because of its stadium-like proportions. For centuries,
poets and painters had come to Caernarfon and gazed in wonder at
this giant among castles. In his diary of 1774, Dr. Samuel Johnson
described it as "an edifice of stupendous majesty and strength."

For me, part of Caernarfon's appeal is its difference from the
castles I grew up with in Kent, like Rochester and Dover. To begin
with, there is no single great tower or keep. Instead, the castle
derives its military strength from a huge circuit of walls. This was
the big departure in castle design in the thirteenth century and, in

this respect, Caernarfon is a "typical" castle of its time. In every other way, however, this mighty fortress-palace, with its polygonal towers, masonry of different colors, and the carved stone figures on top of its battlements, is a truly exceptional building.

As we shall see, Caernarfon is the work of many thousands of anonymous individuals. Ultimately, however, the castle is the accomplishment of one man—the English king, Edward I. It was built to mark, in the grandest way possible, his conquest of Wales in 1283. Edward wanted a castle that was a royal palace and an impregnable fortress, an administrative center for his new dominions, and a grand statement that Wales had become part of a new "British" empire. In Caernarfon, all his wishes were fulfilled.

Perhaps the most remarkable thing about Caernarfon, however, is that it does not stand alone. The castle is "only" the greatest of a whole string of new fortresses, all built by Edward I with astonishing speed at the end of the thirteenth century. The famous castles at Harlech and Conwy, Rhuddlan and Flint, as well as the great unfinished castle of Beaumaris, were all built at the king's command in the wake of his victory. Together they form a group of buildings that still rank among the most impressive engineering achievements the world has ever seen. Not only are they mighty fortresses—a perfect realization of the new ideas of the thirteenth century—they are also works of art, intended to spell out in the most dramatic fashion the achievement of a conquering king.

So what drove Edward I to this excessive display of power? What kind of man was he? As a king, Edward had many great qualities. Physically very big and very strong, he was an expert warrior and a skilled general. He lived up to the image of an ideal Christian ruler by going on crusade. He was also a great legislator, and a faithful husband. But Edward also possessed several less endearing character traits—a dark side, if you like—which earlier historians tended to overlook. Contemporary chroniclers noted that he could be sly and duplicitous. He lacked the ability to see any issue from a point of view other than his own. Most importantly, he was a king who would not tolerate any attacks on the dignity of the Crown.

It is always dangerous to imagine we can read peoples' thoughts and intentions, especially if they have been dead for seven hundred years. But if we were forced to psychoanalyze Edward, and to explain why he was so prickly about his royal dignity, we would probably point to the hard lessons he learnt in his father's reign. Edward's father was Henry III, whom we recently left as a little boy of nine, being crowned after the death of his own father, King John. From the time of his accession in 1216 until his death in 1272, Henry had a long but troubled reign. Although not actively unpleasant, like John (Henry actually comes across as quite an amiable chap) he lacked good judgment and made bad, even inept policy decisions. By 1258, the great men of the realm had had enough of his mistakes, and forcibly deprived the king of power.

By this time, Edward was around. He was, however, still only a teenager, and powerless to assist his father. All he could do was stand in the wings and watch as the king was humiliated. One can easily imagine how angry he felt, and how frustrated he was at his inability to intervene. Just a few years later, Edward did lead the fight-back that restored Henry to power, but by then he had already learnt his hard lessons about rulership. The young Lord Edward was determined never to let such a shameful thing happen again. When he was king, he would defend his royal rights tooth and nail, and accept no challenges to his authority. By God, he was going to be absolute master in his own kingdom, and woe betide anybody who dared to suggest otherwise.

Henry died in 1272, and in due course Edward succeeded him. Of course, once he was crowned, the new king faced political opposition just like any other ruler—occasional conflict between the monarch and his magnates was an accepted part of medieval government. Some English lords did stand up to Edward from time to time, and several of them lived to regret it. The greatest challenge to the king, however, came not from the political heartlands of England, but from the distant hills and valleys of Wales.

At the start of Edward's reign, Wales was a completely separate country from England. Of course, the kings of England had always huffed and puffed about their superiority, and expected Welsh rulers to acknowledge their subservient status. To all intents and purposes, however, these rulers were independent. English kings were able to cope with the reality of the situation because Wales was not a united country. The mountainous landscape made it difficult for any one Welsh ruler or dynasty to establish overall control, and as a result the land was divided into petty kingdoms.

In the thirteenth century, however, things started to change. The rulers of Gwynedd, the tiny kingdom in the northwest of Wales, became steadily more powerful in their own region, and eventually began to establish control over their southern neighbors. From the middle of the century, the Welsh united under the leadership of one man. His name was Llywelyn ap Gruffudd.

Llywelyn saw it as his destiny to lead a united Wales. When he was a young man, however, the prospects of doing so looked very bleak. His grandfather had started to build up a federation of Welsh rulers at the beginning of the century, but it had collapsed during the disastrous rule of his uncle Dafydd; all his grandfather's achievements were undone, and the English invaded large parts of north Wales. As a result, when Llywelyn himself came to power in 1246, he succeeded only to his ancestral lands in Gwynedd and, because of Welsh laws of inheritance, even this meager prize had to be shared with his brothers.

From this unpromising start, Llywelyn rebuilt his family's fortunes. Having defeated his brothers in battle in 1255, he went from strength to strength, driving the English out of north Wales, and establishing ever-stronger links with his southern neighbors. In time, he matched and then surpassed the successes of his grandfather. According to contemporaries, he was not only a skilled warrior, but also a charismatic leader. In the words of one English chronicler, the Welsh followed Llywelyn "as if they were glued to him."

Llywelyn's rapid rise to greatness was helped enormously by the incompetence of Henry III. The events of 1258, as well as molding the character of the young Edward I, had led to a civil war in England that left the country paralyzed in the face of Llywelyn's advances. When the war finally came to an end in 1267, the power of the English Crown was badly shaken. Henry was forced to seek peace with the Welsh, and had no option but to recognize Llywelyn's recent territorial gains. He also went one stage further, and bestowed a new title upon the Welsh leader. When the peace treaty was drawn up at the ford of Montgomery, Llywelyn was named "prince of Wales." He was the first native ruler of Wales to be accorded this title by an English king.

He was also to be the last. The treaty of Montgomery, while it magnified Llywelyn personally and recognized his conquests, also carried the seeds of his destruction. For all the fine words it lavished on Llywelyn, it was, like Magna Carta, an ambiguous document, more likely to provoke further conflict than bring about lasting peace. Although Henry had acknowledged Llywelyn's territorial gains, the English lords who had actually lost lands along the Welsh border were determined to claw them back. At the very end of Henry's reign, a struggle for power began that eventually led England and Wales to all-out war.

The scale and nature of the struggle is best illustrated by mighty Caerphilly Castle. Built by the earl of Gloucester in an effort to assert his right to a disputed part of the border, and completed just as Edward I came to the throne, the new castle was one of the fundamental causes of the conflict that followed. It is, moreover, an ideal castle for illustrating the huge advances that had taken place in castle-building since the twelfth century.

The biggest difference between Caerphilly and castles of the previous generation is that there is no sign of a keep. In the course of the twelfth century, the technology of attack had caught up with great towers, as the rebels at Rochester had learned to their cost. From the end of the century, therefore, castle designers began to experiment with a new idea. Rather than building a keep, they trusted instead to a large circuit of high walls, punctuated by even taller towers. The towers broke the walls at regular intervals, and were thrust forward, enabling defenders to shoot arrows or crossbow bolts right down at the base of the wall. An early example of this new arrangement can be seen at Framlingham Castle in Suffolk, which was built in the 1190s; a similar set of walls was built around the keep at Dover shortly before. In both cases, however, the towers set into the walls are square. In the thirteenth century, the preference was almost always for round ones, as seen at Caerphilly. Without a doubt, this was because round towers were perceived to be stronger.

The weakest point in a castle's walls had always been the entrance, or gatehouse. In the twelfth century, this was typically a single tower, such as the one at Framlingham. In the early thirteenth century, however, a new, far more elaborate design was devised. Castle-builders realized that by building two round towers either side of the entrance, they could produce a much stronger type of gatehouse. Anyone approaching such a building had to pass between the towers, under the watchful gaze of the guards, and flanked on either side by menacing arrow-loops. This new design also created extra space over the gate which could be used for accommodation, usually for the castle's constable. As time wore on, twin-towered gatehouses grew ever larger and more elaborate: so much so that, by the time we reach Caerphilly, the gatehouse is the same size as a twelfth-century keep.

Finally, in the thirteenth century castle-builders developed the idea of "concentricity," or having multiple lines of defense. If you look at Caerphilly, you can see that as well as the main inner walls which form the castle courtyard, there is another set of walls running all the way around the outside. Like the inner defenses, this second line of walls is provided with crenellations (battlements), arrow-loops, and gatehouses. Moving out even farther from the center, there is a third line of defense in the form of the enormous artificial lake which surrounds the castle. Water defenses like this gave all kinds of protective benefits. As well as making it very difficult to storm the castle directly, they also prevented attackers from bringing their siege engines too close, and they made digging a mine under the walls completely out of the question.

At the time it was built, Caerphilly was an absolutely state-of-the-art castle, and one of the largest in Britain. The arrival of such a monster in what he considered to be his own backyard clearly left Llywelyn fuming. On two separate occasions during the building program, the prince overran the area and brought construction to a halt, at the same time complaining to the English king. Henry III, however, was too feeble to stop Gloucester, and the regency government appointed after his death only made matters worse. By 1274, much to Llywelyn's chagrin, Caerphilly was nearly completed. Bitter and resentful, the prince pinned all his hopes on the new English king—Edward. He had just returned from a crusade.

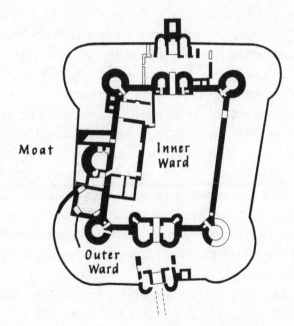

*Caerphilly.*

Edward, to his credit, did not immediately take sides with his English barons: there was little love lost between the king and the earl of Gloucester. There were also good reasons, from Edward's personal point of view, for keeping Llywelyn happy. The king had returned from his crusade with large debts, and the Welsh prince owed him money. In return for the recognition of his title and conquests in 1267, Llywelyn had been charged 25,000 marks (£16,666), and was paying it off in installments. Edward could ill afford to lose such a sum. Indeed, so great were the financial benefits of restoring Anglo-Welsh relations that Edward chose to ignore a calculated diplomatic snub from Llywelyn, when the prince failed to attend his coronation.

So Edward did not take sides; but nor did he solve the prince's problems, and the Welshman remained angry. If we look at the situation from Llywelyn's point of view, 25,000 marks was a lot of money to pay for a treaty that wasn't working. He was supposed to be prince of Wales, for Heaven's sake! If men like Gloucester could build castles like Caerphilly and get away with it, his new title was surely a joke, and everything he had struggled so hard to achieve seemed under threat. Llywelyn grew more and more frustrated, and in his frustration, he made a terrible, fatal error: he tried to coerce Edward I into action. Not only did he withhold money that he owed to the king; he also withheld his homage.

Homage was a symbolic act. To pay homage to someone involved kneeling before them and placing your hands together as if in prayer. You then put your hands between the hands of the other person, and swore to serve them faithfully. It was a public ceremony, intended to advertise that a dependent relationship was being established. When he was invested as prince of Wales at Caernarfon in 1969, Prince Charles carried out exactly the same procedure before Queen Elizabeth II, watched by a TV audience of over 500 million people.

In 1275, Edward I decided it was time to perform this elaborate ceremony with Llywelyn. The prince had been offered several previous opportunities to pay homage to the king, but on each occasion had found an excuse to be elsewhere. So at Easter that year, the king thought he would make things easier for Llywelyn by doing most of the traveling. The English court came to Chester, and members of the political communities of England and Wales convened there in order to watch. In an age before TV and newspapers, Edward's only option for publicity was to pack the place with spectators. We must imagine a day of grand ceremony, just as in 1969; similarly stage-managed, with great solemnity and pageantry. Everyone was going to watch as Llywelyn kneeled before Edward and acknowledged him as his lord and master.

Or at least they would have done, had the prince showed up. Instead, his non-appearance left them confused, disappointed, and bored. Far worse, it left Edward looking foolish, with large amounts of egg on his face, and the blow to his dignity was fatal. In a furious rage, the king returned to Westminster. He was still cross two years later when he wrote to the pope.

"In order to receive [Llywelyn's] homage," he fumed, "we so demeaned our royal dignity as to go to the confines of his land."

From Edward's point of view, it didn't matter what problems the prince had: his homage was absolutely non-negotiable. There were, therefore, to be no more concessions on Edward's part. Llywelyn could come to Westminster, perform his homage, and apologize, or he could face the consequences.

The prince, however, was not for turning either. He refused to budge an inch, and the slide toward confrontation became irreversible. Matters were not helped when, later in the same year, Llywelyn uncovered a plot on his life by some of his own men. When their treachery was discovered, they fled to England, and Edward refused to hand them over. The king, meanwhile, discovered that Llywelyn was planning a marriage alliance with his enemies, and retaliated by seizing the prince's bride-to-be as she was en route to Wales. Eventually, by the autumn of 1276, Edward decided he had had enough. On November 12 that year, in the presence of a full council of magnates at Westminster, he declared that Llywelyn was a rebel. Their personal quarrel was going to be settled by war.

It was not, however, going to be a war of equally matched combatants. In the thirteenth century, the economic and the military power of England vastly outstripped that of its western neighbor. England had major cities, prosperous market towns, and a booming economy. Edward could tap this wealth with taxes and customs, and supplement it with loans from Italian bankers. Wales, with a pastoral economy, few towns, and little coinage in circulation, was going to be no competition.

But at the same time, Llywelyn had one great advantage: geography. His ancestral lands were protected by the impenetrable mountains of Snowdonia. Many times in the past, English kings had attempted to lead armies into north Wales, only to be defeated by the harsh terrain and beaten back by the unforgiving weather. Just twenty years beforehand, Henry III, with young Edward in tow, had tried to advance into Wales, and failed miserably. So the prince remained defiant, confident he could weather any storm that Edward might unleash.

The king launched a three-pronged attack, with one army moving up from the south, and a second driving into mid Wales. Edward himself took command of the third and largest contingent, which headed directly into north Wales. The strategy was an old one: he marched a route that had been trodden by Roman legions as well as his own Norman forebears. The king's intention was to move slowly but surely along the north coast, establishing permanent bases as he went.

The scale of the English war effort, however, was new. By the height of the campaign, the king's force alone numbered fifteen thousand men. As they went, a separate army of eighteen hundred diggers cut a wide new road through the dense forest. The king sent his lieutenants to occupy the island of Anglesey, which supplied the heartlands of Gwynedd with much of its grain. The whole operation, as contemporaries observed, was like the undertaking of some massive siege, the object being to isolate Llywelyn in his stronghold of Snowdonia and starve him into submission.

In the end, there was not very much in the way of actual fighting—by this stage, Llywelyn had lost much of his earlier adhesive appeal. In order to defend his new principality, and pay the annual render to the English king, the prince had been forced to extort large sums of money from all classes of society—churchmen, burgesses, nobles, and peasants. Understandably, his popularity had started to suffer. During the summer, even while the English army was still mustering, many Welshmen had surrendered, and transferred their allegiance to Edward: more than half the king's northern army was made up of men from south Wales. In such circumstances, Llywelyn had little option but to seek terms. On November 2 he met with members of Edward's council at his palace at Conwy. One week later, peace was proclaimed.

The peace that Edward imposed on Llywelyn was humiliating. He did not remove his opponent, or even take away his title "prince of Wales." But by the time the king had finished restructuring the realities of power in the province, it hardly mattered what Llywelyn called himself. All the other Welsh chiefs now had to swear allegiance directly to the king. The prince was left with little more than his ancestral lands in Gwynedd. The united Wales he had been building for twenty years had been broken into pieces.

Edward set about enforcing this settlement by building a string of new castles to hem the prince in. Two were built in the south at Builth and Aberystwyth, but little remains of either castle today. More substantial ruins survive at the two larger and more expensive castles that the king built in the north, at Rhuddlan and Flint. Rhuddlan was most expensive of all, a reflection of Edward's intention that it should be the seat of royal government in north Wales. The castle was built to a typical thirteenth-century design. As at Caerphilly, there are high walls around a central courtyard, round towers, and gatehouses. It is also, like Caerphilly, a concentric castle, but in this instance the moat is dry. In fact, the only major difference between the two castles is one of scale: Edward would not have thanked you for saying it, but Rhuddlan is a lot less impressive than the earl of Gloucester's giant castle in the south. From our point

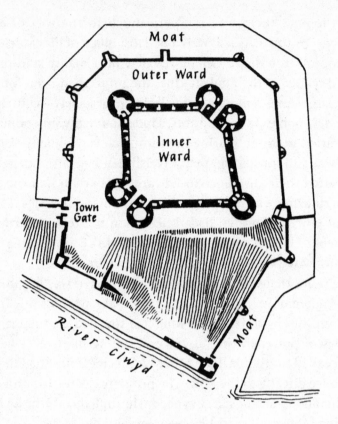

*Rhuddlan.*

of view, however, it does have one great advantage. Because it was built by a king rather than an earl, Rhuddlan shows up in Crown records. Using these documents, we can look in detail at the processes involved in building a thirteenth-century castle.

In comparison with the meager amounts of information from earlier centuries, there is a huge amount of written evidence about castle-building under Edward I. Using original government rolls from the Exchequer, we can find out the names of the builders, the exact costs, the precise dates and more besides. In the case of Rhuddlan, these rolls reveal one especially amazing fact: as well as building the castle, Edward also straightened the River Clwyd.

The location that the king chose for Rhuddlan was in many ways ideal—indeed, the remains of a Norman motte and bailey, which can still be seen to the southeast of the new castle, show that Edward was not the first to identify its strategic advantages. The king did, however, foresee problems in keeping the site supplied. The River Clwyd was far too winding to allow his large cargo ships to reach it. Edward's typically audacious solution was a huge feat of medieval civil engineering. From the fens of Lincolnshire and East Anglia, the king recruited hundreds of diggers, ditchers, and delvers. By September 1277 there was an army of 968 men working on what the records call "the great ditch." Using only picks and shovels, their job was to make perfect what nature had left unfinished: to straighten the three-mile stretch of river that wound its way from the castle to the coast.

Today, using mechanical digging equipment, the canalization of the Clwyd might be achieved in five to six months, and would cost somewhere in the region of £5 million. Even by modern standards, therefore, what Edward had embarked upon was an enormous construction project. And by such feats of engineering, the king left the

*Using satellite photography, it is still possible to make out the original loops and bends that Edward I's engineers straightened seven centuries ago.*

Welsh in no doubt—he was a man who would go to extraordinary lengths to get his own way.

The new castles of Rhuddlan, Flint, Aberystwyth, and Builth were permanent reminders of the humiliating defeat inflicted on Llywelyn in 1277. But the English victory did not end with the planting of fortresses. Edward was also determined to introduce English governmental practices and English law to Wales, and this, more than anything, provoked a widespread backlash. In letters to the archbishop of Canterbury, Llywelyn and his courtiers complained about the unfair ways in which they were treated by English officials and, most of all, the way in which their national identity was being denied.

"All Christians have laws and customs in their own lands—even the Jews in England have laws among the English," they reasoned. "We had our immutable laws and customs in our lands, until the English took them away after the last war."

In addition to these general grievances, there were certain Welshmen who, having supported Edward in the war, came to feel that their service had gone unrewarded. Although they had quickly flocked to the king's banner, they had received only meager handouts, while the richest pickings went to Edward's English commanders. One man in particular who felt unfairly treated was Llywelyn's younger brother, Dafydd ap Gruffudd. He and others like him, having helped bring down the prince's oppressive regime, now found it replaced by the even more onerous and unsympathetic rule of foreigners.

In 1282, these accumulated tensions finally spilled into concerted action. Late on the eve of Palm Sunday, the English lord Roger Clifford, one of Edward's old friends and a major beneficiary of the 1277 settlement, was sleeping soundly in his bed in his new castle at Hawarden. Suddenly and without warning, the castle was stormed by a band of Welshmen, led by Dafydd. Clifford was dragged from his bed and carted off into captivity, while many of his household were killed. The same night, other English castles were attacked. It was clearly a well-conceived and well-executed uprising. Llywelyn, although he claimed not to have authorized the attacks, nevertheless soon assumed the leadership of what quickly became a national rebellion, and joined in the assault on Edward's castles at Flint and Rhuddlan.

When news of the uprising reached Edward, his response was swift. He immediately appointed commanders to three different armies, and ordered a general muster of troops for May. In military terms, it was the same strategy he had used five years before. The king personally led a large army along the north Welsh coast, while the two other armies, led by trusted lieutenants, pressed into mid and south Wales. Politically, however, the ante had been upped massively. Edward was now embarking not merely on an expedition to punish Llywelyn, but on a mission to destroy him. In a letter to his commanders, the king resolved chillingly "to put an end finally to the matter . . . of putting down the malice of the Welsh."

No one, however, was pretending it was going to be an easy operation. To begin with, delays in mustering his armies had left Edward contemplating something that no English king had ever dared to attempt before—a winter campaign in Wales. At first, the king's bold move seemed like a bad decision. The southern army ran into trouble when the earl of Gloucester was defeated, and another commander, William de Valence the younger, was killed in action. In early November, a group of English knights was sent to take Anglesey and create a bridge across the Menai Strait, but they met with disaster when they were ambushed by the Welsh and driven into the sea. Nevertheless, these remained setbacks rather than reverses. The armies on this occasion were twice the size they had been before, and total expenditure on the campaign dwarfed the cost of Edward's earlier Welsh adventure. One modern estimate puts the 1282 figure at £150,000—about seven times that of 1277. Everything indicates that this time, the king was bringing the full power of the English state to bear on his Welsh adversary.

With such enormous resources ranged against him, Llywelyn's future looked exceedingly bleak. In Snowdonia, the Welsh prince watched the relentless build-up of well-provisioned troops with dismay. He began to realize that his only hope of survival was to break free from the snare that Edward was drawing around him. The easiest escape route appeared to be to the southeast, toward an area of the border where English control seemed to be weak.

His break for the border was Llywelyn's last move. On December 11, 1282, within a few miles of the new castle at Builth, the prince and his companions were ambushed by a group of English knights. The Welshmen fought bravely but were ultimately bested, and Llywelyn, who remained unrecognized throughout, fell in the course of the fighting. Later, when his killers realized the significance of their deed, they hacked off the prince's head and in jubilation sent it north to Edward. It was at Rhuddlan, where the northern army had paused in its march, that the two old adversaries came face to face for a final time. Having seen it for himself, the king sent Llywelyn's head to London, for all his subjects to admire. From the start of 1283, and for many years later, it adorned a spike outside the Tower.

As the news spread through Wales, the country despaired. "Is it the end of the world?" asked one Welsh poet. What little resistance still remained now quickly crumbled, and the last native stronghold at Castel-y-Bere fell at the end of April 1283. Two months later, the fugitive Dafydd ap Gruffudd was captured, and treated to a far more elaborate and grisly death than his brother. After the pretense of a carefully staged show trial at Shrewsbury, Dafydd was dragged, hanged, disemboweled, and quartered.

With the native dynasty vanquished, Edward parceled out some of the conquered lands to his followers, and confiscated all the remaining land in northwest Wales for himself. He set about securing his hold on his new territories by building three new castles: Harlech, Conwy, and Caernarfon.

Just by looking at these locations on a map, you can appreciate that the king was choosing the sites for his new castles with care. They are separated by more or less equal distances, each castle being sited no more than a day's march from its nearest neighbor. There was, however, a great deal more to the positioning of Edward's new fortresses than this simple observation implies. For example, in choosing to build at Conwy, Edward deliberately ignored the more obvious site of an earlier English castle just a few miles away at Deganwy. A comparison of the two sites is therefore very revealing, since it shows the way in which thinking about castles had changed, even in the space of Edward's own lifetime.

Today, very little remains of Deganwy Castle. It once sat on the top of a twin-peaked hill on the eastern side of the Conwy estuary. The highest point for miles around, with commanding views over the surrounding landscape, the site is an absolutely stunning defensive location. The site actually has natural crenellations—a series of smaller hills ringing the summit. From the point of view of protecting an army, this would seem to be the perfect spot. The Romans, who built a camp here in the first century AD, clearly thought as much. The princes of Gwynedd thought so, too: Llywelyn's grandfather built a castle here at the beginning of the thirteenth century. And Henry III, Edward's father, also thought Deganwy was by far his best bet. When he seized control of the area in 1245, he built an entirely new castle on the ruins of the old one.

Edward I, however, thought otherwise. Fantastic defensive location it might be, but Deganwy has one very major drawback. Like Rhuddlan, it stands a long way from the sea. There was, however, no question of improving water-borne access on this occasion. The River Conwy lies at the bottom of the hill, hundreds of feet below the castle site. Even as the crow flies, the river and the sea are half a mile away, and the path that winds its way from the shoreline to the castle is considerably longer—almost two miles. The result (as at least one TV film crew can testify) is that Deganwy is very difficult to supply. Being on top of a hill might make it easy to defend, but it also makes it very easy to surround. Once cut off from the sea and the river, it didn't matter how strong the hill-top castle was; a besieging army would only have to wait for the defenders' food to run out, then watch them starve.

Such drawbacks were not acknowledged by Henry III when he began to rebuild the castle in the mid-1240s. They soon became apparent, however, to the soldiers who were stationed there during the initial stages of construction. Writing home, one soldier in the king's army described the terrible conditions that existed in the English camp.

"We dwell here," he said, "in watchings and fastings, in prayer, in cold and nakedness. In watchings, for fear of the Welsh, with their sudden raids upon us by night. In fastings for lack of victuals, since the halfpenny loaf cannot be got for less than five pence. In prayer, that we may quickly return safe and sound to our homes. In cold and nakedness, for we live in houses of linen and have no winter clothes."

When supplies finally arrived, Deganwy's disadvantages were all too apparent, for the English could not reach their own ships. A boat coming from Ireland was inexpertly steered into the Conwy estuary, and became grounded on a sandbank. The English and the Welsh fought over the beached vessel for twenty-four hours, but eventually it was the Welsh who gained the upper hand and made off with its precious cargo. Such handicaps ultimately led to Deganwy's destruction. In the autumn of 1263, the castle's inadequacy was underlined for a final time when Llywelyn (then enjoying his glory days) captured the castle and razed it to the ground. The castle lies in ruins today largely because of the prince's comprehensive demolition.

So, when Edward I marched into the area in 1283, he decided that there was absolutely no point in following the ancient tradition of fortifying Deganwy by rebuilding his father's castle. Like Napoleon, Edward understood that his soldiers marched on their stomachs. As the letter written in 1245 testifies, they also needed warm clothes, strong tents, and plenty of ammunition. The English king had conducted a successful winter campaign in 1282 and 1283 precisely because he had managed to keep his armies supplied with such basic necessities. If he was going to hold on to his conquests, he knew he had to keep his supply lines open. Deganwy was therefore left to decay, and a new site was selected. Forgoing the superb defensive position on top of the hill, Edward opted for a location on the opposite bank of the river, right on the shoreline. The result was Conwy—a castle whose walls are lapped by the sea, enabling Edward to bring his cargo ships right up to the gate.

Edward sited all his castles in this manner so that they could be kept supplied at all times. Conwy, Caernarfon, and Flint all stand by the sea today. Harlech, although it now appears land-locked, was not always so isolated. The land below the castle has been reclaimed—the sea once ran right up to the base of the cliff. At Rhuddlan, we have already seen how the king canalized the river for exactly the same logistical reasons. By building castles where the water could lap at their walls, Edward made it impossible for the Welsh to deploy their traditional tactics. No longer could the king's fortresses be blockaded and destroyed. From now on, the English would have a permanent foothold in Wales.

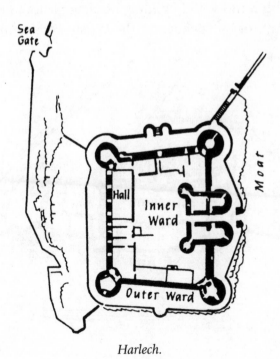

*Harlech.*

In certain cases, choosing the optimum strategic position for a castle also enabled Edward to make a political point. When it came to grandstanding, the king was a master showman, with a ruthless eye for detail. As is well known, when he later invaded Scotland, Edward seized all the symbols of native power, including, most famously, the Stone of Destiny. It is less widely appreciated, however (precisely because, in this instance, the king was more successful), that he did exactly the same thing a generation before in Wales. After the conquest of 1283, Edward seized all of Llywelyn's regalia—his crown, orb, and scepter—and had them sent back to Westminster. Similarly, he confiscated the prince's seal-matrices and had them melted down to make a silver chalice.

But it is Edward's castles that provide the most outstanding testimony to his determination to impose a new identity on Wales. Neither Caernarfon nor Conwy were built on virgin sites; both towns had been popular destinations for Llywelyn's court. Edward flattened these settlements, removing or destroying the great halls of the Welsh princes, and building his new castles in their place. The old days of independence, the Welsh were to understand,

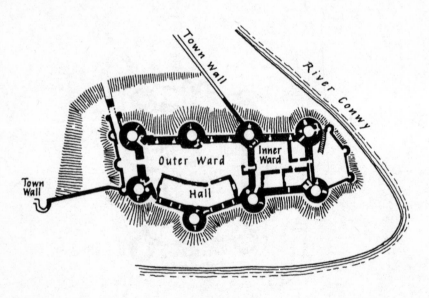

*Conwy.*

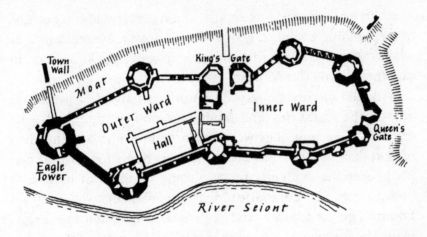

*Caernarfon.*

were now over; a new and more powerful authority was rising in its place. At Conwy, there had once stood a great Cistercian abbey, founded by Llywelyn's grandfather and the last resting place of the prince's ancestors. Edward leveled the building, and built Conwy Castle directly over their bones. With calculated callousness, the king literally erased the memory of Llywelyn's family from the face of the earth.

Construction at Harlech, Conwy and Caernarfon started in the summer of 1283, in each case within days of the arrival of Edward's army. The first task at all three locations was establishing the castle site and making it secure. At Harlech and Caernarfon, this meant cutting ditches around the perimeter; no mean feat at Harlech, since this involved hacking through solid rock. Such work, like the "sea-ditch" at Rhuddlan, required armies of laborers, and they were drawn from all over the country. Like those who built castles in the twelfth century, these men were paid a daily wage, mostly at the rate of one or two pence a day. The work, however, was backbreaking and dangerous, and for this reason many men had to be forcibly persuaded to accept the king's offer of a job. The belief that large numbers were pressed into service is borne out by an entry on one of the building accounts, which records three mounted sergeants who were paid to escort three hundred diggers from Yorkshire, "in case they should flee while on the road."

With the ditches underway, a wooden palisade was put up around the castle site, and temporary wooden buildings were erected. These buildings were not just the medieval equivalent of Portakabins; they included suites of rooms for Edward and his household, evidently built to some standard of luxury. At both Conwy and Caernarfon, separate chambers were built for Edward's queen, Eleanor, and gardens were laid out for her enjoyment, the turf being shipped in specially. Although all the timber buildings would eventually be replaced by stone, the investment in wooden walls was nevertheless enormous—twenty shiploads of timber were sent from Liverpool to Caernarfon in the first few weeks of building.

But the essential commodity, of course, was not timber, but stone. As we saw in Chapter Two, it made good sense to source the bulk of the material as locally as possible, but the expensive stone needed for window frames and fireplaces had to come from further afield. In the case of Edward's castle at Aberystwyth, built after the first Welsh war, high-quality stone was shipped all the way around the Pembrokeshire coast from Bristol. Other commodities had similarly long journeys. Lead for roofing and plumbing the castles was mined in the mountains of Snowdonia and brought overland to the construction sites. Iron and steel were ordered from Staffordshire, and ropes were sent from Lincolnshire.

Again, we know these kinds of details because the processes of construction are detailed clearly in surviving records. The same records also give us the precise number and kind of workmen on each site. Most of the labor force were of the unskilled variety, press-ganged in the counties. There were, however, scores of skilled artisans on every site, including carpenters and plumbers, and in the later stages, glaziers. When work at Harlech was at its height in the summer of 1286, in addition to the 546 general laborers, there were 115 quarriers, 30 blacksmiths, 22 carpenters, and 227 stonemasons.

Stonemasons were the key to the whole operation. They were skilled workers, and paid at the accordingly high rate of three to four pence a day. They were sometimes known as freemasons, not because they dressed up in aprons and indulged in arcane ceremonies, but because they had the ability to carve the more expensive "freestone," which could be chiseled in any direction without splitting. Working any kind of stone was a slow process, especially if the patron demanded that every inch of a building was finished to the same high standard. Typically working in teams, masons traveled the country from one project to the next, and worked mostly in the warmer months of the year.

The written records, for all their exhaustive detail, are rather inexpressive when it comes to the actual processes involved in the construction of a castle. To understand these, we have to turn to the illustrations in contemporary manuscripts. These provide a wealth of additional information: how scaffolding was erected, how stone was carved, and how blocks of stone were moved around the site. Heavy blocks were either dragged on sleds, or wheeled from place to place in carts. The method of lifting them off the ground and up to the level of the builders was particularly ingenious—at each site, carpenters constructed several windlass cranes, powered by men in a treadmill. One such crane survives at the top of the spire in Salisbury Cathedral.

Because the castles had to fulfill a vital military role, Edward drove construction on at lightning speed. Astounding as it seems, the records show that Conwy Castle was substantially completed in just four years. Harlech scarcely took longer, and was finished by 1289. Only at Caernarfon did work drag on into the 1290s and beyond. The speed and scale of construction meant that these castles were not cheap. Harlech, with a price tag of £10,000, was the least expensive of the three. Conwy, being larger and more sophisticated, cost something in the order of £15,000. When the builders finally put down their tools at Caernarfon, the project had absorbed at least £27,000.

*The treadmill crane at Salisbury Cathedral.*

So, from the summer of 1283, we have to imagine thousands of men being conscripted from all over England, marched to northwest Wales, and beginning to build Conwy, Harlech, and Caernarfon. The big questions that remains is, who was in charge? Edward himself was of course the prime mover, but who masterminded the layout and design of the new castles, supervised the workforce, and ordered the materials? Today we would expect these jobs to be shared by a number of individuals—an architect would come up with the initial design, a surveyor would inspect and assess the site, a foreman would take charge of the labor force, and so on. In the Middle Ages, however, all these tasks fell to one man. He was the master mason, a uniquely skilled and talented individual.

All kinds of jobs might fall to the master mason. He was responsible for sourcing the stone and devising the machines for lifting the blocks. He carried with him the "moulds" or templates that were used to mark the uncut pieces of stone. Unlike a modern architect, he had no formal professional training; his skill with stone and his knowledge of geometry and mechanics were all acquired on the job. Master masons worked their way up from the ranks of ordinary masons, and started their careers cutting blocks just like the rest. Moreover, although his skills might elevate him above his peers, a master mason was never entirely removed from the workplace. Even though he might conceive of the design for a whole building, and have hundreds of men working under him, he was not confined to an office; he might still be found, chisel in hand, working alongside his fellows.

Who was Edward I's master mason? Until recently, all that historians had to conjure with was a name: Master James of St. Georges. He first occurs in the records in the spring of 1278, when he appears at Flint and Rhuddlan "to ordain the works of the castles there." After the second Welsh war, he is styled "master of the king's works in Wales," and receives the very high salary of three shillings a day for his efforts. Clearly this is our master mason. But who was he? He appears in 1278 out of nowhere. Where had he come from? Nobody could say until, in the mid-twentieth century, a historian called Arnold Taylor became Chief Inspector of Welsh Monuments (1946–55), and set out to solve the mystery.

In the course of his work, Taylor came to know Edward's Welsh castles inside out. He soon became puzzled by some unusual and apparently unique features. In the first place, he noticed that there were small square holes in the sides of the towers. This in itself was perfectly normal; you find such holes in the sides of castles everywhere. They were for the wooden scaffolding supports or joists to fit into while the castle was being built, and are known as "putlog holes" because (wait for it) they are the holes where they put the logs.

Something, however, was not quite right about the ones at Conwy and Harlech. Normally they wrapped around the walls or towers of a castle at the same horizontal level. At Edward's Welsh castles, however, the holes spiraled around the towers, suggesting that the original scaffolding had been sloped, rather like the slide on a helter-skelter.

There were other oddities. Conwy and Harlech had several archways that were perfectly semicircular. This might not sound especially strange, but Taylor knew from his experience of other castles in England and Wales that such archways were not to be found elsewhere in the UK on buildings of this date. Similarly, Taylor realized that the windows in the great gatehouse at Harlech, as well as being exceedingly large and handsome, were apparently unique. Despite his extensive knowledge of castles, he had never seen anything like them. And then there were the toilets. Nothing unusual there, you might think. Taylor, however, was intrigued by the peculiar projecting funnel-shaped design he saw at Harlech. Again, he'd never seen anything else quite like it.

Could these clues—putlog holes, archways, windows, and toilets—help reveal the identity of Master James of St. Georges? Taylor decided to find out. The evidence in the architecture seemed to suggest that, whatever else he might be, Master James was certainly not British. And so, in the autumn of 1950, Taylor left Britain on a quest to find him. Following what was no more than a strong hunch, he headed for Switzerland, and the tiny alpine province of Savoy.

Today, Savoy is a region shared between Switzerland, Italy, and France. In the thirteenth century, however, it was an independent state, ruled by a dynasty of counts. Although small in size, its position made it powerful. The counts of Savoy controlled the Alpine passes between France and Italy, and therefore controlled traffic and communication between the kings of England and France to the west, and the emperor and the pope to the east.

Even so, it might seem an odd place to go looking for clues about Welsh architecture. Taylor, however, had done his homework. He knew, for example, that since the middle of the thirteenth century, there had been strong ties between the counts of Savoy and the English royal family. Precisely because of their powerful role as brokers of international relations, Henry III had married into the Savoyard family and, for a time, his court was dominated by his relatives from Savoy. Edward grew up in the company of Savoyard uncles and cousins and, when he was king, continued to cultivate the connection between the two dynasties. Many of his best friends were from Savoy, including the great Otto de Grandson, whom Edward put in charge of north Wales after the conquest.

Having reached Savoy, Taylor headed for the eastern edge of Lake Geneva, and the castle of Chillon. As Taylor says in his writings, "It is easier to remember than to communicate one's impressions on visiting this marvelous building for the first time." The castle stands on a small island right by the edge of the lake, and seems to rise directly out of the water, like a ship in harbor. Unlike Edward's castles, it has been much restored and rebuilt since the thirteenth century, but what it occasionally lacks in medieval authenticity it more than compensates for in overall ambience. Seen from the west, framed by the snowy peaks of the Swiss Alps, the castle and its setting are nothing less than breathtaking.

The castle at Chillon was originally established in the first half of the twelfth century, but most of the existing walls and towers were

*Windows at Harlech (left) and Chillon (right).*

built in the middle of the thirteenth century, at the command of the then count, Peter of Savoy. It was here that Arnold Taylor made his first major discovery. Several of the windows, although much restored in the late nineteenth century, were identical in design to those in the gatehouse at Harlech. Not only were they a similar shape; they were exactly the same size. When Taylor measured them from top to bottom, he found that they differed in height from their Welsh equivalents by just a quarter of an inch. Two sets of windows, a thousand miles apart, but with less than half an inch between them—a big clue, surely, that Taylor was on to something.

Other discoveries soon followed. Heading further into the Alps, Taylor came to two smaller castles at La Batiaz and Saillon. Both were built in the thirteenth century by Peter of Savoy as part of his struggle with the bishops of Sion to control the Rhône valley. As castles, neither is as striking as Chillon, but their locations are similarly stunning. La Batiaz is perched dangerously on top of a spur of rock, many hundreds of feet above the small town of Martigny. It was here that Taylor found his second major clue. On the side of the castle walls is a pair of projecting garderobes, built to exactly the same funnel-shaped design as the solitary example at Harlech. Subsequent investigations have uncovered no similar examples. In other words, Taylor had stumbled across another rock-solid, utterly distinctive architectural parallel between the castles of Wales and Savoy.

The final pieces of architectural evidence were located a few miles up the valley in Saillon. A marvelous little place, the town still has an authentic medieval feel, and is built at a ridiculously steep angle on a small foothill of the Alps. Little remains of Peter of Savoy's castle today—just a single round tower. The town walls, however, were also built at that time, and contained all the clues Taylor needed. The towers along the walls had the same spiraling putlog holes as those at Conwy and Harlech, and the arches of the town gates were of the same semi-circular design as the Welsh ones. Furthermore, beyond the clinching evidence of these identical features, the appearance of the walls as a whole gave Taylor

*Garderobes at Harlech (left) and La Batiaz (right).*

an unmistakable feeling of déjà vu: seen from a distance, they are entirely reminiscent of the town walls at Conwy.

All the unusual features of Edward I's Welsh castles, therefore, had identical counterparts in medieval Savoy. What was the connection? The counts of Savoy, like the kings of England, kept detailed financial records of their building projects, and luckily these records still survive in the archives at Turin. It was there that Taylor found the answer. When he unrolled the fragile accounts for the 1260s, he found that Peter of Savoy's castles had been built by two men, a father and son team, called Master John and Master James. The later accounts showed Master James working alone and, in particular, working on a brand new castle site, owned by the counts of Savoy but located over a hundred miles away near the French city of Lyon. The name of this castle was St. Georges-d'Esperanche. This, Taylor recalled with delight, was the very place that, in 1273, Edward I had stopped on his way back from crusade to visit his Savoyard cousin. It seems very likely, since work on the castle was still underway at the time, that the king may have been introduced to a skilled master

*Archways at Saillon (left) and Harlech (right).*

mason and castle-builder par excellence, who went by the name of Master James of St. Georges.

Arnold Taylor's hunch had paid off—he had discovered the true identity and origins of Master James, and proved beyond question that he was one of the world's greatest architects. Not only was he responsible for the great royal castles in Wales; he was also the designer of a string of castles in Savoy. When you look at his early handiwork, you can see how Edward I, traveling through the Alps in 1273, must have been impressed, not to say envious. It is always slightly galling when you drop in on relatives and discover that their new house is quite a lot nicer than yours. Sitting in the magnificent chambers of Chillon Castle, gazing at Lake Geneva through the "Harlech" windows, one is tempted to think the unthinkable. Was Edward really driven by necessity and outraged honor, as he would always claim? Or did he just want a lovely new set of fabulous castles in the mountains, like his cousins?

We will never know. What we do know is that when Edward formulated his castle-building plan in 1278, there was only one man for the job. The king summoned Master James and put him in charge of the entire operation. Since the results were Conwy, Harlech, and Caernarfon, we can say with some confidence that his faith was not

*The town walls at Conwy (top) and Saillon (bottom).*

misplaced. Edward was clearly delighted with the castles because, as well as paying his architect a handsome salary, he also gave him a wonderful gift. In 1290, he appointed Master James as constable of Harlech Castle. What better reward for the architect than to live in the magnificent gatehouse that he himself had created?

Harlech is in some respects Master James's most striking castle, owing largely to its situation on a great outcrop of rock, with views out to sea to the west and vistas of Mount Snowdon to the east.

Impressive as it is, however, the castle was intended to house only a garrison and resident constable—it would have been a little pressed to accommodate the king and his court. At Conwy and Caernarfon, though, the story was different. These were castles built as palaces, where Master James designed and built spectacular suites of rooms for the king, his family, and the royal household.

The best place to appreciate the luxury of Master James's designs is at Conwy, since its royal apartments still survive. Domestic comfort has taken several steps forward since the twelfth century and its great towers. Not only do we find plenty of grand fireplaces, but also many more toilets—even the tiny watching-chamber for the king's chapel is thoughtfully provided with en suite facilities. The biggest advance, however, is in terms of windows. Although the windows on the outside of the castle are few and tiny, the windows on the inner courtyards are large and stately, and would have been fitted throughout with stained glass of many colors.

At Caernarfon, meanwhile, you can appreciate the military sophistication of Master James of St. Georges' design. On the exposed southern side of the castle, two passageways run through the curtain wall for its entire length, one above the other, punctuated at regular intervals with crossbow-loops. The garrison, therefore, with archers and crossbowmen shooting from within the walls as well as behind the battlements on top, had triple the defensive force. On the north side of the castle, the arrangement of the defenses is even more ingenious. What from the outside seems to be a bank of five conventional crossbow-loops is revealed on the inside to be a cunning arrangement of interlocking slots, with each loop capable of being shared by up to three archers. The result, combined again with the potential number of men shooting from the battlements and the towers, has been justly called "one of the most formidable concentrations of 'fire-power' to be found in the Middle Ages."

The best place, however, to stand and admire the military might of Caernarfon Castle is at the main entrance, the so-called King's Gate. Any would-be attacker trying to get in this way was faced

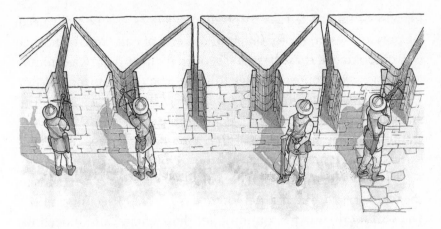

*Soldiers using the crossbow-loops at Caernarfon.*

with a daunting set of obstacles. In the first place, there was the great ditch in front of the gate, which could only be crossed by means of the drawbridge. If, by some miracle, the attacker managed to get past that, he was confronted by five sets of sturdy oak doors, alternated with no fewer than six portcullises. Above his head were holes in the ceiling, called *meutrières* or murder-holes, conventionally believed to have been for boiling oil or rocks, but now generally (and rather boringly) considered to have been water chutes, for use if a fire was started in front of the gates. Even if we grudgingly accept this new hypothesis, we can still draw comfort from the fact that the gatehouse is liberally provided with crossbow loops and flanked by the other mural towers and wall-walks on this side of the castle. Boiling oil or no boiling oil, our would-be assailant was going to have a hard time getting in this way.

The King's Gate is unquestionably a mighty piece of military thinking, but its functions are not purely practical. Above the doors is a carved statue of a king, which makes Caernarfon the earliest example of a castle with an ornamented gatehouse. As with the forebuildings on our twelfth-century castles, this is an entrance designed to impress the friendly visitor as well as deter the attacker. Some of the military paraphernalia can also be read in this way. One portcullis, for example, is a jolly good idea, and two portcullises might likewise be interpreted as very prudent. But does anyone really need six portcullises or, for that matter, five sets of oak doors? Another way of looking at these barriers is to see them as part of a ceremonial procession route. We have to imagine a distinguished visitor entering the castle, and being treated to the spectacle of doors swinging open and portcullises being raised in an intentionally elaborate ballet. It seems clear that a deliberate degree of theatricality has been incorporated into the architect's design.

The sense of drama at Caernarfon's King's Gate in fact extends to the whole castle. The fashion for towers in the thirteenth century, you will recall, was for round rather than square, and indeed we have seen round towers at Caerphilly, Flint, Rhuddlan, Harlech, and Conwy, as well as at Chillon, La Batiaz, and Saillon. Caernarfon's towers, however, are neither round nor square, but polygonal. Some of them have eight sides, and one has a total of ten. Moreover, in the Middle Ages it was typical to finish the walls of a castle with whitewash. At Conwy and Harlech you can still see traces of this original finish (and imagine how different and glorious they would have looked in their heyday). Once again, however, Caernarfon was unusual. Instead of being covered over, the castle's walls were left bare, in order to expose to the outside world the different colored bands of stone in the masonry.

Why was Caernarfon Castle so different to all the others? The answer, it seems, lies in Edward's love of chivalric literature. The king was a big fan of the legendary King Arthur, and on several occasions we can catch him indulging his passion for all things Arthurian. In 1278, despite having plenty of other pressing business, he personally attended the disinterment of two bodies at Glastonbury Abbey, which the monks swore blind were those of Arthur and his queen, Guinevere. After the conquest of Wales in 1283, Edward was ceremonially appeased with a bauble known as "Arthur's Crown," which he subsequently presented at the high altar of Westminster Abbey. The following year, Edward organized a "round-table" tournament in Wales; and the great round table on display in Winchester Castle has recently been scientifically dated to Edward's reign. King Arthur, we should note, was according to legend not simply a king of England, but the king of a united island of Britain, and this alone would have made him an attractive role model for a conquering king like Edward. When he later wrote to the pope to justify his right to rule Scotland, it was the historic precedent of Arthur that Edward cited in his defense.

Edward's enthusiasm for the mythical British past was evidently keenly felt, and without a doubt he had heard an ancient Welsh tale called *The Dream of Macsen Wledig*. It was first written down in the fourteenth century, but had already been current for several hundred years. The story recounts how Macsen (or Maximus), a Roman Emperor, dreamed of traveling from Rome to Wales, until he came to a point where the river met the sea, and saw a great castle, "the fairest castle that mortal had ever seen." The location of this castle, the poet later reveals, was Caernarfon. Edward, therefore, by choosing to build his new castle there, was not only building on top of yet another hall of the Welsh princes; he was making this ancient legend come true by building his own fairy-tale castle, like the one in Macsen's dream. Macsen's status as a Roman emperor is reflected in the decoration of Caernarfon's largest tower, which is topped with stone carvings of imperial eagles, and appropriately called the Eagle Tower.

The cleverest part, however, is the message hidden in the banded masonry and the polygonal towers. According to the same Welsh legends, the Emperor Macsen was the son of the Emperor Constantine, celebrated not only as the first Christian emperor, but also as the founder of the new imperial capital of Constantinople (modern Istanbul). There is no indication that Edward ever visited this city, but someone in his entourage clearly knew what the walls there looked like. They have banded masonry, and polygonal towers. Caernarfon, even though it stands at the opposite end of Europe, is an unmistakable echo of Constantine's imperial city.

The big question is, of course, who came up with these ideas? It is totally unanswerable and therefore all the more intriguing. We might be tempted to ascribe all the invention to Master James, but

*Polygonal towers and banded masonry:*
*Caernarfon (top) and Constantinople (bottom).*

it was clearly Edward himself and not his master mason who was inspired by King Arthur. We might imagine Master James coming over from Savoy with a set of sketches tucked under his arm, but again this is highly unlikely. At Harlech, Conwy, and Caernarfon, each castle is built to fit the platform of rock on which it stands, and therefore much of the design had to be worked out on the spot.

The great tower at Rochester, seen from inside the castle's bailey, showing its prominent forebuilding. *Photo credit: Jeremy Ashbee.*

ABOVE: Conwy. *Photo credit: GailJohnson/Bigstock.com.*

BELOW: Harlech, with the mountains of Snowdonia in the distance. *Photo credit: Marc Morris.*

ABOVE: Caernarfon. *Photo credit: Marc Morris.*

BELOW: Beaumaris. *Photo credit: Marc Morris.*

ABOVE: Bodiam. *Photo credit: WyrdLight.com.*

BELOW: Chillon. *Photo courtesy of Chillon Castle.*

ABOVE: Threave—the fourteenth-century tower house with its fifteenth-century artillery wall. *Photo credit: mobil61/Bigstock.com.*

BELOW: Urquhart, with the Grant Tower in the distance. *Photo credit: johnbraid/Bigstock.com.*

Craigievar. *Photo credit: Circumnavigation/Bigstock.com.*

Raglan—the main gate. *Photo credit: Cadw: Welsh Historic Monuments.*

ABOVE: A victim of the Civil War: Pontefract as it appeared on the eve of the conflict. *Photo credit: Wakefield MDC Museum.*

BELOW: Pontefact—a view of the site today. *Photo credit: Bob Yarwood, WYAS Archaeological Services.*

Moreover, there is no indication from his work in Savoy that Master James had ever designed or built a twin-towered gatehouse before he came to England. The fact that he constructed such gatehouses at Harlech and Rhuddlan suggests he was open to new ideas, or tried hard to incorporate his patron's wishes. Later, when Edward was at war with the Scots and needed a castle at Linlithgow, he wrote a letter to Master James telling him precisely what kind of design he wanted, specifying (among other things) the depth of the ditch and the number of towers. There is no doubt that Edward had similarly strong views about what he wanted in Wales, and gave equally detailed orders to his master mason.

At Conwy and Caernarfon, Edward ordered Master James not only to build new castles, but also to lay out whole new towns. In each case, large new settlements were created, surrounded by handsome sets of town walls. These walls, which still stand today to a remarkable degree of completeness, were built in the earliest stages of the construction process, in order to protect the workers from attack while the rest of the work was carried out. Their impressive scale is reflected not only in their present appearance, but also in their original cost. The Caernarfon walls alone cost £2,100.

Edward wanted new towns in Wales for several reasons. On the one hand, building new boroughs was an attempt to make his castles self-sufficient. With a prosperous town on the doorstep importing goods from all over Europe, a garrison could be kept supplied with food, wine, and other essentials throughout the year. Most of the things that English soldiers wanted or needed could not be bought locally, and this itself was a symptom of the larger problem that the new towns were intended to remedy: the Welsh. Seen through the eyes of thirteenth-century Englishmen, the Welsh were an utterly barbarous bunch. For example, rather than getting down to the serious business of cultivating fields and growing crops, they preferred to stand around all day tending sheep. Consequently, rather than enjoying a civilized English diet (which included, among other things, wine and bread), the Welsh had only meat and milk. Likewise, when it came to religion, they had Christianity so back to front that they could hardly be considered Christians at all. From an English point of view, the conquest was just about the best thing that could have happened to Wales. It was, admittedly, a strong medicine for the Welsh, but one that would eventually make them better people.

Towns, it was felt, were the best way to begin improving the moral fiber of the natives—even the archbishop of Canterbury heartily endorsed the idea. Once exposed to civic life, the Welsh would come to experience English standards of decency, understand the way normal people behaved and, in time, it was hoped, start to act like upright Englishmen. This did not mean, however, that the Welsh were expected to actually live in the towns—good heavens, no! Edward's new boroughs were inhabited exclusively by English colonists, who were given generous tax breaks to induce them to come and set up shop in Wales. The Welsh, it was intended, would come into the towns only to buy or sell goods, encouraged by laws that made it illegal to trade anywhere else. To any right-thinking person, this seemed to be a win-win situation. The English burgesses had a monopoly that would guarantee their prosperity, and the Welsh had no excuse not to come into town and be dazzled by the bright lights of civilization.

What it meant in practice, of course, was that the Welsh came to hate the towns. Obliged to trade within their walls, yet at the same time denied any of the privileges of the English mercantile elite, the Welsh quickly singled out the towns as the source of their oppression. If the subtler symbolism of polygonal towers, banded masonry, and imperial eagles was lost on them, the overall message sent out by the castles and their attendant towns was abundantly clear: Wales was now a conquered nation, ruled by an arrogant alien power. Inevitably, it was a message they chose to resist. In 1294, the Welsh rose again as a nation, venting their fury on both the towns and the castles. In the winter of that year, Edward's iron ring of fortresses was put to the ultimate test.

———

This revolt had a leader of sorts—a distant cousin of Llywelyn ap Gruffudd called Madog ap Llywelyn, who began styling himself as prince of Wales. Madog, however, was only small fry; the rebellion he claimed to lead was actually much bigger than he was. It was a true national rising, a series of carefully coordinated attacks on the new English settlements. Harlech, Conwy, and Caernarfon were all targeted. The Welsh scored a major victory when the walls of Caernarfon, still not finished, were breached and thrown down. Both town and castle were overrun, the burgesses and royal officials massacred, and the fabric of the castle despoiled.

Edward, as you can well imagine, was livid when he heard the news. Apart from the fact that Caernarfon was his pride and joy, he was busy getting ready for a fight with the king of France; the Welsh uprising meant that this new war would now have to wait. However, with large numbers of men and equipment already mustered, the English king was well equipped to deal with the Welsh revolt. His response was, in fact, the largest deployment of troops in Wales so far, with numbers even exceeding those of the conquest campaign of 1282. A total of thirty-five thousand men were re-routed and sent west. From Chester, the king set out at the head of a northern army of sixteen thousand, determined to retake his castles.

Everything went smoothly until the king reached Conwy, at which point disaster struck. The English supply lines, which stretched all the way back to Chester, were cut by an attack from the Welsh, trapping Edward and his large army in the town and in the castle. For the first time in decades, the Welsh had the upper hand, and it looked like the unthinkable might happen: the English king who never backed down might be forced into a humiliating surrender.

Edward tried to improve his chances of survival by dismissing half his army, but this purge still left him with eight thousand hungry mouths to feed. With the majority of men living in tents, in close quarters with animals and without proper sanitation, there was also the risk of losing hundreds, even thousands, to disease. To make matters worse, it was starting to turn bitterly cold. According to contemporary chroniclers, the winter of 1294 was particularly appalling.

One chronicler, Walter of Guisborough, describes how, as the dead of winter approached, supplies of wine had almost run out. When only one barrel remained in the castle, the soldiers set it aside for the king. Edward, however (great guy that he was) would have none of it, and ordered instead that it be shared out among his men. The story is typically heroic stuff and probably a fabrication (Walter is a great storyteller, but his tales are notoriously tall). It does, however, serve to underline the increasing desperateness of the king's situation. The days and weeks that Edward spent at Conwy must have been dark ones. As he sat in his new great hall, trying to jolly his knights along, he must surely have remembered his father's failures in Wales. Castles like Deganwy, then only recently constructed, had been besieged and destroyed. English troops, ill equipped and ill supplied, had frozen and starved to death. Royal armies, surrounded on all sides by hostile forces, were forced into ignominious retreat. Was history about to repeat itself? Were he and his army about to suffer the same fate?

The answer, in the end, was no—though in the early days it was a close-run thing. The king and his army ultimately survived for two reasons. In the first place, Edward could command enormous resources from the rest of his empire. It was a huge logistical exercise for his government ministers, but ships eventually sailed into Conwy harbor carrying grain and vegetables, wine, chicken, and fish. They came not just from English ports like Bristol and Chester, but from the king's colonies further afield in Ireland and Gascony. Secondly, the ships on this occasion could actually get to the troops, because both the town and castle of Conwy were located right on the seashore. Edward's choice of site, when put to the test, proved to be a very good one. After three months cooped up in a city of tents, rather than suffering, the king's troops actually ended up with more than they could eat. By the start of the spring, the town's quayside was awash with unwanted food. Huge piles of grain had been dumped there and, having become wet in the April rains, had sprouted shoots; they now resembled little hills. The harbor stank of rotting fish that nobody wanted to buy, even at knock-down prices. Logistically, this is still extremely impressive stuff. Edward had fielded a total of thirty-five thousand men, and no one had gone hungry.

In the spring, the king's army rode out to find the revolt practically over. Most of the fighting had been done by the other commanders while Edward was holed up in Conwy. The king ordered the execution of the ringleaders—though not, surprisingly, Madog ap Llywelyn: he was carted off to London, destined for imprisonment in the Tower. Harsh penalties were inflicted on local communities, with hundreds of hostages being taken and heavy fines imposed.

The community that suffered most from these repercussions was the town of Llanfaes. Situated on the eastern tip of the island of Anglesey, it had been the most prosperous native settlement in Wales. It had also been one of the centers of the rebellion, a fact that the townspeople had highlighted when they lynched their English sheriff at the start of the revolt. Anglesey had exposed itself as the weak link in Edward's chain of defenses, and the king responded accordingly. He decided to build one last great fortress, and made a deliberate point of destroying Llanfaes in the process. The result was Beaumaris—Master James of St. Georges' most perfectly conceived castle.

The name Beaumaris, which literally means "pretty marsh," is an indication of the principal problem that the new site presented to the master mason. Unlike Caernarfon, Conwy, and Harlech, which all offered rocky platforms on which to build, the flat and marshy land around Llanfaes offered few natural advantages. It did, however, mean that there were no restrictions when it came to shape, and so Master James was able to create a perfectly symmetrical building. In the eyes of many, Beaumaris is the ultimate concentric castle, with two great gatehouses, drum towers on each corner, and

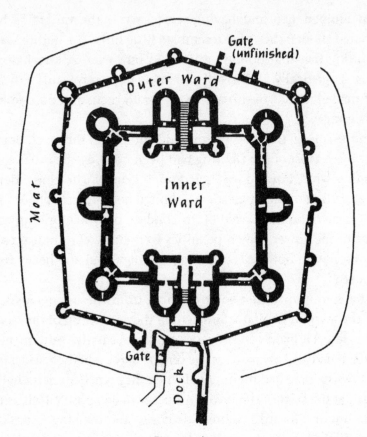

*Beaumaris.*

an outer wall that runs for a quarter of a mile. The architect compensated for the absence of rock-solid foundations by surrounding the whole structure with a moat. He also provided the castle with its own deep-water harbor, so that ships of up to forty tons in weight could get supplies right up to the watergate.

In terms of construction, Beaumaris was the biggest challenge to date. Not only did Edward demand that building was carried out at relentless speed; the castle's island location meant that most of the stone had to be delivered by water, which caused costs to soar. In the first six months of building, the work absorbed £7,800, and over a quarter of this sum was spent on transportation of materials. At one point there were almost three thousand men working at

Beaumaris, the biggest workforce yet deployed by a king who had already smashed all previous records.

By the late 1290s, Edward's massive resources were stretched to the breaking point. As well as pouring more men and money into Wales, the king was also engaged in wars against the Scots and the French. Fighting on so many fronts at once brought opposition from his subjects in England, who had become tired of footing the bill for such costly campaigns. Although Edward weathered the political storm, it left Master James trying to cope with an ever-worsening cash crisis. In February 1296, the architect wrote to the officials of the Exchequer in Westminster with a desperate plea for more money.

"If our lord the king," he began, "wants the work to be finished as quickly as it should be, and on the scale which it has been commenced, we could not make do with less than £250 a week."

Anticipating the objections of the money-men, he reminded them that he had to pay four hundred masons, two hundred quarrymen, thirty smiths, and three thousand others, including carpenters, plasterers, and general laborers. Moreover, fear was starting to get to these men. With Wales only recently pacified, they were surrounded by a deeply hostile population. Despite the presence of ten mounted sergeants, twenty crossbowmen and one hundred footsoldiers, Master James still had doubts about their safety.

"As to how things are in the land of Wales, we still cannot be sure," he said. "As you know, Welshmen are Welshmen." Having put down his pen, the mason picked it up once more to add a heartfelt postscript. "My lords, for God's sake be quick with the money," he scribbled. "Otherwise everything done up to now will have been to no avail!"

The letter obviously did the trick. Edward made sure that Master James got the money he needed, and building work at Beaumaris went on. At the same time, repairs were under way at Caernarfon— over £1,000 was spent rebuilding the town's damaged walls, and the building of the castle continued apace. Notwithstanding the distractions in Scotland and France, and despite cutbacks in all other areas, the king continued to pour men and materials into Wales. Year by year, his two greatest castles grew steadily more grand.

By 1305, Edward's imperial vision had almost been realized. He had conquered Wales, eliminated its rulers, and crushed all trace of rebellion. Six great stone castles stood finished, and two more were nearing completion. By this date, Edward had also added Scotland to his dominions. The northern kingdom, after nine years of spirited resistance, had finally been bludgeoned into submission. Londoners who had grown bored gaping at Llywelyn ap Gruffudd's skeletal features could now venture down to London Bridge, where William Wallace's freshly severed head was the latest grisly attraction. To us, his actions may make Edward seem like a bloody tyrant, a Caligula or a Stalin. But many contemporaries saw it differently. For patriotic Englishmen, Edward had become what he had always aspired to be—a new Arthur, ruling over a united kingdom of Britain.

It was, however, a fleeting vision. Even as the king clutched at his dream, it slipped through his fingers. In 1306, the Scots rose in rebellion. Edward moved north to crush it, but he grew ill in the course of the summer and, although his armies had some notable successes, the revolt was not extinguished. Christmas was spent at Lanercost, and the following spring Edward crossed to Carlisle, planning to lead a fresh expedition into Galloway. At that point, however, time caught up with the sixty-eight-year-old king. On July 7, at Burgh-by-Sands on the Cumbrian coast, Edward himself was conquered.

Just eighteen months later, Master James of St. Georges, the genius behind the king's Welsh castles and one of the greatest architects of the European Middle Ages, followed his employer to the grave. Neither Caernarfon nor Beaumaris was ever finished. Work at both castles ground on for another two decades, but the vast river of money no longer flowed as freely. By the 1320s, it had slowed to a tiny trickle, and ten years later it stopped completely: building on both sites was abandoned forever. Today the castles still stand incomplete, their appearance much as it was seven centuries ago. At Caernarfon, the majestic outer walls conceal an interior only half-realized. The royal apartments intended for the upper ward were never built, and the gatehouses, so imposing from the outside, have the feel of a movie set when viewed from behind. At Beaumaris, the inner walls, which had grown to about half their intended height, simply stop at the same horizontal level. You can almost picture the workmen packing up their tools and going home.

In one sense, Edward's great chain of castles did their job. As tools of conquest, they were supremely successful. The Welsh never drove the English out, and their country continued to be ruled by foreigners. As royal palaces, however, Edward's castles can only be viewed as failures. Their great halls, intended for feasting and revelry, stood empty. Their suites of chambers, designed for luxurious living, were never finished. The king had imagined royal visits on a grand scale; Beaumaris was to have accommodation enough for five separate royal households. But future kings and queens of England stayed away, preferring their comfortable homes in southern England to Edward's windswept white elephants in northwest Wales. Within a few generations, the castles were falling into ruin, reduced to the role of administrative outposts in a failing English empire. Ultimately, despite spending enormous sums of money on huge armies and spectacular castles, Edward's dreams died with him.

Never again would a king of England attempt to build a castle on the scale of Caernarfon. In the fourteenth century, Edward's successors learnt to accept that, in reality, their power in Britain stopped at England's borders. Instead of expanding northward and westward, they turned their attentions south and east, and began once again to exercise their ambitions on the Continent. The result was endless war in France, unbroken peace at home—and a brand new breed of castle.

# CHAPTER FOUR

# AN ENGLISHMAN'S HOME

—⟨∿∿⟩—

B odiam Castle is one of the most famous, most photogenic, and most visited castles in Britain. One look at it and it is easy to see why: it is what you might call a pin-up castle. Ravishing good looks have made it a firm favorite with calendar compilers and magazine picture editors; it has charmed its way onto the cover of many a book. A stunning setting in the middle of a mirror-like moat, especially magical on cold mornings when the mist hangs around the walls, has guaranteed top billing in pop videos, TV series, and Hollywood feature films. Some castles can look tough, others can look homely, but few can manage both at the same time. Bodiam can, but then Bodiam has star quality—it's a true celebrity.

All this attention would have much gratified the castle's builder, Sir Edward Dallingridge, who, in his own day, was just as much of a celebrity as his castle is now. Just as Bodiam is a great example of a castle from the late Middle Ages, so Edward Dallingridge is a perfect example of a late medieval castle-builder. Castles in the fourteenth and fifteenth centuries tended to be built not by kings, dukes and earls—who, after all, had plenty of them already—but by men like Sir Edward: individuals who stood on the lower rungs of the aristocracy, but were determined to climb higher.

Bodiam and Dallingridge belong, essentially, to Chaucer's England. It is an age we associate with good times, largely because of the lively characters, vivid colors, and bawdy humor of Chaucer's *Canterbury Tales*. Chaucer's England is "Merrie England"—a golden age, yet to be tarnished by the dynastic struggles of the fifteenth century, or the religious upheavals of the Tudor period. Yet in fact, these times were far from trouble-free. The story of Dallingridge and Bodiam is played out against a backdrop of invasion threats, revolting peasants, and rebellion against the king.

More important, Edward Dallingridge was not a fuzzy idealized character like Chaucer's knight in the *Canterbury Tales*. He was a real flesh-and-blood individual, with genuine ambitions and legitimate anxieties. He and his friends and family lived in an age which has left a rich seam of documentary evidence, enabling us to view their lives inside and outside the castle in a way that is impossible for earlier periods. We know not only what they ate and drank, but the exact recipes they followed, the actual songs they sang, even some of the things they believed in.

In some respects, Bodiam is similar to the castles featured in the previous chapter. Both Edward Dallingridge and Edward I asked for castles built to an enclosure design; at Bodiam, as at Beaumaris, there is no trace of a keep. There is, however, one very important difference, and it springs from the contrasting priorities of the two Edwards. The king's castles were constructed as weapons of conquest, and it is quite clear that military considerations were uppermost in the master mason's mind. Caernarfon, Conwy, and Harlech were made all the mightier by being built to fit platforms of rock. All three castles therefore have irregular ground plans and, as a result, some rather unusually shaped rooms. Take, for example, the great hall at Conwy Castle, which is banana shaped. This peculiar layout, one imagines, was not an essential part of Edward's design brief. Clearly what happened was that the castle's exterior wall was given top priority, and the great hall was built to follow a predetermined curvy profile. At the king's other castles, the halls and chambers were similarly squeezed inside restrictive military straitjackets.

At Bodiam, however, the thinking was the other way around. Far from being a peculiar shape, the castle is very regular and symmetrical; seen from above, it looks almost perfectly square (in fact, it's rectangular—the east and west walls are 10 percent longer than the north and south). The chambers, hall, and chapel are all well proportioned, and arranged to serve each other perfectly. It therefore seems that more importance has been attached to the accommodation than to the exterior walls. The starting point was a well-ordered courtyard, and the castle walls were simply wrapped around the outside. In fact, if you look at the plan of Bodiam, and ignore the gatehouse, towers, and turrets, it starts to look very much like a courtyard house.

The courtyard design originated in the fourteenth century, and was first used by the builders of manor houses and colleges. It soon became the most popular shape for castle designers, too, and in this respect Bodiam can claim to be a "typical" castle of its time. There were, however, plenty of alternative models for castle-builders to follow. In the fourteenth and fifteenth centuries, masons were having so much fun experimenting with form that it becomes very difficult to generalize about their designs at all. We find courtyard castles up and down the country, at places like Maxstoke (Warwickshire), Sheriff Hutton (Yorkshire), and Cooling (Kent); they are especially common in the south of England. We also find great towers making a spectacular comeback at places like Tattershall (Lincolnshire), Ashby de la Zouche (Leicestershire) and Raglan (Monmouthshire—see Chapter Six). Other castles built in this period simply defy classification; try as we might, it is impossible to pigeon-hole castles like Nunney (Somerset), Old Wardour (Wiltshire), and Warkworth (Northumbria). Bodiam belongs to an age of great variety and individualism.

However, the big question that has been raised about many of these castles is this: Are they really castles at all? Bodiam itself has been one of the main battlegrounds for debate. For more than a century now, the building has taken a heavy pounding from harsh critics, who have sought to expose its weaknesses and undermine its military reputation. At the same time, it has been staunchly defended by legions of doughty admirers. If you are writing about Bodiam, therefore, you have no choice—you must strap on your armor, and step bravely into the fray.

On first inspection, the castle's defenders seem to have the upper hand. Bodiam, surely, must be a castle. After all, it appears to have everything: towers on every corner, a fine pair of gatehouses, battlements along every wall, and, of course, a splendid moat. If you made a list of features you might expect to see in a castle, Bodiam would get a check in almost every box.

Ah, yes, say the critics, but do these features work? If you take a circular stroll around the castle and, like a hostile attacker, look for weak spots, they are many and obvious. The southern and eastern walls of the castle are punctuated by two huge windows—equal in size to the palatial windows at Conwy but, crucially, on the outside. Nor are they the only weak points. The rest of the windows may look small in comparison (perhaps suggesting a concern with defense), but they are windows nonetheless, not arrow-loops. Arrow- or crossbow-loops are conspicuously lacking at Bodiam: there is little sense of the castle taking the fight to the enemy, as there is at Caernarfon. Bodiam does not even score very highly when it comes to passive defense. The walls are nowhere more than a few feet thick, and the parapets, with a thickness of barely twelve inches, are positively weedy.

It is the castle's moat, however, which has been the focus of the critics' attack. Moats of an earlier age were conceived as defensive barriers—intended, as at Caerphilly and Beaumaris, to impede access to the walls and to frustrate attempts at undermining. The moat at Bodiam is a less convincing obstacle. At six feet deep, it is no puddle, and looks sufficiently broad to deter the average medieval house-breaker; but in fact, it would have been far easier to deal with than the massive water defenses of thirteenth-century castles. The chief problem is that it could be easily drained. The castle is built on sloping ground, which falls away from north to south, and the moat is held in place by a man-made bank at the southern end. This bank is all that stops the water flowing away to join the River Rother at the bottom of the hill. As barriers go, it is not particularly thick or strong; the sides are not reinforced with stonework. It is argued, therefore, that a small group of men working with picks and shovels could have cut through it in the space of a day (or a long night, if they wanted cover of darkness). Deprived of its moat, the castle would be an easy (if rather muddy) target. Mud, however, was not really much of a hindrance—using tree-branches and planking, an organized attacker could quickly lay a carpet of makeshift duckboards and create a path to the foot of the walls.

So is there anything to be said for Bodiam's defenses? The castle, seen from the north, would certainly have us think so. While getting into the building today is literally straightforward (a wooden bridge runs directly from the north bank of the moat right up to

*A gun-loop in Bodiam's main gatehouse.*

the gatehouse), in the Middle Ages it was a good deal more com-plicated. Medieval visitors had to start on the west bank and cross a long bridge in front of the castle. This led to a small octagonal island where they turned through ninety degrees to face the castle directly. The approach was, however, protected by a barbican (an outer gatehouse). Only having passed through this could visitors proceed toward the castle's main gate.

This gatehouse, on first inspection, has all the paraphernalia of military might that we saw at Caernarfon—oak doors, portcullises (three of them), and murder-holes. What's more, because it was built a hundred years after Edward's great Welsh castles, it also has a couple of new tricks up its sleeve. In the first place, there are gun-loops. Guns and gunpowder arrived in western Europe in the fourteenth century, and Bodiam is one of the earliest English castles to make provision for this new type of weapon. The castle's other up-to-date feature is at the top of the gatehouse. Here the masonry stands proud from the wall, as if the building is wearing a crown. It is a feature known as "machicolation," and is a stone version of the wooden hoardings that were built around the tops of earlier towers. Rather like murder-holes, machicolation offered the defenders another vantage point from which to drop things on to the heads of people standing underneath.

So it seems that full marks go to Bodiam's architect for making the main gate secure. Or do they? A more careful inspection of this impressive entrance raises all kinds of questions. For example, looking at the gatehouse from outside, you might think the gap between the bridge and the castle was crossed by means of a drawbridge. I certainly assumed as much on my first visit to the castle, because the front of the gatehouse is recessed as if to accommodate a drawbridge in the upright position. Look closely, however, and you discover that there are no holes in the stonework for the all-important drawbridge chains. Look closer still, and you realize that there is no room in the gatehouse to house a drawbridge mechanism. The gap, we are forced to conclude, must have been bridged by something much less elaborate and much weaker—a simple removable wooden gantry.

The drawbridge problem is merely the clearest example of how the gatehouse's swagger in fact conceals a weak design. Other features are similarly duplicitous. The masonry only allows for thin wooden doors, and provides no means for effectively barring them. The murder-holes look rather too small and mannered to be effective, and would hardly deter a determined intruder. The gun-loops and the machicolation might have offered some protection, but they only defend the gatehouse itself—the rest of the castle remains totally unprotected.

What really undermines our confidence in the main gatehouse, however, is its smaller counterpart on the opposite side of the castle. The rear entrance not only shows the same structural weaknesses— no drawbridge, thin doors, and puny murder-holes; it doesn't even bother with the elaboration of the main gate. The bridge ran directly up to the doorway, there is only room for one portcullis, and there are no gun-loops at all. This is the real clincher—why go to all the trouble of securing the front door if you are going to leave the back door unlocked? We can only conclude that all the elaborate features on the north of the castle, including the complex bridge arrangements, were intended not to keep out undesirables but to impress distinguished guests.

In this respect, there is no doubt that Bodiam must have worked a treat. For all its apparent weaknesses, the gatehouse is very impressive—tall, dramatic, and menacing. Despite its evident vulnerability, the moat still glistens and shimmers in the sunshine, and the castle's appearance is greatly enhanced by its reflection in the water. The walls and towers may be thin and indefensible, but they are tall and sheer, their height exaggerated by a host of tiny battlemented turrets and chimneys. Moreover, Bodiam's determination to strike a pose extends beyond its walls and moat. The castle once stood at the center of a carefully planned and skillfully sculpted landscape of gardens and ponds. The ponds have now disappeared, their banks long since broken. Recent topographical surveys, however, have revealed their true extent—an elaborate series of water features, created to increase the castle's dramatic effect.

The lack of viable defenses at Bodiam is quite typical of late medieval castles. So why were they so weedy? It was, in part, because of a change in military tactics. When politics in England broke down in the twelfth and thirteenth centuries, the first response on all sides was to rush to castles and try to hold them against the enemy. Warfare revolved around castles, and resulted in spectacular sieges like Rochester (1215), Dover (1216), and Kenilworth (1266). By the fourteenth century, however, the goalposts had shifted. With advances in siege technology, fewer and fewer commanders were willing to put their trust in castles, however strong they might appear. Instead, they preferred to fight pitched battles in the open field. Such encounters were liable to be far more decisive than before, because they had become far more bloody. By the start of the fourteenth century, the chivalric taboo on killing a defeated opponent had been quietly forgotten (largely thanks to Edward I, if you ask me).

The biggest reason, however, for the decline of serious fortification in England is that there was not really much fighting going on. Although the fourteenth century got off to a disastrous start during the reign of Edward II, and despite the bad press it has often received, late medieval England was fundamentally a peaceful place to live. In such circumstances, huge, elaborate, and expensive fortifications became unnecessary.

Bodiam, then, might talk tough, but it would not have been much good in a real fight. It is a castle that is more concerned with dazzling us with its good looks than it is with keeping us out.

Does this mean, then, that we should not describe it as a castle? As I said in the introduction, I really don't think so. Bodiam's status only becomes a problem if we adhere to the old-fashioned view that a castle must be built with defense in mind. If, on the other hand, we pay less attention to our own definitions, and ask what contemporaries thought, the problem disappears. Edward Dallingridge clearly believed he had built a castle and, more importantly, so did his contemporaries. It hardly mattered to them whether or not Bodiam's defenses worked. The fact that it had them was enough.

However, this does beg a whole host of other questions. If defenses were becoming unnecessary, why bother building them? Why construct a castle, when you could have had a nice little courtyard house or, for that matter, a grand palace? The answers to these questions are tougher and more complicated. The best way to answer them is to look at the needs, lifestyles, and personalities of late medieval aristocrats, and try to work out why they still wanted to build castles.

By 1385, Sir Edward Dallingridge wanted to build a castle. He was around forty years old, and had just about everything else he could possibly want—a rich wife, a strapping son, bags of money, and plenty of political influence. A prosperous Sussex knight, he mixed with the great and the good in his county, and was beginning to make his mark on the national stage. All he needed now, he reasoned, was a fabulous new home, and so that year he began to build Bodiam.

The Dallingridge family, however, had not always had it so good. A century before, they had been little more than prosperous peasants. Edward's great-grandfather had been a mere forester, possessing a few acres at a place called Dalling Ridge (near East Grinstead). When he died at the end of the thirteenth century, he left his descendants little more than the family name.

Over the next three generations, however, the Dallingridges pulled themselves up by their bootstraps by making really good marriages. Edward's grandfather John did very well for himself when he married the daughter of a local knight. By the time he died in the autumn of 1335, the family's fortunes had substantially improved, and John had taken to advertising his newfound importance with a coat of arms, borrowed from his father-in-law. Edward's father, Roger Dallingridge, did even better. He married not once but twice, first a rich heiress and second to a rich widow. By the middle of the fourteenth century, the Dallingridges had become thoroughly respectable. Roger served as both a justice of the peace and sheriff of Sussex, and ended his days as a member of Parliament.

But it was Edward himself who made the last and biggest leap forward. In 1364 he married Elizabeth Wardieu, a very wealthy young lady indeed; she was heiress not just to lands in Sussex, but also to estates in Kent, Northamptonshire, Leicestershire, and Rutland. When her father died in 1377, Edward acquired the lot, and three years later he entered into his own paternal inheritance. Edward also outperformed his ancestors by becoming the first Dallingridge ever to take up the distinction of knighthood.

You can see how much pride Edward took in his family's achievement when you look at the front of Bodiam Castle. Above the doors of the main gatehouse are three carved shields.

The one in the middle is Edward's own coat of arms, inherited from his father and acquired by his grandfather. To the left and right are the coats of arms of Edward's wife, Elizabeth, and his mother, Alice. Together, these three shields celebrate how far the Dallingridges had come in just a hundred years.

While Edward was rich, however, he wasn't super-rich. His estates were worth at least £200 a year, but that placed him on only the lower rungs of the aristocracy. He was a prosperous knight, but still a knight and not a titled nobleman. Men like him generally had to content themselves with manor houses rather than castles, because castles cost thousands and thousands of pounds. This, then, is the first part of the mystery—how could Edward Dallingridge, knight, afford to pay for Bodiam Castle?

Several options were open to him. It is quite possible that he borrowed some money, either locally from friends or from moneylenders in London. We know that from 1381, as part of his drive to develop the Bodiam estate, he began to sell off his wife's properties in the Midlands, and this would have raised quite a lot of cash.

Edward had also made plenty of money from another source. Once again, the clues lie in the castle's heraldry. Around the back of the castle, above the doorway of the rear gatehouse, are three more stone shields.

Those on the left and right are blank, but the angled one in the middle has a heraldic design carved onto it. It is the coat of arms of Robert Knowles, perhaps the most notorious individual of his age. Born and bred in Cheshire of peasant stock, Knowles, like Dallingridge, had taken the quick route to fame and riches. His rapid rise was due to his skill as a soldier—a soldier of fortune. He owed his reputation to his own savagery; even in a brutal age, Knowles stood out as a man more brutal than any other. His fortune had been gained through making war in France—raiding cities, towns, and villages, burning and destroying, plundering and looting, ransoming and killing. French peasants, it was said, would throw themselves into the river at the very mention of his name.

His arms are displayed over the postern gate at Bodiam because, for a time, he was Edward Dallingridge's captain in a conflict known as the Hundred Years' War. Edward had been in France with Knowles, indulging in the same get-rich-quick schemes, and committing the same atrocities. Pretty little Bodiam, England's favorite fairy-tale castle, was built with blood money.

The Hundred Years' War is not, obviously, a contemporary term. It was, like most convenient historical tags, invented in the nineteenth century by a French historian to describe a series of intermittent wars between England and France in the late Middle Ages. As such tags go, the Hundred Years' War is tolerably accurate (the wars started in 1337 or 1340, depending on your viewpoint, and lasted until 1453) and perfectly serviceable.

The origins of the conflict can be traced as far back as the Norman Conquest. William the Conqueror may have been king of England, but he was also duke of Normandy, and he and his successors continued to hold extensive lands in what is now modern France. These reached their greatest extent under Henry II who, through a combination of great skill and sheer good luck, ended up with more lands in France than the king of France himself. King John, with characteristic incompetence, managed to lose most of his father's Continental possessions, and from the start of the thirteenth century English kings controlled only a narrow strip of coast in the area of southwest France known as Gascony.

By the reign of Edward I, even holding on to Gascony was starting to become difficult. As king of England, Edward bowed to no one, but as duke of Gascony, he was in theory answerable to the king of France. From the end of the thirteenth century, the kings of France began to get designs on Gascony, and sought every excuse to interfere in the duchy's politics on the grounds of their legal superiority.

From an English point of view, the situation looked insoluble; then, abruptly, the picture was transformed. France had been blessed with an unbroken succession of kings since the tenth century, but in 1328, the French suddenly found they had run out of candidates. In the event, they neatly stepped around the problem, anointing a cousin of the old king as their new monarch. This maneuver, however, involved overlooking the claims of another candidate, King Edward III of England, who was the nephew of the late French king. For Edward, this was great news—the perfect answer to the problem of his Continental lands. Never mind his ancient right to rule Gascony; he now had a claim to rule all of France.

It is one thing to lay claim to France; getting hold of it is much more difficult. But to everyone's surprise (not least that of the French), Edward did remarkably well, roundly defeating his opponents in major battles at Crécy (1346) and Poitiers (1356). The high point of the English king's campaigns came in 1360, when he was recognized as independent ruler of most of south-western France.

It was at this juncture that Edward Dallingridge made his first appearance in the war—or at least, so he claimed. Giving testimony as a witness in a court case in 1386, Dallingridge stated that he had been with Edward III's army when it was camped outside Paris in the winter of 1359–60. He also stated for the record that his age was forty, which would have made him just thirteen at the time of his Parisian debut. This sounds rather fishy. Either his evidence was bent, or vanity got the better of him. The first official record we have of Edward crossing the Channel comes eight years later in 1367.

If, however, we take Sir Edward at his word, and suppose that his baptism of fire was indeed in 1359–60, he would have had the opportunity to join Robert Knowles during the most profitable period of his career. After the battle of Poitiers in 1356, the French royal government had totally collapsed, and the whole of the country was given over to anarchy. Such circumstances offered untold opportunities for men like Knowles, and Dallingridge, to make themselves a fortune. Banding together in large well-organized gangs (known as the Free Companies), they moved through the French countryside looting, plundering, and killing as they went.

"They would order villages great or small to ransom themselves," wrote one French monk, "and buy back the bodies, goods, and stores of every inhabitant, or see them burned, as they had been in so many other places. The people appeared before the Englishmen, confused and terrified. They agreed to pay in coin, flour, grain, or other victuals in return for a temporary respite from persecution. Those who stood in their way the English killed, or locked away in dark cells, threatening them daily with death, beating, and maiming, and leaving them hungry and destitute."

From 1360, England and France were nominally at peace, but this hardly mattered to Knowles and his gang. According to the contemporary French chronicler Jean de Froissart, the mercenary Englishman would boast that he fought for neither the king of France nor the king of England, but for himself. Setting up camp in Brittany in western France, Knowles continued to lead raids into the interior for a further twelve months. He returned to England in 1361, having already made a vast fortune. The Free Companies, however, continued to operate in his absence, and Knowles himself returned to the fray in the 1370s and 1380s when war was officially resumed.

In such circumstances, there was plenty of opportunity for Edward Dallingridge to make a mint, regardless of when his career actually started. We know from English Crown records that he crossed the Channel to fight at least six times during the 1360s and 1370s, participating on one occasion in a five hundred-mile march from Bordeaux to Calais and seizing a French ship, *La Seinte Anne*, on another. Doubtless there were other equally profitable occasions that went unrecorded. As well as terrorizing peasants and townsmen, he would also have had the occasional opportunity to go for the real jackpot—the capture and ransom of a French aristocrat. We know that later in his career Edward had at least one prisoner in his custody, and he may have had others. Even if the French nobles themselves evaded capture (by dying or escaping), it was still possible to turn a tidy profit by selling their armor, which by the fourteenth century had become very sophisticated and accordingly expensive. A full suit could fetch as much as £400—twice what Dallingridge earned in a year from his estates.

By the time Edward Dallingridge returned from the Hundred Years' War, therefore, he was a made man. With his own inheritance, his wife's fortune, and his recent ill-gotten gains from France, he had the wherewithal to invest in a splendid new home—a building appropriate to his newfound wealth and status. The early 1380s were doubtless years of sounding out architects, discussing different designs, and talking specific costs. At the same time, Edward was also trying to get his hands on a very special and specific document; a piece of parchment sealed by the king. In 1385, his wish was granted. On October 20 that year, the king sent him the following letter:

> *The king to everyone who sees this letter, greeting. Know ye that, of our special grace, we have granted and given license, as far as we can, to our dear and faithful Edward Dallingridge, knight, that he may crenellate and strengthen with a wall of stone and lime his manor house of Bodiam, next to the sea in the county of Sussex, and may make and construct it into a castle, in the defense of the country roundabout and in order to resist our enemies.*

This letter—a so-called "license to crenellate"—is the central piece of documentary evidence about Bodiam Castle. Not only does it help us date the building; it also helps to explain why Edward Dallingridge wanted a castle in the first place. Like the castle itself, however, the license has proved to be very deceptive. Its meaning seems to be perfectly clear, but if you read between the lines, it tells us a different story about Bodiam and its owner.

Taken at face value, the document confirms that castles are dangerous weapons. This much seems obvious from the very fact that the king felt he had to license them. The ownership of castles, like the ownership of guns or dangerous dogs, needed to be monitored and restricted by the government. If the king did not exercise such control, who knows what he might face? In the wrong hands, castles might be used against him—just think of the trouble King John had with Rochester. Only in very special circumstances, therefore, would permission be granted to build one. But if there were extenuating circumstances, the king might choose to extend his "special grace and favor" and give you a license.

This fits very well with the known facts about Bodiam. In the 1370s and 1380s, the Hundred Years' War was not going at all well from the English point of view. The French had begun to strike back, attacking the south coast of England, raiding and burning towns like Rye, Southampton, and Plymouth. In 1385 (the very year Dallingridge got his license) the people of southern England were seized with panic when they learnt that the French had assembled a huge armada, and were making ready to invade. In such circumstances, what king could refuse one of his leading subjects the right to build a castle? The license itself specifically links Bodiam to the raids. The castle was to be built "in the defense of the country" against the French ("our enemies").

This interpretation also seems to be supported by the fact that Dallingridge was not acting alone. Other men with lands in southern England, especially the counties nearest the coast, were applying for and receiving licenses to crenellate at exactly the same time. In the 1380s new castles were under construction at Cooling, Penshurst, Hever, and Scotney. Their owners, like Dallingridge, evidently wanted to protect their lands and their families; and they also wanted to make it clear that they were doing their bit for everyone. Dallingridge, his license tells us, was building Bodiam to help defend the country in general. John de Cobham, who built Cooling Castle from 1381, similarly wanted us to know that he was motivated by public-spirited altruism. When his castle was finished, he took the trouble to have a little metal charter made, and fixed it over the gatehouse. It is still possible to make out the words: "Knowyth that be-th and schul be / That I am mad[e] in the help of the cuntre." What could possibly be clearer? An authentic voice from Edward Dallingridge's day, addressing us directly, and telling us that Cooling (and, by extension, Bodiam, Hever, Scotney, and others) was built for the common good in the face of threatened invasion.

There is only one tiny problem, which is this: these noble sentiments are completely contradicted by the castles that were actually built. If Cooling really was "made in the help of the country," as Cobham's plaque proudly proclaims, why did it have towers with open backs, and why was it so badly defended on the side that faced the coast? Likewise, if Edward Dallingridge really built Bodiam "in the defense of the country," as his license to crenellate would have us believe, why is it built in such an untenable position, halfway down a hill and overlooked by higher ground to the north? As we saw earlier, the castle was not really built with defense in mind, and would hardly have been up to keeping out aggressive burglars, nevermind an invading French army. We can only assume, since the castles they built were so puny, that Edward Dallingridge, John de Cobham, and their ilk were not actually very frightened by the prospect of French raids at all. This, in Dallingridge's case, is hardly surprising; Bodiam, despite what it says in the license, is not actually very close to the sea at all; it's a good ten-mile walk to the nearest beach.

So why did Edward Dallingridge and others like him need to get licenses for their castles if they didn't intend to build useful military bases? The simple answer is that they didn't actually *need* licenses at all. Plenty of castles, some of real military value, were built without the king's say-so. Historians, it seems, have for a long time had the whole idea of licensing completely back to front backward. Dallingridge and other would-be castle-builders sought licenses from the king not because they *had* to have them, but because they desperately *wanted* them. It was not a matter of getting planning permission; more a case of getting listed building status. Building without a license was perilous, not because the king might turn up one day and pull your castle down, but because people might not acknowledge that your new home was a proper castle at all. Suppose, for instance, you did what Edward Dallingridge did, and built yourself a really splendid little castle—bristling with towers and battlements, decked out with portcullises, murder-holes, and machicolations—and your neighbors referred to it as your house! Imagine the humiliation!

It might sound funny, but it was no laughing matter for the upwardly mobile knight Sir William Heron. In 1338 he began building a new home at his manor of Ford in Northumberland, and took the trouble to get hold of a license to crenellate. Two years later he seems to have realized that this in itself was not going to be enough to impress the locals, so he wrote to the king again. His new crenellated house at Ford—could he please, um, call it a castle as well?

Edward Dallingridge, as his license shows, got it right the first time: the wording of the grant leaves no doubt that he would be entitled to call Bodiam a castle. In fact, it is now assumed that references to the clear and present danger from France were Dallingridge's own invention—a cunningly worded case for castle ownership, intended to improve his chances of getting the royal stamp of approval. The king might not have been worried about castles being built from a military point of view, but there was nevertheless a social dimension to be considered. Castles were for kings, dukes, and earls; you did not want any Tom, Dick, or Harry coming back from the Hundred Years' War and starting to build one. Edward Dallingridge, descended from a family of foresters, was still very much on the fringes of the nobility; it was not his God-given right to live in a castle. In order to justify his entry into the charmed circle of castle-owners, he needed to dress up his private desires as communal needs, and pose as a genuine defender of England's south coast. It hardly mattered if he then went on to build a castle that was not up to the job. Once he got his hands on the license, he calculated, the document itself would confer greatness upon him.

The actual license has not survived, but it would have been a grand affair, handsomely written and sealed with the king's great wax seal. Such documents spoke of great honor. It is important to note that it was not addressed to Edward personally, but to "everyone who saw it"—it was not a private letter, but a public one, intended to be read out loud in the county court of Sussex, and perhaps put on display afterward. It was really more like a certificate—something Dallingridge could wave under people's noses to prove that Bodiam was indeed fit to be called a castle. From what we know of Sir Edward, the only surprise is that he didn't go as far as John de Cobham, and have a little metal version made to go over his front door.

The Hundred Years' War, therefore, explains how Dallingridge and others like him (for example, John Fastolf who built Caister in Norfolk, and the Beauchamps who rebuilt Warwick) were able to pay for their castles. It also explains how, despite his fairly humble origins, he was able to justify it. The turning tide of the war in the 1370s and the attacks on the south coast of England provided the crafty knight with an ample excuse. But what the war cannot adequately explain is why Sir Edward wanted a castle. As their licenses to crenellate suggest, Dallingridge and his neighbors wanted castles for social reasons rather than military ones. Castles were noble homes, and this alone made them desirable for upwardly mobile knights. But this, by itself, hardly seems sufficient explanation for the sudden burst of castle-building that occurred in southern England in the 1380s.

In fact, there seems to have been a quite specific reason for the boom. Men like Dallingridge might not have feared the French, but they did have good grounds for concern about an enemy closer to home. Ever since the Black Death in the middle of the fourteenth century, English peasants had been getting uppity. The great plague had wiped out a third of the population more or less overnight, and the result was massive social upheaval in the decades that followed. Labor was suddenly in short supply, and peasants therefore found themselves in a much stronger bargaining position. Landowners found it increasingly difficult to enforce their traditional demands for unpaid "customary" services—though the resistance they encountered did not, of course, stop them from trying. In 1381, the situation exploded. The peasants of Essex, Kent, and Sussex rose up against their superiors. Manor houses and castles were attacked, agricultural tools were destroyed, and manorial accounts were burned. This was the famous Peasants' Revolt—the biggest mass uprising in the English Middle Ages.

The Peasants' Revolt confirmed what the governing classes of England had been suspecting for a long time—that society was going to the dogs. The French war was going badly, the peasants were getting ideas above their station, and the proper order of things was starting to collapse. Men like Dallingridge responded by helping to put down the rebellions in 1381, and keeping a watchful eye on their communities in the years that followed.

It is arguable, however, that they thought that this in itself was not enough. What they needed to do was actively reassert the fundamental order of society, to stress their authority and their right to rule. So, when they invested in buildings, they went not for manor houses, but castles—a deliberate "back to basics" in architectural terms. Portcullises, gatehouses, and crenellations might not be necessary to keep the peasants out, but they were essential as traditional symbols of power. The peasants were supposed to understand that people who possessed such homes were their natural superiors, and entitled to a bit more respect than they had been getting of late. Of course, whether the peasants themselves actually fell for such unsubtle propaganda is another matter. The rather desperate protestations of public utility that John de Cobham tacked on to the front of his gatehouse suggest that the people in his neighborhood saw right through him and his new castle.

Bodiam may, therefore, have been part of a general trend among the minor aristocracy of southeast England as they struggled to reassert their authority in the wake of the Peasants' Revolt. There is no direct evidence to suggest that Dallingridge's own property was attacked during the uprising, but there can be little doubt that, as a substantial landowner, he must have suffered losses. Sir Edward was certainly active in putting down the revolt in East Sussex, and like others he may have thought a castle would send out the right kind of signal to the peasants in his locale. But he may also have had a much more specific and personal reason for wanting a castle in 1385. Rather than being directed downward at the peasants, Edward's message seems to have been aimed considerably higher. Dallingridge may have made a fortune by 1385, but his relentless rise had also made him an enemy, in the shape of a man called John of Gaunt.

Gaunt was the duke of Lancaster—a very rich magnate in the super-league of English landowners, and this fact alone made him a force to be reckoned with. He was also a man with an international reputation. A younger son of King Edward III, he had royal blood flowing in his veins. By the 1370s, he had acquired a crown of his own; his marriage to a Spanish princess gave him a claim to be king of Spain. Most importantly, when his royal father died in 1377 and the English crown passed to the young Richard II, Gaunt became the power behind the throne. As uncle to the ten-year-old king, it was Gaunt who held the strings of power; he was arguably the most important person in the kingdom.

He was, in short, not a man to cross lightly; as Edward Dallingridge must have appreciated—before he set out to do just that. In 1372, Gaunt acquired large estates in Sussex, which made him the overlord of a number of Sussex gentry, including Dallingridge. This, at first, may have served to bring the two men closer together—the following year, Edward participated in a notorious expedition through France under the duke's command. However, their relationship deteriorated rapidly. Unlike the previous landowner, Gaunt proved to be a very strict overlord in Sussex, and his officials were zealous in their interpretation of their master's rights. Dallingridge, who had flourished in the east of the county precisely because he had been free from this kind of interference, found his ascendancy blocked and his existing rights under attack.

The audacious Sir Edward therefore began a campaign of intimidation to try to persuade the duke's agents to back down. He seems to have started off on a small scale. In 1377, he began to trespass on Gaunt's estates, deliberately hunting in his parks and poaching his deer. This tactic apparently had little effect, and so from in the early 1380s Edward really began to up the ante. His principal target throughout the dispute was a private court that Gaunt had revived in the Dallingridge heartlands; as far as Edward could see, this, more than anything else, was undermining his own authority. In May 1381, he burst into the court while it was in session, seized the court rolls, and forcibly compelled the duke's steward to swear never to hold the court again. Once again, however, Gaunt was prepared to turn a blind eye to the matter. Although he was powerful, he did not enjoy much support in Sussex, and Dallingridge was able to pose as a local hero resisting the pretensions of an interfering outsider.

Then, in March 1384, things came to a head when Dallingridge was involved in an attack which ended in murder. The victim, one William Mouse, was Gaunt's sub-forester in Ashdown Forest. Gaunt retaliated by taking Dallingridge to court (which is how we know about all this, because the court records have survived). The duke used his influence to get the jury rigged in his favor, and Dallingridge responded to this obvious bias with a brilliantly theatrical performance. On two separate occasions during the proceedings he threw down his gauntlet, challenging his accusers and one of the witnesses to a duel. Refusing to plead to the charges against him, he was found in contempt, and committed to the sheriff of Sussex for imprisonment.

So this is how we find Sir Edward Dallingridge on the eve of applying for his license to crenellate in 1385: faced with imprisonment—which, in the event, was only temporary. However, it was still a nasty knock-back for a man trying to achieve respectability. Physically, Dallingridge had emerged from his run-in with Gaunt unscathed; his lands and livelihood were still intact. His reputation, however, had been left badly bruised.

Bodiam Castle, therefore, may well have been Edward Dallingridge's response to his experiences in 1384. The castle was a fine way to announce that, despite his defeat in court, he was still top dog in Sussex. In wishing to make a statement by building a castle, of course, Sir Edward was no different to generations of men who had come before him. William the Conqueror, Aubrey de

Vere, Henry II, Edward I—just about everybody in this book, in fact, wanted castles in order to say something about their power, authority, and standing. However, the difference in the case of men like Dallingridge is that, because of the peaceful times in which they lived, they did not have to worry about building castles that actually worked. However much Sir Edward might have relished the prospect of a straight fight with John of Gaunt, he knew the duke was not going to turn up at his house with siege engines; there was simply no point wasting money on huge defenses such as those at Beaumaris, Rochester, and the Tower of London. All he needed was a building that looked the business—and Bodiam is certainly that.

Dallingridge's run-in with Gaunt is a temptingly specific explanation of his sudden desire for a castle; it seems to fit perfectly with the known facts about his life, and also the flamboyant but weedy castle that he eventually built. However, even if we are wrong in making Edward's wounded ego the main reason for building Bodiam, the Gaunt episode can nevertheless help us to understand the nature of the castle he constructed.

As well as having powerful enemies by 1385, Dallingridge had powerful friends. Even as he was squaring up to John of Gaunt, Edward was snuggling up to another great magnate—Richard Fitz Alan, earl of Arundel. The connection between the Dallingridges and the Fitz Alans had been established a generation earlier—Edward's father had been a leading servant of the previous earl. Edward, however, continued to build on the family tradition. From 1376 on, when Richard succeeded his father as earl, Edward was frequently in his service. Like Gaunt, Arundel was a major landowner, with large amounts of property not only in southern England but also in the Welsh marches, and castles at Lewes and Shrawardine, as well as Arundel itself. In the 1380s the earl put Dallingridge in charge of his Welsh estates, and in 1385 Edward accompanied him in an expedition against the Scots. Both in war and peace, Dallingridge proved to be indispensable to Arundel.

And, in the event, the earl proved to be indispensable to Sir Edward. There was no way that Arundel could intervene directly when Dallingridge was dueling with Gaunt. The earl was rich—possibly the richest man in the country—but he lacked Gaunt's political influence, and also the control the duke exercised over the young king. However, shortly after Edward's imprisonment, Gaunt left England for France to negotiate a peace treaty, and his absence gave Arundel an opportunity to intervene. The earl invited the king to stay at Arundel Castle, and it seems highly likely that he used the opportunity to have a quiet word on behalf of his imprisoned friend. Soon afterward, Edward Dallingridge was once again at large, restored to his place at the top of Sussex society.

So, Sir Edward seems to have got off the hook because he was well connected. His liberty was not due to any retrial or review of the evidence; it was entirely down to the patronage of the earl of Arundel. With friends in high places, you could go far in the fourteenth century. When Edward Dallingridge began to build Bodiam Castle the following year, it was not as a serious fortification to keep out the French. Nor was it just a symbol of his right to rule, a bold claim in the face of challenges from peasants and dukes. It was a tool to help him play the patronage game. It was a place to entertain his friends and delight his betters—men like Arundel and perhaps, one day, the king.

As we established at the start, Bodiam is built much like a courtyard house, or the quadrangle of an Oxbridge college. Rather than being dotted around a bailey area, all the rooms necessary for a medieval household (or a college community) are packed around the four walls, and cleverly arranged in order to serve and supply each other. Today, Bodiam's interior is quite ruinous, but careful examination reveals the purpose of each room, and the way they functioned together to provide for the Dallingridge household.

As in the twelfth century, the biggest problem with an aristocratic household was keeping it fed. At Bodiam, food and drink came in via the back door—it made much more sense to use the shorter

*The screens passage at Bodiam.*

and more direct route into the castle. Stepping out from the tower of the rear gatehouse, you would have found yourself in a narrow passageway known as the "screens passage," so called because of the wooden and stone screens that stood on either side. The wooden screen that would have been on the right is no longer there. The stone screen, however, has survived. As you can see from the picture above, it was provided with three doors. The one on the left led into a small room called the pantry, used for storing bread (and derived from the French word for bread, *pain*). If having a whole room reserved just for bread sounds rather excessive, bear in mind that Dallingridge had a large household to feed, and everyone, from his immediately family down to the lowliest servant, needed their daily bread. Even the dogs of the household would have been fed large quantities as part of their diet, and quite often thick, dried slices of bread, known as trenchers, were used instead of plates.

The doorway on the right of the screens passage led into a similar-sized room called the buttery, used for storing the other absolute necessity—no, not butter, but alcohol in the form of wine and ale (it derives from the word *bottle*). Since it was quite unsafe to drink water, these were drunk with every meal. It was still possible to ride a horse in a straight line afterward: the alcohol content of the regular ale (known as small beer) was low. It was drunk by the whole household, and was made on site (although perhaps not inside the castle). Just as bread had to baked every few days, so ale had to be brewed regularly to keep it fresh. Wine, on the other hand, kept indefinitely, and was as potent then as it is now. It would normally have been reserved for Edward's immediate family and friends, and typically imported from southern France.

The third doorway in the screens passage led to a narrow corridor between the pantry and the buttery, which opened out on to

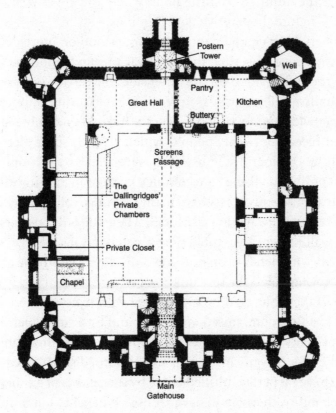

*A floor plan of Bodiam Castle.*

the kitchen. Bodiam's kitchen is quite cleverly arranged, making ingenious use of the space available. A great fireplace for cooking is built into the thickness of the exterior wall and connected to a crenellated chimney on the roof (yes, he even did the chimneys). In one corner of the room a stairway led down to the bottom of the southwest tower, where there was a well—of sorts. Today it is filled with water from the moat, but this can't have been the case in the fourteenth century; apart from anything else, the moat serves as a sewer for the castle's many toilets. One possible solution is that the "well" was in fact a water tank, lined with lead to isolate it from the moat, and actually filled with rainwater from the roof. At the top of the same tower was another feature designed to keep the kitchen supplied. It was once a dovecote, and you can still see the hundreds of little holes where the doves would have nested—before they were baked into pies.

Kitchen, buttery, and pantry therefore stood on one side of the screens passage. Together, their job was to supply food and drink to the room that stood on the other side: the castle's great hall. As great halls go, Bodiam's is quite dinky, measuring only twenty-four feet wide and forty feet in length. It could probably seat only around fifteen or twenty people, which gives us some idea of the size of the Dallingridge household. Nevertheless, the room is laid out according to all the conventions expected in Sir Edward's day (which are also still preserved in many Oxbridge colleges). Two long tables ran lengthways down the hall, where the ordinary members of the Dallingridge household (like the students in a college) would have sat. With benches on one side only, diners faced one another across the hall, and the servants enjoyed unrestricted access to the inside of the tables as they approached with plates of food. At the far end of the room, raised off the ground by a small platform to emphasize its importance, was a third table. This, the high table, was where Sir Edward, his family, and his most distinguished guests would have sat (a role fulfilled today by the fellows of a college). In all probability, they would have sat not on benches but individual chairs. In keeping with its high status, this end of the hall was lit by a very large, south-facing window. Interestingly, the room has no fireplaces, despite the fact that there are dozens of others throughout the castle. Instead, the hall was lit by an open hearth in the center, with a vent in the roof above to allow the smoke out. This arrangement—having a great fire in the middle of the hall, providing light and warmth to the whole household—can be traced right back to the Dark Ages, and continued to be used well beyond Dallingridge's day.

While some traditions were preserved, however, others were gradually being abandoned. By the late fourteenth century, for example, aristocratic households were beginning to spend less time traveling. As a market economy continued to develop, noblemen could rely on getting a greater percentage of their produce locally. Indeed, they might even take steps to encourage the process. In 1383, Dallingridge obtained permission from the king to hold a weekly market in the village of Bodiam, as well as an annual fair. In addition, a knight like Sir Edward would have kept his own stocks of animals in order to feed his household. Meat of all kinds was expensive and high-status food, and therefore formed the principal part of an aristocratic diet. As well as keeping herds of animals for grazing, Dallingridge and his family would have supplemented their diet by hunting. Precisely because they were beasts associated with the chase, deer and expensive game birds like pheasants and partridges were regarded as especially noble dishes. They could be especially delicious, too—Dallingridge's venison would have tasted twice as nice if he had personally poached it from under John of Gaunt's nose.

Of course, the bad thing about medieval aristocrats, as everybody knows, is that they did not eat their vegetables. Stuff that came out the ground was the food of peasants, and therefore not highly prized by well-to-do knights. Dallingridge would probably have turned up his nose had you offered him cheese, too, unless it was of a particularly fine variety. Fish, however, came a close second to meat as a dish of distinction, and was also an essential alternative to meat during Lent. It could be stored salted or pickled in barrels, but Dallingridge had plenty of ponds around the castle to keep him supplied with freshwater fish on a day-to-day basis. He might have splashed out from time to time for something a bit more fancy if the occasion demanded it: larger fish like pike or bream were viewed as suitable delicacies for top table. And if Sir Edward had a hankering for a bit of fresh seafood—well, that was hardly going to be a problem. After all, Bodiam (as he no doubt reminded whichever skivvy he sent to fetch the shopping) was right next to the sea.

This, as their household accounts testify, was the diet of the English nobility in the Middle Ages. Moreover, by the time we reach Edward Dallingridge's day, we know not just what the aristocracy ate, but also how they cooked it. In the 1390s, Richard II asked his master chef to compile a book of recipes, and the manuscript has survived. Known as the *Forme of Cury*, it is nothing less than the first English cookbook. There was more to medieval cooking, it transpires, than putting a pig on a spit and garnishing its mouth with an apple. As well as recommending simple dishes like "Chykens in Gravey" and "Makerel in Sawce," the book also contains wonderfully inventive recipes, calling for expensive spices and rare ingredients. One of my favorites (having tasted it) is the "Hastelet of Fruyt," a joke dish of almonds and raisins, strung together and fried in batter so as to look like deers' entrails. The book also indicates that English cooking was far from insular. Richard's chef betrayed his knowledge of Italian cuisine with Lumbard Mustard, and could also serve up peas, German style (Peson of Almayne). Even pasta might have found its way on to the king's menu—the *Forme of Cury* has a recipe for "Macrows" (i.e., macaroni).

We can imagine, therefore, similar dainty dishes being set before Sir Edward and Lady Elizabeth as they sat down to dinner in their great hall at Bodiam; though, in fact, if they were throwing a major party, they might not have used this hall at all. To the north of the castle, 300 yards or so up the hill, is a grassy platform, now known as the Gun Garden, and for this reason long assumed to have been an artillery earthwork dating to the seventeenth century. Recent excavations, however, have revealed traces of a large medieval building, almost certainly contemporary with the castle. Its position, as well as its size, is very suggestive; from this point, the castle, with the river valley behind it, looks particularly splendid. The vanished building, it has been plausibly proposed, was once a banqueting hall, where Sir Edward could entertain honored guests in grand style and, as they were eating, invite them to gaze on his achievement.

So, let us picture the scene back at Bodiam Castle at the end of the fourteenth century. Sir Edward Dallingridge has given a feast, as great as his pocket can bear. He has invited a number of distinguished guests, including his friend and patron the earl of Arundel. His lordship's presence has pushed the numbers up, so the evening's entertainment has taken place in the banqueting hall up on the hill. The meal has been served, the sun has started to set, and everybody has taken their cue and said how nice the new castle looks in its river valley setting. They have broken their bread, quaffed their ale, and slurped their wine. At one point they were horrified to see deers' entrails being carried into the room, but were relieved to discover it was just another hilarious joke dish. Minstrels have been hired especially for the evening, and the guests have listened attentively to their plaintive songs, and have had a dance to one or two of the more jaunty numbers. But now, the evening is finished, and everyone is very tired. Slowly they begin to filter out of the hall and make their way down the hill, where they can see the castle and its reflection clearly in the moonlight. Nevertheless, that wine was very good, and it is therefore with exaggerated carefulness that they make their way across the bridges, into the castle courtyard, and mount the stairs to bed.

It is at this point that Sir Edward's castle comes into its own. The amount of accommodation crammed inside the walls is one of the major differences between Bodiam and castles of an earlier generation. No longer were people expected to find a space on the floor of the hall at the end of the evening; anyone of any importance staying overnight at Bodiam was shown to his or her own room. Most of the chambers are squeezed into the towers, stacked vertically on top of one other, and therefore quite small and low roofed. All of them, however, are very well appointed; each has a fireplace and a window (with a window seat), and all have en suite toilets. Sadly, the castle's interior is too ruinous to say exactly how many of these chambers were bedrooms; but the extent of the hospitality potentially on offer can be gauged from the surviving architectural details—altogether, there are no fewer than thirty-three fireplaces and twenty-eight toilets.

Such lavish facilities give a strong indication of the role that Dallingridge envisaged for Bodiam. This was not a castle for keeping a garrison of soldiers, but for entertaining honored guests. In order to play the role of the great lord he was becoming, it was essential for Edward to exhibit the virtue of generosity. "Mi castillo es su castillo," he might well have said, for the architecture of the castle itself said as much. Observing its ponds teeming with fish, its well-stocked deer parks, its now-vanished banqueting hall, and especially its many, many suites of bedrooms, a visitor to Bodiam was intended to understand that guests were always welcome chez Dallingridge.

The best private rooms, of course, were reserved for the Dallingridges themselves. Most of the east side of the courtyard is occupied by suites of grand chambers for Edward, Elizabeth, and their children. As well as their bedrooms, there were great chambers where the Dallingridges could, if they wished, dine in private, or receive especially honored guests. Although they are very dilapidated today, we must imagine these rooms as being richly decorated; perhaps not with tapestries (a bit too expensive, even for Sir Edward) but with painted wall-hangings. As for other furnishings, we know from surviving wills and inventories the kinds of things that fourteenth-century aristocrats valued most highly. Fur-lined cloaks, silks from the Mediterranean, and bedding were all treasured and passed on, and so too was silver plate. In the Dallingridges' private chambers, we can picture all these things. Perhaps, too, we can picture Sir Edward's most prized possession hanging above the fireplace in his chamber. The mantelpiece in this room is carved, and you can still make out the little battlements on top. This, surely, was the perfect place to display a license to crenellate.

Close scrutiny of Bodiam Castle, therefore, reveals a charming picture of medieval domestic bliss. It was a place where Dallingridge and his family intended to enjoy the good things in life. However, no sooner had Sir Edward conceived this vision than it was thrown into jeopardy. In 1386 the earl of Arundel, in alliance with several other magnates, planned to seize control of the king's government. Dallingridge, as Arundel's right-hand man, backed the earl in his endeavor. If they succeeded, they knew, the rewards would be unimaginable; if they failed, it would cost them dearly. One false move, and Edward stood to lose everything: his castle, his family, and even his life.

Arundel was prompted to act in 1386 by the policies of Richard II. The young king had been welcomed to the throne with much rejoicing, but the feel-good factor had quickly evaporated. As Richard had grown older, he had turned into a foolish, haughty, and self-obsessed king. From the point of view of Arundel and his allies, however, Richard's biggest problem was his attitude to war; basically, he didn't like it. As soon as the king was old enough to influence government policy, he began to negotiate with the French for peace. For war-profiteers like Arundel and Dallingridge, this was not good news. Toward the end of 1386, in the charged atmosphere created by the expectation of a French invasion, Arundel and his hawkish colleagues ousted the king's existing councilors, seized control of government, and set about prosecuting the war with renewed vigor.

A pro-war strategy, however, is only popular if you win convincing victories, and the new regime had little success. Arundel, with Dallingridge by his side, led two separate expeditions to France, both of which ended in failure. At home, meanwhile, the opposition of the king's friends drove the new government to increasingly desperate measures. Having defeated Richard's allies in battle, Arundel and his associates cornered the king and threatened to depose him, and shortly afterward they sentenced four of his former councilors to death. With the war going badly, and the new government looking increasingly discredited, sympathy for Richard's position grew. In 1389 the king managed to split his opponents, and on May 3 that year he declared he was resuming personal power. Arundel and his allies were ejected from the council, and anxiously awaited their fate.

Dallingridge, however, proved once again what a skilled survivor he could be, even when the odds were stacked heavily against him. In the very week that Arundel was dismissed, the crafty Sir Edward quietly detached himself from his patron's side and sought the protection of the royalist earl of Huntingdon. The king, who was hardly in a position to refuse support from any quarter, graciously overlooked Edward's recent opposition, and accepted him among his new councilors. Even as his old master's ship was sinking, Dallingridge, with remarkable nimbleness, had hopped on board the royal barge.

Having pulled off this breathtaking political stunt, Edward set about making his position secure through sheer hard work. Surviving royal records from the early 1390s show that he was the most frequent attendee of council meetings. Also revealing is a wonderful little expense account submitted by Dallingridge to the Exchequer in 1393, covering the costs that he had incurred in the previous year. As well as proving that he spent no less than 207 days in the king's service, the roll also exposes the extent of his movements. Dallingridge seems to have acted as a liaison between the king, who still habitually toured the country, and the council, which for the most part met in Westminster. Destinations ranging from London to Stamford and Dover to Nottingham show that Edward was rarely out of the saddle. His assiduousness, however, paid off. After only a few weeks in the king's service, Dallingridge was permitted to purchase new lands in Sussex, and was granted a royal pension of a hundred marks (£67) a year.

The downside, naturally, was that Edward was not getting much free time to spend at his new castle (which by now must have been very nearly finished) or, for that matter, with his wife. Sadly, we do not have much specific information about Elizabeth Dallingridge; women have left fewer traces than men in the records of medieval royal government. The Dallingridges probably wrote personal letters to each other, just as the famous Paston family of Norfolk would do a century later, but none have survived. Similarly, there are no wills or prayer books, no inventories or epitaphs that can shed any light on Elizabeth's personality or tastes. Nevertheless, using sources like this for other women of her age and upbringing, we can start to imagine what the life of Lady Dallingridge must have been like.

During Edward's long absences, Elizabeth would almost certainly have been in charge of running both the household and the Dallingridge estate. Although she would have delegated much of the humdrum work to a professional estates steward, he would have been answerable to Elizabeth, and she may well have overlooked his accounts. Likewise, the domestic staff—the cook, the huntsman, the chaplain, and the butler—would all have looked to her for their orders. Elizabeth's ability to act as lady of the manor during her husband's long absences may have been part of her original appeal to the dashing Sir Edward. Of course, we should not kid ourselves here—the eligible young lady's principal attraction, from Edward's point of view, was undoubtedly her huge tracts of land. But it would be a mistake to imagine that men only married to get their hands on property, or because they wanted to produce an heir. While these were very important considerations, men like Edward also married for companionship and love. Chivalric romances are full of young knights doing quite ridiculously dangerous things to win a lady's heart, and many of the most successful careers in the Middle Ages were built by a husband and wife team supporting each other and working together.

Elizabeth, therefore, would have been an educated woman, able to read not just English, but also French and Latin. The spur to her literacy, however, would not have been its administrative usefulness, but its ability to bring her closer to God. The fourteenth century was a period when religion among the aristocracy was becoming a much more personal, introspective affair. Encouraged by the introduction of confession in the thirteenth century, men and women who could afford them were increasingly buying books of hours and prayer books so they could practice their devotions in private.

This increasingly personal and private piety is reflected in the design of the chapel at Bodiam castle. Of course, chapels in castles are nothing new; even the earliest earth and timber castles had chapels within their bailey walls, and there are chapels at the Tower of London, Colchester, and Rochester. The chapel at Bodiam, however, differs from these in two ways. First, it flaunts its vulnerability. As we noted right at the start of this chapter, the chapel is provided with a very large three-light Gothic window, which pierces the castle's east wall. In addition, the chapel is the only room in the castle that interrupts the otherwise perfect symmetry of the overall design. Both effects are quite deliberate; the Dallingridges wished to advertise their devout Christianity. Such was their devotion, the architecture suggests, that they were willing to expose themselves to attack and to compromise the shape of their castle. Defense and consistency pointedly take second place to religious considerations.

The second important innovation at Bodiam can only be seen from inside. By the start of the fourteenth century, it had become common for the main part of the chapel to be overlooked by a small, private room, so that privileged individuals (usually the castle's owner) could observe the mass in private. At Bodiam, a door in the Dallingridge master bedroom led into a small closet that looked down directly on to the altar. Like the increasing use of personal books of religious devotion, and the tendency to employ confessors in aristocratic households, this arrangement at Bodiam speaks eloquently of the increasingly private religious life of the fourteenth-century nobility.

Strange as it may seem at first, the movement toward a more personal form of worship was led by men like Dallingridge—men who had been soldiers in France, with quite bloody reputations. These, however, were the men who, as they grew older and closer to God, had the most on their consciences. Henry, duke of Lancaster, for example, a veteran from the early campaigns of the Hundred Years' War, picked painfully at his conscience in his *Livre de Seyntz Medicines*, describing the sores that afflicted his soul on account of the killings in his youth. Sir William Beauchamp, another old soldier, sought similar atonement by becoming an enthusiastic sponsor and devotee of new religious cults. Even the brutal Sir Robert Knowles, Dallingridge's one-time captain, eventually repented of his earlier atrocities. Later in life he founded a church at Pontefract, and sought absolution from the pope.

Likewise, when Dallingridge joined the ranks of the kings' councilors, he started to mix with another group of individuals who advocated a more contemplative, personal form of piety. The literati who gathered at the court of Richard II, like the king himself, were much given to such introspective musings, and shared Richard's anti-war sympathies. Sir John Clanvowe, who like Dallingridge was a frequent attendee of council sessions and also a chamber knight, wrote poems deriding the ideals of chivalry, and condemning men who went to war for profit. John Gower, another court poet, echoed these views. "In the present day," he wrote, "chivalry is maintained for pride and foolish delight."

Another individual at court whom Dallingridge would certainly have met was Geoffrey Chaucer, who was already entertaining the great and the good with early drafts of *The Canterbury Tales*. At one level, their lives had strong parallels, even before they met in the king's household. Both were born in the early 1340s and both fought in the French wars from 1359. Chaucer, like Dallingridge, had briefly been in the service of John of Gaunt, and had also served as a member of Parliament at the same time as Sir Edward. But their careers had taken quite different turns. Dallingridge belonged to the gentry; Chaucer was the son of a merchant. Edward made money in the wars, but Geoffrey was captured on his first expedition and had to be ransomed. As he grew older, Chaucer increasingly took up his pen as a clerk and poet; Dallingridge continued to rely on his sword to cut a path to greatness.

So what did the writer make of the fighter? Some modern authors suggest that, like Clanvowe and Gower, Chaucer was very critical of contemporary knighthood. Others contend that he has nothing but sincere praise for it. Others still maintain that the poet was trying to reconcile the two contradictory positions. Ultimately, it all depends on whether or not Chaucer is being ironic, and this we have no way of knowing; he is simply too subtle a writer.

A more important issue for us, and equally unfathomable, is how Edward Dallingridge regarded himself. Did he, like Clanvowe and Knowles, regret the killings of his youth, and seek absolution? Or did he not regard them as misdemeanors at all, but a necessary part of his chivalrous calling? Did he come to view himself as a medieval mercenary, or still regard himself a very "parfit gentil knight"? When, suddenly, he died late in the summer of 1393, did he go with his sins on his head, or repenting them? We do not know. Nor, frustratingly, do we know how or why he died. Probably in his late forties, he was not exactly old, even by medieval standards. Perhaps it was a lingering war wound, sustained on the battlefields of France. It could have been a sudden heart failure, brought on by his high-fat, low-fiber diet. Tentatively, as the hardest-working royal councilor, perhaps it was sheer exhaustion from all those long hours in the saddle that finally laid Sir Edward low.

They may have been private in their devotions, but when it came to being buried, medieval aristocrats liked to be seen in public. Although they were hardly ever seen praying inside their local parish churches, they nevertheless lavished money on rebuilding them as a point of pride, and were often interred inside, encased in grand tombs. The tomb of Edward's parents, Roger and Alice Dallingridge, has survived in the parish church of Fletching, then the center of the family's power. Although the stonework was sadly disfigured and destroyed in places during the Reformation, the carved coat of arms still survives, and matches the one on the front of the castle. Moreover, the lid of the tomb still has its fine monumental brass, depicting Roger and Alice in all their finery.

This memorial, of course, was probably commissioned by Edward, and shows how the Dallingridges wanted to be commemorated in death. Both figures are portrayed as pious, with their hands pressed together in prayer. Roger, however, is decked out in full military gear, his helmet on his head, and his sword by his side. Here, at least, we see no contradiction between the ideals of a military life and a Christian one.

Fate did not deal squarely with Sir Edward. He rose fast and achieved his goals quickly, but he was cut down with equal suddenness. As a leading adviser to the king, he stood for a moment on the cusp of greatness, ennoblement and immortality seemingly within his grasp. But his premature demise means that today we find no mention of a Lord Dallingridge in our dictionaries of the peerage. Death may even have cheated him of a role in Shakespeare. Other royal councilors got to star in Richard II, but Dallingridge missed his cue.

Posterity has been equally unkind to this meteoric man. There is no epitaph in any chronicle to explain how, through brilliant soldiery and astute political maneuvering, Dallingridge climbed to the top of the social and political ladder. Nor is there any effigy to mark the end of this knight's tale. Edward and Elizabeth were buried with great solemnity in the abbey of Robertsbridge, but it was dissolved and destroyed four and half centuries ago.

Sir Edward's memorial, however, does not lie hidden inside a parish church, or concealed in the pages of a chronicle. It is tucked among the rolling hills of East Sussex, in a little river valley, at the center of a sparkling moat. Lasting fame may have ultimately eluded him but, many centuries after his departure, it has come to rest on his magnificent home.

## CHAPTER FIVE

# SAFE AS HOUSES

———◈———

Edinburgh and Stirling are, with good reason, the most famous castles in Scotland. Both stand on top of great outcrops of rock, looming majestically over the streets and houses below. They look proud, invincible, and defiant—appropriately, given the pivotal roles that both have played at the crucial turning points in Scotland's history. William Wallace won his famous victory over the armies of Edward I at Stirling Bridge, and proceeded to recapture the castle; Robert the Bruce's troops seized Edinburgh from the English before going on to defeat them at Bannockburn. Their participation in the great events from Scotland's past has secured lasting celebrity for both castles. Edinburgh, of course, has a slight edge on its northern cousin. Its location at the heart of the nation's capital, as well as the great military tattoo that takes place there every year, ensures that Edinburgh Castle continues to top the league as Scotland's most famous historic monument.

But while they can justly be called famous, neither Edinburgh nor Stirling can be described as typical. As the property of the nation's rulers, they have been endlessly modified by a succession of kings and queens, eager to adapt and improve the two most prestigious castles in their possession. More importantly, many of the buildings we see today within the walls of both castles were put up in the sixteenth century, at a time when the court of Scotland was closely linked to the court of France. They were constructed by Continental masons, following the European fashion for Renaissance courtyards, rather than local craftsmen adhering to native Scottish traditions. Moreover, both castles underwent major renovation and redevelopment in the eighteenth and nineteenth centuries, transforming them out of all recognition. In short, these two castles are the exceptions, and not the rule.

In Scotland, the rule was not courtyards but towers, and it is the tower, or "tower house" design that has given Scottish castles their unique and enduring identity. From the middle of the fourteenth century, hundreds and hundreds were built in every corner of the country, from the Borders to the Shetlands, from Aberdeenshire to the Outer Hebrides. As well as being totally different from the courtyard castles that were being built in England at the time, they also outlived castles south of the border. Whereas castle-building in England and Wales was in decline from the end of the fifteenth century, Scotsmen continued to build tower houses right up until the middle of the seventeenth century.

So why did Scotland do its own thing in the late Middle Ages? And why did Scotland enter a new and dynamic phase of castle-building when in England and Wales, it was drawing to a close? If you take an old-fashioned view of castles as primarily military buildings, the answer is quite obvious. If Scotland has more castles than England and Wales, it must be because Scotland was a more violent and war-torn place. This view of castle architecture certainly seems to fit with the traditional view of Scottish history in the three-hundred-year period when tower houses were being built. The coming of the tower house coincides with the coming of a new and notorious dynasty of Scottish kings—the Stewarts.

The Stewarts took their name from one Walter, who was steward to the king of Scots. They came to the throne in 1371 and held it right up until the late seventeenth century. Their rule is seen as traumatic and bloody; almost all of them came to a sticky end. James I was stabbed to death; Mary Queen of Scots was executed; James II, James III, and James IV were all killed in battle. In addition to their propensity for dying horribly and being called James, the Stewarts have a reputation for being bad rulers—utterly useless, dangerously violent, or irrepressibly lazy, and sometimes a mix of all three. As such, history's judgment on them tends to be that they got what they deserved.

The Stewarts' notoriety is exceeded only by that of the people they governed. The Scottish nobility, according to one historian in the last century, "were probably the most turbulent, rapacious and ignorant in Europe." The lords of Scotland, according to this line of thinking, were in fact so utterly despicable that the merely deplorable kings seemed almost good by contrast. Scottish history under the Stewarts therefore reads like one long-drawn-out fight between the kings and nobles. Locked in an endless round of bloody power struggles, they both slugged it out for centuries, until eventually the kings won the day.

If this was the reality for the Scots in the late Middle Ages, small wonder they chose to shut themselves away in strong stone towers. But is this really what life was like in medieval Scotland? The answer, which you probably saw coming, is no. When you start to look closely at the castles themselves, and the careers of the men who built them, a very different picture of Scotland emerges—one that stands the old version of the story completely on its head.

Until the middle of the fourteenth century, castle-building in Scotland was much the same as it was in England and Wales, although the timing was somewhat different. Motte-and-bailey castles arrived in Scotland slightly later than in England, coming with Norman settlers in the early decades of the twelfth century. Also, perhaps because castles (and Normans) arrived late, Scotland never witnessed the building of great keeps. By the thirteenth century, however, Scottish castle-building had caught up, and the new castles that were being built were almost indistinguishable from those south of the border. Leading Scottish noblemen, often related by marriage to their English counterparts, built great curtain-wall or enclosure castles; like the castles of Edward I in Wales, these were characterized by circuits of high walls, round towers, and imposing gatehouses. Good examples include the mighty castle at Bothwell (near Glasgow) and the somewhat smaller Caerlaverock. Both were built in the second half of the thirteenth century.

A particularly fine example of a great curtain-wall castle is Tantallon in East Lothian. It was built by Sir William Douglas, probably to mark his elevation to the peerage as the first Earl Douglas in February 1358. He economized somewhat by choosing to build on a spur of land that stuck out into the sea. With sheer cliffs on all but one side, the site required only one great stretch of wall for protection, and the result is a very dramatic and unusual-looking castle. Nevertheless, Tantallon clearly belongs to the same tradition as Bothwell and Caerlaverock. The great curtain wall has a large gatehouse, and once had two round towers (both of which have now partly collapsed and fallen into the sea).

For all its former splendor, however, Tantallon was the last of a dying breed. Scottish nobles had given up building castles on this scale. Even as Sir William was putting the final touches to Tantallon, his cousin, Archibald Douglas, was busy on the other side of Scotland, building to a different design—one that would endure for the next three centuries. Archibald, known to his contemporaries and to posterity as "Archibald the Grim," had also been promoted. In September 1369 he was made lord of Galloway in the extreme southwest of Scotland. But rather than build a curtain-wall castle like his cousin, Archibald had decided to mark his elevation by building a tower house.

Archibald's tower, known as Threave Castle, is a grand affair. Now slightly diminished in stature, it once stood around eighty feet high. At such a size, it is reminiscent of the great towers of Norman

England, and it might therefore seem that Archibald simply resurrected an old and unfashionable design that had been around for at least three hundred years. In fact, if he was following any form of fashion, it probably originated closer to home. Some historians are inclined to see the origins of tower houses like Threave in the *brochs* of Dark Age Scotland.

There is, however, enough to distinguish the tower house of the fourteenth century from any of its suggested ancestors. Some of the differences are stylistic. Tower houses tend to have one or more barrel-vaulted ceilings, rather than the wooden floors typically found in Norman keeps. Those who cling to the blood-and-guts view of Scottish history say that this was because your average tower-house owner lived in perpetual fear of attack, and built stone ceilings to stop his tower being torched; but the difference may have been for more mundane reasons. Wooden flooring requires a lot of very large oak trees, which were less readily available in Scotland than stone. Another minor difference is that Scottish towers, especially later ones, did not have portcullises. Instead, entrances were barred with a simple but sturdy iron gate, called a "yett." Furthermore, some tower houses, especially later ones, are entered by a door on the ground floor, whereas keeps are always entered on the first floor.

The major difference, however, between a Scottish tower house and a Norman keep is one of function. Keeps were not intended to be self-contained and (as we saw in Chapter Two) may have been intended more for ceremonial use than day-to-day living. While they typically contained accommodation, they needed to be supported by a range of additional buildings in the bailey, not least a kitchen and a hall. Tower houses, on the other hand, were built to be self-contained. In every case, a tower house contains not only bedrooms, but also a hall, a kitchen, and storerooms.

This difference of function has colored people's view of tower houses. Because they are self-contained, they have been seen as "closed up" and "inward looking." While keeps are seen as being proud, assertive, defiant, and often architecturally exuberant buildings, tower houses, by contrast, have been seen as plain, dark, and forbidding. Keeps, built in towns or villages, dominate and overawe their surroundings. Tower houses are often as not built in isolated locations. Cut off on rocky peninsulas, stranded on lonely hills, they seem to speak not so much of domination but retreat. They are seen, in short, as the product of a mind-set that regarded itself as under threat, and constantly in danger of attack. The tower house is the paranoia of the Scottish medieval nobility, expressed in stone.

This idea certainly seems to be borne out when one looks at Threave. A great, forbidding tower, unadorned and unwelcoming, the castle stands alone on an island in the middle of the River Dee. Even today, it is only accessible via a mile-long footpath and a boat ride across the river. It is hard to imagine a building being more remote. As if this is not proof enough, another feature suggests a permanent siege mentality—around the base of the tower is an artillery platform: a strong wall of stone with towers at each corner, designed both to carry cannon and to protect the castle from bombardment. All in all, Archibald's tower appears to have been as grim as the man himself.

First appearances, though, can be deceptive. When you start to dig a little deeper, a very different picture emerges. This is exactly what Chris Tabraham and a team of archaeologists did in the mid-1970s. What started out as a straightforward job of preserving and consolidating the masonry of the artillery wall soon expanded to become one of the more remarkable archaeological digs of recent times—one which blew the idea of Threave as an isolated military outpost clean out of the water. The major discovery was that the artillery wall had been built over the foundations of a set of earlier domestic buildings. Adjacent to the tower were the remains of a very large rectangular block, almost certainly a great hall. At right angles to this building stood another stone structure, longer but narrower, interpreted as a second suite of rooms, possibly including a chapel. On the basis of their smaller archaeological finds, Chris and his colleagues concluded that they must have been constructed at the same time as the tower. And these stone buildings were not the only ones on the site: spreading out from the castle, and filling almost all the habitable part of Threave Island, was what amounted to a small village of lesser buildings made of wood. These could be reached by means of a causeway that ran from the southern tip of the island to the opposite bank of the river.

So Threave had a very different appearance in Archibald the Grim's day. It was not an isolated tower, but a whole complex of castle buildings, surrounded by a bustling community. The nature of this community was further revealed by the fantastic small finds—one of the most important archaeological collections of medieval Scottish artifacts. Some of the finds, like the excavated buildings, were high status; they included a seal-matrix and an extremely well-preserved silver locket. No less valuable, however, were the everyday items that were uncovered in the castle's harbor. Because of the muddy, water-logged conditions, all kinds of ordinary wooden and leather items (which in normal conditions would have perished) were preserved at Threave. Several shoes were unearthed, some of them so small that they had obviously once belonged to children. Wooden tableware was also discovered, including bowls and plates stamped with the symbol of the Douglas family, the Bloody Heart (Archibald's father, James Douglas, had carried the heart of Robert the Bruce on crusade with him, in accordance with the late king's wishes). Even a small wooden gaming counter was found, very well carved and evidently part of a set used for playing draughts or backgammon.

Such a hoard of everyday items is a useful reminder that castles, even Scottish castles, were homes to their owners 99 percent of the time, and were rarely put to military use. They indicated that in the late fourteenth century, Threave was not a castle full of grizzled soldiers, but a community of men, women, and children going about fairly humdrum business, and leading perfectly ordinary lives.

If this sounds like a rather poor exchange for the blood-and-guts version of Scottish history we have all come to know and love, you will be pleased to know that we can only push this archaeological evidence so far. Even if we concede that the castle was not "closed up," that the women wore silver lockets, the children wore shoes, and everybody enjoyed the odd game of checkers, certain other facts about the castle and its history are inescapable. Most obviously, the main building is almost eighty feet tall. It has (or had) a battlemented roof, and you can still see holes for joists that would have supported a wooden hoarding or fighting platform around the top of the whole tower. Even if we picture the castle stripped of its artillery platform, and imagine instead the vanished stone buildings standing nearby, it still seems very clear that this was a building designed to hold its own in wartime. No amount of imaginative recasting is going to turn Archibald the Grim's tower house into a holiday home.

The political circumstances of his promotion to the lordship of Galloway are also worth remembering. In the late fourteenth century, Galloway was a war-torn region. The loyalty of its people to the kings of Scotland was highly doubtful; in recent decades they had sided with the English against the Scottish Crown. Archibald was a veteran of the wars against the English, sent to Galloway to control and pacify the area. He was a man with a fierce reputation, and had not earned his nickname by playing board games.

Archibald could have chosen to build at Threave for any number of reasons. To some extent his choice of location may have been symbolic. The island is said to have been the seat of power for the native rulers of Galloway since the eleventh century. If so, then Archibald had in part chosen the site to make a statement: not quite so bold and imperious a statement as William the Conqueror or Edward I ("I came, I saw, I conquered"), but nonetheless a significant statement of authority ("There's a new sheriff in town").

Likewise, the decision to build a tower can be read in other ways. Towers were becoming fashionable, and tall buildings are always popular with those who wish to express domination and power. However, whatever deeper meanings we ascribe to the castle and its location, we must not ignore the old-fashioned functional considerations. Threave Island is wonderfully well defended by nature, and Archibald's tower is also well equipped to withstand a military assault. So yes, Archibald was making a statement with Threave. It may not be an isolated and inward-looking building and, yes, he built a castle that scores of people eventually regarded as home; but whichever way you look at it, Archibald the Grim was clearly expecting trouble.

The other major stumbling block to a more mellow interpretation of Threave is its present appearance. Even if we grudgingly allow that Archibald the Grim had a jolly time on the island, we have to account for the fact that, at some point after his death (he died at Threave on Christmas Eve, 1400), someone felt the need to demolish the more peaceable parts of the castle, dig a great ditch around the tower, and build a stone platform designed to withstand and carry guns.

That someone, it is now believed, was either William Douglas or his younger brother, James. They were the last of Archibald the Grim's descendants, the so-called Black Douglases. After Archibald's day, the power of his family grew greater and greater, making them by far the most powerful noble family in Scotland. In 1440, William Douglas inherited lands all over southern Scotland, as well as several highland estates. This was good news—until an especially nasty Stewart king decided it was time to take the Douglases down a peg or two.

King James II was a little younger than Earl William. He was only seven years old when he ascended to the Scottish throne in 1437, and it was not until 1449 that he came to rule in his own right; and then the trouble began. At the time, there were plenty of public professions of goodwill between the new king and his greatest subject. Douglas declared himself ready to be "ever servable" to his lord and master, while James declared himself delighted with the earl's "singular favor, love and zeal." Behind the smiles and the handshakes, however, the rot had already set in. Driven by a greed for more land, and encouraged by the anti-Douglas members of his council, James took advantage of William's absence on pilgrimage and led a military progress through the earl's lands. He aimed to undermine the Douglas family's power and win away their supporters but, much to his annoyance, the earl returned and successfully reasserted himself. For a brief while it was all false smiles again. In February 1452, however, the king hit upon a new idea. He invited William to dinner at Stirling Castle and, after a hearty supper and a few glasses of wine, personally stabbed him to death.

James Douglas, suddenly and unexpectedly made earl, was less than impressed. His brother had been promised a safe conduct by the king, only to be literally stabbed in the back. He responded by mounting a show of defiance in Stirling, the site of his brother's murder, taking six hundred men to burn the town, and parading the king's letter of safe conduct in contempt. There followed a tense three-year stand-off between the king and the new earl, the one trying to muster enough support to finish the Douglases off once and for all, the other trying to rebuild his late brother's shattered lordship.

It was around this time that Threave Castle was altered out of all recognition. The wooden domestic buildings were pulled down, and the great stone hall and chapel buildings were leveled. In their place, using the same stone, the artillery platform was built around the tower house. Somewhat frustratingly, it is not clear which of the two Douglas brothers actually instigated the rebuilding. The archaeological dig in the seventies revealed evidence to suggest the artillery platform dated to around 1450, but we can't be sure exactly when. It could have been William Douglas before his death in 1452, sensing that the wind was beginning to blow against him. Equally, it may have been the work of James Douglas, a defiant response to his brother's death and a preparation for a final showdown. Certainly one of the two Douglas boys changed Threave from a cozy community to a fortress intended to withstand cannon.

And with good reason. James II, in addition to his obvious flair for other forms of violence, was especially into guns. Artillery had come a long way since its introduction in the early fourteenth century, and James, as well as having a good many smaller, anti-personnel guns, was in possession of the latest in gunpowder technology. These were huge great things called bombards—guns designed and built expressly for the purpose of destroying castle walls. The best example in Britain is Mons Meg, a present to James II from his father-in-law (and fellow gun-enthusiast), the Duke of Burgundy. Meg, now residing in Edinburgh Castle, did not arrive in Scotland until after the king's battle with the Douglases, but the king had plenty of other cannon of equivalent size that were quite capable of wreaking similar havoc and destruction.

In 1455 James II turned his guns on the castles of the earl of Douglas. At the start of March he laid siege to the castle of Inveravon, and soon reduced it to rubble. The following month he reached the castle of Abercorn, which held out for a month before falling in the face of the king's assault. James personally conducted these sieges, and clearly enjoyed the experience immensely; he wrote a letter to the Duke of Burgundy, giving him a blow-by-blow account of his artillery bombardment. By the start of the summer, the royal army had drawn up outside Threave, now the Douglas family's last remaining castle. James arrived ahead of his artillery train—for all their devastating power, bombards were cumbersome beasts and moved extremely slowly, never more than three or four miles a day. Although the siege lasted over two months, it was all over before the king's greatest guns had arrived. Probably bribed into submission with the king's gold (and no doubt also encouraged by the imminent arrival of his artillery), the garrison inside the castle decide to cut their losses and surrender. The earl of Douglas, who was not present at the siege, fled to England. He never returned to Scotland again, and ended his days in exile.

The story of the struggle between the Black Douglases and the Crown demonstrates the enduring theme of Scottish history in the first half of the fifteenth century. A sorry tale of treachery, stabbing, bombardment, and exile, it could be (and for centuries has been) taken as good evidence that the lot of the Scottish nobility had become far worse by this time. James II was far from being the only dangerously violent Stewart king. For most of the century, Scotland was ruled by extremely unpleasant men of dubious character. James II's father (James I) was no less greedy and vindictive than his megalomaniac son. Having spent the first twenty years of his life in captivity in England, he returned to Scotland in 1424 with a colossal chip on his shoulder. Holding his cousins, the Albany Stewarts, chiefly responsible for his lengthy sojourn south of the border, he began his reign with a jolly round of family executions. A short, fat, pushy man, his rule came to a sudden end when a member of the royal household stabbed him to death in 1437. Later in the century, James II's son (James III) was, if possible, an even less likeable individual. Irresponsible, vengeful, and above all just plain lazy, the third King James hoarded money and debased the coinage to pay for his ill-conceived foreign policy schemes. Imperious and unjust in dealing with his subjects, he had so alienated his nobles by 1488 that they defeated him in battle and hacked him to death. And if, incidentally, you are wondering what became of James II, you may be pleased to know that he also got a fitting comeuppance. Laying siege (for a change) to the border town of Roxburgh in 1460, the king stood far too close to one of his great guns. The bombard exploded on firing, and the king was killed instantly.

Surely with such rascals on the throne, the canny nobleman would look to his own protection and build a castle? Such an idea seems to find support in the explosion of castle-building that took place in the fifteenth century. More tower houses were built during the reigns of Jameses I, II, and III than in any other period. Some of them, moreover, were positively enormous. Take Borthwick Castle, which stands on a spur of land some twelve miles southeast of Edinburgh. At an exceedingly lofty 108 feet tall, it is the biggest and best-preserved tower house in Scotland. Significantly, perhaps,

*Borthwick Castle.*

there is absolutely no question of any other buildings surrounding the castle, as was once the case at Threave: at Borthwick, all the domestic space is packed inside the tower. Surely, then, the lord who built it was deliberately shutting himself away, no doubt in the expectation of troubled times ahead?

Well, probably not. The lord in question, Sir William Borthwick, even though he lived during the reigns of James I and James II, seems to have had other things on his mind. Take a look at the license he was granted in 1430, and watch for the twist in the tale:

*The king [James I] grants to William Borthwick, knight, special license to build a castle in the place which is commonly called the*

*Motte of Locherwart, near Edinburgh, and permission to erect
and fortify the same castle or fortress, to surround it with walls
and ditches, to have a door of bronze or iron, and for the top to
have defensive ornaments* (ornamentis defensivis).

And there you have it. For all its fighting talk of walls, ditches, and
doors, the license recognized that the castle's wall-head defenses
were going to be purely ornamental. Whereas the top of the tower at
Threave was provided with post-holes to enable the construction of
wooden hoarding (a proper fighting platform), Borthwick is decked
out with eye-catching machicolations in the latest fifteenth-century
fashion. As defenses, they are almost entirely useless, because they
come at the expense of crenellations—there are no battlements
on the top of the tower to offer any cover to a defender. So the
machicolations, for all that they look pretty, actually compromise
the castle's defensibility.

Borthwick, in fact, has no functional military hardware at all—no
arrow-loops, no gun-loops, no murder-holes. Most tellingly, where
the architect had the opportunity to capitalize on the defensive
advantages of his design, he conspicuously chose to ignore them.
Consider, for example, the castle's wings. From the start of the fifteenth century, it became increasingly common for tower houses,
rather than being simple, single blocks (like Threave), to have one
or more additional wings. Such buildings are commonly referred
to as L-plan or Z-plan tower houses, because of the shape of their
floor plans.

A conventional (blood-and-guts) theory of castle development
would say that such wings were developed in order to provide
flanking fire across the castle's entrance. According to this logic,
the best place for the entrance at Borthwick would be on the west
side, nestled safely between the two great wings (unusually, both
wings at Borthwick are on the same side of the tower). The builder,
however, completely ignored the defensive opportunity this presented. Instead, he located the doorway on the castle's north face,
in a completely exposed position.

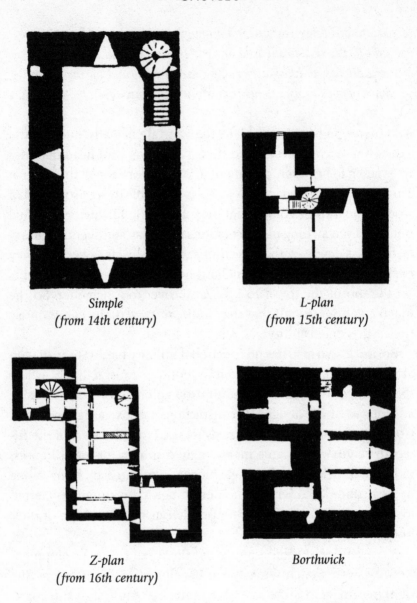

*Simple*
*(from 14th century)*

*L-plan*
*(from 15th century)*

*Z-plan*
*(from 16th century)*

*Borthwick*

To be fair, Borthwick Castle does have a certain inherent strength because of its height—when a building is this tall, you need thick walls to support the weight of the floors above. But it is impossible to read Borthwick as an overtly warlike building, constructed in the face of hostile threat from a dangerous dynasty of bad kings. Apart from anything else, it was the king who gave Sir

William permission to build in the first place. What the royal license tells us (with unusual explicitness) is that contemporaries, including the king, recognized that anyone building a castle in fifteenth-century Scotland was likely to have motives other than defense, and that ornamentation (showing off) was a crucial factor. William Borthwick was, in fact, a man in much the same mold as that other castle-builder, royal licensee, and all-round show-off, Sir Edward Dallingridge. Like Dallingridge, Borthwick wanted a castle because he wished to stress his newfound importance, rather than because he lived in constant fear of attack. The son of a reasonably well-to-do knight, Sir William amassed a small fortune after succeeding to his father's estate in 1414, perhaps as a result of being the king's customs collector early in his career. Later a rising star at the Scottish court, what he needed was a grand building in which to offer the king hospitality, rather than a fortress to keep him out.

When it came to accommodating people, Borthwick was well up to the job. The wings of the castle serve not to flank the entrance, but to provide more rooms for guests. This is quite apparent to anyone who pays a visit to Borthwick today; the castle now functions as a hotel. Inside the castle, the walls, which may once have been plastered or painted, now stand stark and bare. This reveals the outstanding quality of the castle's construction. Inside and out it is finished with blocks of top-quality ashlar, each piece laboriously cut and shaped by a stonemason before being assembled. This is good evidence of how wealthy William Borthwick must have been, but the stonework also provides other clues about the nature of Borthwick Castle.

In the Middle Ages, stonemasons would leave a mark on every block they cut—not as any mysterious sign, just as a useful way for workmen and their employers to keep tabs on productivity. Masons' marks are normally visible to some degree on almost any castle you care to visit. I don't think, however, I have ever visited a castle with so many marks on display as Borthwick. The only obstacle to comparing them is the castle's present décor—most of the wall-space is covered with pictures, swords, and suits of armor—but if you persist, the results are very illuminating. Painstaking investigation of the castle has revealed over sixty different masons' marks, which means that sixty different masons were working on the project (not counting carpenters, glaziers, smiths, quarriers, general laborers, and other assorted skivvies). Interestingly, identical marks are found on fireplaces, lintels, curved blocks, and flat ones, which suggests that the masons didn't specialize—each one was actually very versatile. Most importantly, however, comparing the marks reveals identical sets spread right throughout the building, from the basement to the rooftop. The workforce, then, was the same for the whole building project—individuals might come and go, but by and large the men who started the project were also present when the final blocks were heaved into place.

The conclusions drawn from the masons' marks, the design of the castle, the wording of the license, and the position of William Borthwick invite us to reflect on Borthwick Castle as a whole. For a start, as the grandest tower house in Scotland, it cannot have been built in a hurry. Even with sixty masons on the job, it would have taken at least a decade, and possibly a lot longer, to complete. The quality of its construction, as well as its scale, indicate a huge investment of capital over a long period. The castle is far more preoccupied with ornamentation and display than it is with defense. Now, it may sound obvious, but people do not normally pour money into building undefended houses unless they can be reasonably certain that they will get a return on their investment. Borthwick was part of a major building boom, and building booms rarely occur in war zones. Sir William's tower house is an expression of confidence—a project prompted not by feelings of insecurity, but by the expectation of a secure future ahead.

So it seems that at mighty Borthwick, as at Threave, first appearances can be deceptive. Both buildings, when subjected to close scrutiny, start to tell a different story about late medieval Scotland. Tower houses did not always stand alone, and were not built in opposition to the Crown. They could stand at the center of communities during peacetime, and could be built with the king's permission. As much ornate status symbols as fortresses, they must have required many years of peace and stability to construct in the first place.

So where, you may be wondering, does this leave the dastardly Stewart kings or, for that matter, their good-for-nothing nobles? The history books tell us that they were always at each others' throats, stabbing each other to death and getting killed by exploding cannon. Surely we can't explain them away so easily?

All Scottish castles have to have at least one legend (apparently the Tourist Board is very strict about this). Ghosts are an obvious favorite for pulling in the punters; bloody battles and grisly murders come a close second. Borthwick is blessed with two such tall tales. Its ghost story is remarkably humdrum (local girl, pregnant by laird, killed with sword, still wails at night, and so on—the only true mystery is why she was never mentioned before the late twentieth century). The other legend, however, is wonderfully inventive, and makes cunning use of the castle's unusual architecture. In the Middle Ages (that is, the Bad Old Days), the lords of Borthwick Castle were a contemptible bunch. When they were not out getting the local lasses in trouble, and felt unable to face *another* game of backgammon, they would amuse themselves by playing with their prisoners. These poor wretches, held captive in the bowels of the castle for reasons that history does not relate, were from time to time led to the top of the tower. Once up on the roof, allowed a taste and a view of liberty, they were offered a cruel choice by their gloating captors. They could, if they wished, leap across the gap between the two wings of the castle—a yawning chasm some twelve feet wide, and once apparently complemented by a set of iron spikes at the bottom (with a drop of over a hundred feet, this seems a trifle unnecessary; no doubt the Borthwicks reasoned that, if you're going to be villainous, you may as well go whole hog). Since the prisoners had their hands tied behind their backs, the odds were stacked heavily against success and strongly in favor of a major cleaning job. If, however, they succeeded in making this death-defying leap, they were rewarded with that prize most treasured by legendary medieval Scots—their freedom!

It must have been fun to be the kind of mischievous Victorian grandfather who made up stories like this (I for one certainly look forward to the day when I can inflict lasting trauma on my own grandchildren with such gruesome tales). When such yarns are presented to us, freed from the constraints of evidence and probability, we are able to recognize them as the work of inspired inventors, and distinguish them from the narrative of proper history. Or are we? What if such tales are woven into the history of a nation, and have become so ingrained, so well known and so self-evident, that questioning their authenticity seems tantamount to heresy?

In actual fact, many of the stories told about the Stewart kings belong to the same category of old wives' tales. Only recently have historians started to unpick the strands of truth from the rich tapestry of history and legend. For example, the idea that for centuries on end, the Stewarts were locked in an epic struggle for supremacy with their leading subjects has been shown to be false. How, then, you may ask, did we end up with the idea that it ever happened in the first place? Step forward, if you please, storytelling grandfather extraordinaire, Sir Walter Scott.

Walter Scott is rightly revered as Scotland's most famous literary son. Born in 1771, he overcame a host of personal misfortunes (polio, insolvency, and romantic rejection among them) to become the most prolific and popular writer of his age. Esteemed in his own day (he was created a baronet in 1820), he was commemorated after his death by the great monument that still stands on Prince's Street in his home town of Edinburgh. As a writer, his specialty was making history dramatic. As well as a clutch of historical novels, he also wrote a popular history of Scotland entitled *Tales of a Grandfather*. Like any granddad trying to hold the attention of his young audience, Scott packed his history with lots of exciting detail: dramatic reported speech, feats of derring-do, and struggles against impossible odds. The only drawback was that much of this detail was made up. To be fair to Scott, this was not entirely his fault; for the most part, he was just skillfully reworking tales that had been in circulation for centuries. Most of them were first told in the sixteenth century, by writers with very definite political agendas, who had good reason to pour scorn on the rulers of the not-too-distant past. Walter Scott's unique contribution was to take these biased histories and make them digestible, memorable, and hugely popular. Countless editions of the *Tales* were churned out, including specially abridged versions for use in schools. Just as for generations of English people Shakespeare was the only history they ever read, so Walter Scott provided Scotland with a gripping and dramatic version of medieval and early modern past. Neither author, however, got even remotely close to what had really happened.

So how can we find out "what really happened"? The problem facing historians of late medieval Scotland is the appalling state of contemporary written evidence. For Walter Scott, the lack of chronicle material was in itself sufficient proof of his basic point: "Everybody was too busy fighting to write anything down," he reasoned. There is, however, enough evidence to nip the more outrageous myths in the bud. Take, for example, the struggle between James II and the Black Douglases. Walter Scott would have us believe that the Douglases at one point raised forty thousand men against the king; the contemporary Auchinleck chronicle puts the size of the earl's force at Stirling at just six hundred. Such information has led to a drastically revised picture of the realities of power in late medieval Scotland. The Walter Scott version suggests a king in danger of being eclipsed by his turbulent nobility. The reality was a king who, in spite of his violent and plainly unjust methods, enjoyed wide-ranging support from the political community as he set out to destroy one of his great noble families. But kings teetering on the edge of destruction make for more gripping reading than kings doing just fine. Grisly stories always make the front pages and help keep the grandchildren quiet. The reality of the matter was that the Stewart kings worked in partnership with their nobles in the business of governing Scotland.

Indeed, the kings of Scotland would have been hard pushed to rule in any other way. To a large degree, the extent of their power was limited by the Scottish landscape. A country crossed with mountains and lochs is far harder to govern directly than a land of rolling hills and fields. Communication and travel was arduous, not just for the king and his armies but also for his ministers. Even the most energetic monarchs found it difficult to make their presence felt across the kingdom. In addition, Scottish kings had no regular tax base; on the rare occasions that they did try to mulct their subjects, they encountered hostility. As a result, despite their deepest desires to cut a dash on the European stage, the Stewarts were poor cousins in the international family of princes. To take an obvious example, the kings of England in the fifteenth century could count on at least £50,000 a year from taxes and customs. A Stewart king would count himself extremely lucky if he managed to raise a tenth of this sum.

So, geography and poverty limited the extent of the Stewarts' power. It obliged them to work with their nobles, not against them. It meant that they had to rule through consensus and cooperation, and accept the fact that large chunks of their authority had to be delegated for others to exercise.

Nowhere was this more true than on the northern and western fringes of the kingdom—the point where the lowlands met the highlands. Nowadays, of course, the highlands provide the corporate identity for all of Scotland: the image of the tartan-clad clansman is the predominant motif of the Scottish heritage industry. It will hardly come as groundbreaking news that this is invented history—surely everyone now knows that the modern kilt was invented by a nineteenth-century factory owner? The Heritage Highlands are almost entirely the work of nineteenth-century enthusiasts, and once again the chief culprit is Walter Scott. Through his romantic novels (especially *Rob Roy*), and also in his other capacities (he was, for example, Master of Ceremonies during the royal visit of George IV to Edinburgh, an occasion which demanded the rapid invention of a lot of "traditional" festivities and costumes), Scott helped to devise and perpetuate the image of the highlander as a "noble savage." Under the weight of these fantasies, the true identity of the medieval highlands was buried.

There is, however, more than enough evidence to resurrect the real highlanders of the late Middle Ages. In the fourteenth and fifteenth centuries, power in the north and west of Scotland rested with the Lords of the Isles—the Clan MacDonald. They governed these areas as independent rulers in all but name, occasionally paying lip-service to the Stewart kings. Descended from ancient Gaelic and Scandinavian tribes, their power was on the increase starting in the middle of the fourteenth century. At the height of their power in the fifteenth century, they could muster an army of ten thousand men.

There was much more to these clans, however, than just fighting, as even a cursory examination of their culture will reveal. The extent of their literacy can be appreciated by the large number of written documents that have survived, drawn up in both Gaelic and Latin. The men of the Isles used their great galley-ships more often for trading, especially with their Gaelic relatives in Ireland, than they did for raiding. Highland society took unchecked violence and disorder seriously, and attempted to combat it through a network of local courts. In other words, the Lords of the Isles in the fifteenth century had a reputation for good government.

"In thair time," wrote one sixteenth-century Scottish historian, "thair was great peace and welth in the Isles throw the ministration of justice."

The men and women of the Isles were not savages, but rather the eventual losers in a clash of cultures—a clash that had been on the cards for some time. By the end of the fourteenth century, lowland chronicler John of Fordun acknowledged the culture gap when he described the northerners as "wild Scots."

The highlanders, for their part, had come to regard their southern neighbors as weak and effeminate, and hardly worth taking seriously. They had, for example, started to drink a rather effete new draught called "whisky," rather than drinking red wine like real men. But despite occasionally trading punches, the gloves only really came off at the end of the fifteenth century. The seeds of trouble were sown in 1462, when the Lord of the Isles, John MacDonald, entered into a secret treaty with the exiled earl of Douglas and the king of England—an agreement in which they conspired to carve up the kingdom of Scotland between them.

Although it came to nothing, King James III took a very dim view of the plan when it came to light in 1475. He charged MacDonald with treason, confiscated his properties on the Scottish mainland, and compelled him to acknowledge his status as a vassal. John himself proved willing to submit, but the rest of the Clan MacDonald, and in particular John's son Angus, resented both the territorial losses and the humiliation. For the next twenty years the Isles were divided by this bitter internal dispute, and the struggle left them fatally weakened. In 1490, shortly after defeating his father in battle, Angus was murdered. Three years later, the king of Scots intervened and imposed his authority. The days of the Lords of the Isles, he declared, were over—all their lands and power were forfeit to the Scottish Crown.

The king in question was James IV, who was rather a good king. Although apparently unpleasant in his youth, he matured into a highly capable ruler, a man who understood the realities of power in Scotland and knew how to work the system to his best advantage. More than competent as a military leader, and highly assiduous when it came to traveling his realm and dishing out justice, James IV's real strength lay in his ability to delegate power to the right people. His decision in 1493 to intervene in the Isles was his first political act as an adult, but he was already old enough to appreciate that he would need plenty of help in enforcing the confiscation of the lordship. Even his less capable ancestors had encouraged their lowland nobles to build castles along the highland-lowland divide, entrusting them to bring order to the region.

It was under James IV, however, that the greatest amount of castle-building took place, as Crown and nobility worked together to tackle the problem of reducing the north-west to obedience. The major beneficiaries of this joint-stock enterprise were the Gordon family, earls of Huntly, and the Campbells, earls of Argyll. However, few of the castles built by these men survive today; in fact, the best architectural example of the collaboration between the Scottish Crown and its aristocracy was provided by someone a little more lowly.

Castle Urquhart is one of the most dramatically sited buildings in Scotland. It stands on a rocky spur on the shores of Loch Ness. The site has been fortified since ancient times, but the first castle was built to an enclosure design in the thirteenth century. Because of its position on the highland-lowland fault-line, control of Urquhart was long contested by the Stewart kings and the Lords of the Isles, and the castle was taken and retaken several times by both sides during the fifteenth century. Following the forfeiture of 1493, however, James IV was determined to hold on to it. And so, paradoxically, he gave it to someone else—a minor nobleman called John Grant of Freuchie.

The king's gift of Urquhart to John Grant in 1509 was a big thank-you for more than twenty years of loyal service to the Crown. It made permanent an arrangement that had existed since the last years of the fifteenth century, under which the Grants had held the castle on a series of temporary leases. Nevertheless, the perpetual custody of a former royal castle was a terrific prize, and as such it came with several conditions attached. In return for holding Urquhart in perpetuity, the Grants were obliged to keep the castle in good repair, and bound to restore the damaged buildings to their former glory. According to the text of the charter that confirmed the king's gift, the Grants were "to construct within the castle a hall, chamber and kitchen, with all the requisite offices, such as a pantry, bakehouse, brewhouse, oxhouse, kiln and dovecote."

Most importantly, the king wanted them to construct a tower house on the site. They were "to repair or build at the castle a tower, with an outwork or rampart of stone and lime, for protecting the lands and the people from the inroads of thieves and wrong-doers."

The line about thieves and wrongdoers is the real catch, and goes to show that there is no such thing as a free castle. The king could have got anyone to agree to rebuild Urquhart had it not been located on the fringes of hostile territory; the real job was going to be holding on to the castle in the face of attacks from the disinherited and disgruntled Clan MacDonald. Unsurprisingly, the Lords of the Isles did not take too kindly to being told that their authority was forfeit. In the fifty years after 1493 they endeavored to win it back, making frequent raids on the mainland, and often sweeping up the Great Glen to try and reclaim Urquhart. On All Saints Day 1513, just four years after John Grant took "permanent" custody, they succeeded. The Grant family were driven out of the castle, and were unable to return for a full three years. When John Grant later listed his losses before the king's council, it was clear that the clansmen had taken everything but the kitchen sink. Pots, pans, kettles, beds, sheets, blankets, and pillows had all been carried away as booty. All the castle's stores of fish, bread, ale, cheese, and butter had been similarly confiscated or consumed. Moreover, the lands around the castle had been completely devastated; three hundred cows and a thousand sheep had been comprehensively rustled. Altogether, John Grant estimated his losses at over £2,000.

Small wonder, then, that the Grant family, when they eventually got a moment's peace, built one of the more defensible tower houses of the sixteenth century. Although it is now very ruinous, having suffered at the hands of a great storm in the eighteenth century, the Grant Tower still exhibits certain features of real warlike intent. The machicolations around the top of the castle are, for the most part, purely decorative (there are no holes), and may in fact date to a later rebuilding. Over both the entrances, however, they suddenly get serious, standing discreetly but distinctly proud of the wall. Equally subtle but no less murderous in intent are the pistol holes secreted under most of the windowsills. It should also be remembered that, in addition to the tower, the Grant family rebuilt the rest of the castle, as the conditions of their tenure demanded. The strength of the restored fortifications indicate that, come what may, they were determined to cling on tight to the castle the king had given them. And so they did. In spite of repeated attacks, it was not until 1911 that the family finally surrendered their castle, this time into the friendly arms of the state.

John Grant of Freuchie was favored in 1509 in the expectation that he would defend the area around Urquhart from attack. His role, however, was not simply a military one. He was also expected to govern the region in peacetime, and to this end he was entrusted with extensive police powers. This hardly made him exceptional— even a good, energetic king like James IV, who hardly stopped touring his country to hear court cases, was only able to exercise a loose, supervisory jurisdiction over his kingdom. Most of the decisions and judgments that affected people's everyday lives were in the hands of men like John Grant.

People who fell foul of the law in John Grant of Freuchie's neighborhood could expect to end up in the prison at Castle Urquhart. Cold, dank, and windowless, its facilities (or lack of them) are typical of castle prisons at the time. Apparently the long narrow cell once had a latrine chute at one end, which must been a source of some consolation to both jailed and jailer. Because Urquhart is an older castle and had its tower house added later, the prison is situated in the old thirteenth-century gatehouse. With tower houses built from scratch, it was more common for prisoners to be kept in the basement of the tower itself, as was the case at Threave and Borthwick. Prisons in towers like this were, quite literally, pits. Accessible only from a hatch above, they lacked even the basic sanitary facilities once on offer at Urquhart. The only solace for a detainee in such circumstances was that his or her incarceration would probably not last long: days or even weeks, but probably not years. Imprisonment in the Middle Ages was rarely used as a form of punishment. Rather, a prison was used like a cell in a police station or a remand center—somewhere to hold the accused until it was time to go to court.

Court was never very far away—sometimes just a walk upstairs. At Urquhart it was a short distance across the courtyard to the castle's great hall. Today little remains of this; only low ruins of walls and cellarage are now visible, but in its day it would have been an all-purpose room, used for public business as well as for dining and entertainment. When occasion demanded, it would also have served as a courtroom for John Grant. Lords in England and Wales would use their castle halls in much the same way, but there was a big difference in the powers they possessed. South of the border, the jurisdiction of a local lord in his manor court would only extend to minor matters—drunkenness, brawling, and so on. Everything else was the responsibility and preserve of the king, and lords who exceeded their remit were in turn punished severely. In Scotland, the opposite was true. Even at the lowest level of the baron's court, lords had the right to fine, mutilate, and even execute criminals. An English lord could have you clapped in the stocks, but John Grant of Freuchie could send you to the gallows.

John Grant's powers over the life and death of offenders in his locale may seem remarkable, but they are far from being the most startling aspect of justice in his day. Beyond the court and prison lay another route, at once more ancient and more commonplace: the blood feud. The word itself conjures up the worst images of medieval Scottish society—the bloody feuding of Walter Scott legend: marauding clansmen armed with claymores, sweeping down from the hills and laying waste to villages; rival families slugging it out for generations . . . an endless cycle of mindless violence. Like boisterous schoolboys left to play unsupervised, the turbulent nobles of Scotland apparently knew no better.

It would be silly to pretend that there is not some truth in this. Fighting between clans could indeed be drawn out and bloody. The Grants of Freuchie had their fair share of scraps with their neighbors, the Farquharsons; they would frequently make off with each others' cattle or grain, and raids could end in mutilation and murder. Such a view of feuding, however, gives only half the picture. Blood feuds could also be a way of limiting violence and ensuring peace in a society where the power of the state was weak. The documentary record reveals that individuals and communities would go to extraordinary lengths to restore order when the peace was broken. In October 1527, for example, John Grant of Freuchie made his last datable appearance in a written agreement with the Farquharsons. As chief of the Grants, and accompanied by his sons and other leading members of the clan, he met with Finlay Farquharson and family, his former enemies. Both sides had come together to lay down their weapons and put aside their differences.

"Deploring of the taking ill, and the cutting off, and the plundering," the document began, and went on to say that both sides desired "so far as human weakness can, to redeem, satisfy and amend the disgraceful crimes towards God and each other."

Later in the same document, there are elaborate clauses as to how this restitution of wealth and salving of injured pride is to be achieved. The really interesting part, however, comes in the middle. Here, both sides are anxious to spell out that the decision to stop fighting is mutual. Neither side has been pressured into the agreement by some greater power, like a judge, bishop, or king. Both the Grants and the Farquharsons, it says, were acting "in themselves; neither induced by force nor fear, uncompelled and unconstrained, of their own mere and free wills."

Agreements such as this were quite common, and prove that there was more to feuding than just fighting. Feuding was also about doing justice, even though to us the whole concept might sound very unjust. A system like this often meant that no one was punished for a particular crime; you could quite easily get away with murder. Without a higher authority waving the sword of justice, you could not expect judgment and demand retribution. The best that both parties could hope for was that the balance would be restored to society, and that the losses on each side would be compensated.

This could result in arrangements that sound quite astounding to modern ears, such as the oft-quoted example of Catherine Patrick. Placed at a disadvantage when her father was murdered in a feud, she was eventually compensated by being married to the murderer's son. It sounds almost farcical, but the fact of the matter was that an agreement like this was conceived to heal divisions between two kin groups. Catherine had to look on it not so much as losing a father as gaining a husband.

On the one hand, the example of Catherine Patrick shows that, at a very basic level, the victims of crime could expect some form of justice. On the other hand, the justice was rough, and the fact that her father was murdered by one of his neighbors can only indicate that late medieval Scotland was not an especially peaceful place to live. John Grant of Freuchie, having fought with the MacDonalds and feuded with the Farquharsons, could also have told you as much. At the same time, however, he could also have told you about his efforts to combat disorder and bring stability to the region around his castle. As a judge, he sat in the courtroom of his great hall, handing down verdicts with an authority delegated to him by the king. As a powerful individual in his own right, he often acted as an impartial arbiter, bringing an end to the feuds of others. As a man who ultimately wanted peace for his friends, family, and tenants, he buried the hatchet with his neighbors, and swore to try and live in peace.

Men like Grant built castles like Urquhart in anticipation of troubled times ahead. But the warlike appearance of these buildings can also blind us to the fact that many of them were built in a spirit of cooperation. Constructed with encouragement from the Crown, they are evidence that both the Stewarts and their nobles desired a more peaceful and prosperous society. Scotland in the late Middle Ages was not the romantic but anarchic wasteland depicted by Sir Walter Scott; neither was it a society that never knew peace. When Sir John Grant accepted James IV's gift of Urquhart, he not only proved that kings and nobles could be perfect partners; he also accepted responsibility to administer justice in the region—to act as policeman, judge, and peacemaker. In the words of the charter that the king gave him, he was there "to protect the lands and the people."

There was one area of Scotland, however, where one could always count on violence in the late Middle Ages, and that was the border with England. This was not, as it is today, a neatly drawn line on a map—it was a frontier zone where two countries collided. Even when the governments of England and Scotland were nominally at peace, the Borders were a lawless region. Attacks were expected and dreaded; banditry and cattle rustling were a way of life.

This had not always been the case. Throughout the thirteenth century the English and Scots had actually got on rather well, and this was reflected in their domestic architecture. Recent research has shown that, throughout the century, the dwellings in both northern England and southern Scotland were becoming steadily less defensible, and by the century's end the preferred form of building was the first-floor (or even ground-floor) hall.

All this changed when Edward I attempted to conquer Scotland starting in 1296. The peaceful conditions that had been developing for decades were shattered, and the bloody struggle that followed lasted half a century. The physical effects reduced an area that had only just started to enjoy the benefits of peace into a desolate wasteland. The psychological effects, of course, lasted a lot longer— thanks to Edward I, the English and the Scots quickly learned to hate each other again. When the wars came to an end in the second half of the fourteenth century, a slow economic recovery began in the Borders, but the mutual hostility between the lowland Scots and northern English lasted for the rest of the Middle Ages and beyond. There was no question of building halls—for both sides, towers were the only option.

The difference came to lie in the types of towers they built. While lowland Scots built tower houses of high quality, it seems that their counterparts in northern England could only afford a humbler type of tower, called a "bastle" or a "pele." Why there was such a marked division is unclear. It has been suggested that most Scots nobles were richer because they managed their land directly, whereas many farmers in northern England were obliged to pay rent to the Crown. It could equally be that the Scots had the best of the fighting and made off with more of the moveable wealth. A third possibility is that bastles and peles were once more numerous on the Scottish side of the border, but have since been destroyed. A cluster of Scottish bastles remains around the town of Jedburgh, with an especially well-preserved example at Mervinslaw.

At first sight, Mervinslaw Pele seems quite grim. It lies well off the beaten track in the middle of a field of sheep, and from a distance you might mistake it for a large cowshed or at best a deserted farm building. It is hard to imagine human beings living comfortably inside. However, this dilapidated little tower was once quite homely, and has fundamental similarities to other grander members of the tower house family. It is a two-storey building and, as with larger towers, the main entrance was on the first floor, accessible via a vanished wooden stair or ladder. The main room on this level was hardly luxurious, but a pair of windows on the south side allowed it to be lit during the daytime. While there is no trace of a fireplace, it is possible that flagstones were once placed against the wall at the

*Mervinslaw Pele.*

opposite end of the room, and that a degree of heartiness was there-fore also achievable. Like larger tower houses, the pele at Mervinslaw did not stand alone—it is surrounded by the foundations of other buildings, which were probably the homes of tenants. The ground floor of the tower was used for storage, and probably for locking up the most expensive livestock at night. The doorway at this level was once heavily secured: there are holes in the stonework to indicate that the door could be barred twice, bolted, and may have also been reinforced by an iron yett (the poor man's portcullis). Mervinslaw lies just a mile from the English border, so such high levels of security made sense if you wanted to hang on to that prize bull.

In its own humble way, therefore, a pele tower was probably up to the job of protecting a man, his wife, and their favorite cow, if they had the questionable good fortune to live on the Scottish border five hundred years ago. Nevertheless, one can only imagine how frightening it must have been to hear a warning cry go up, or perhaps glimpse horsemen on the horizon, and know that a raid was about to take place. If you acted quickly, you might just have time to pen up the sheep, drag Billy the Bull inside, and lock yourself and your family upstairs. As you sat there and awaited the inevitable, anxiously fingering your pistol and wondering if your tiny stone tower was as strong and secure as you hoped, you could cling doggedly to one cheery thought: come the morning, your friends and neighbors would be round, helping you to assess the losses and repair the damages—and get ready to offset both with a raid into England the following evening.

For such was life on the borders. "Contynuall intercoorse of win-ninge and loosinge of goods do ebb and flowe like the sea," wrote one sixteenth-century English border commissioner. Raiding and rustling ("reiving" as it was known locally) was the norm, and the situation looked unlikely to change so long as England and Scotland remained rival nations.

Starting in 1603, however, this was suddenly no longer the case. In that year, King James VI of Scotland became King James I of England as well. With the two governments cooperating at last, a conscious effort was made to police the borders properly, and it was highly successful. Levels of cattle rustling fell away almost overnight. Very soon bandits and border reivers were the stuff of song and legend.

Nor was it just the Borders that benefited during the reign of James VI. This was something of a golden age for Scotland as a whole, and a welcome relief at the end of a disastrous sixteenth century. Things had got off to an exceedingly bad start in 1513, when the popular James IV had confidently marched a united nobility to meet an English army at Flodden, only to experience the most cataclysmic military defeat in Scottish history. By the end of the day, not only the king but most of the Scottish aristocracy lay dead in the field. James was succeeded by his son, James V, then a strapping lad of eighteen months. By the time he reached adulthood there was just enough time for him to repeat his father's mistake. After a crushing defeat in battle in 1542, James died a broken man, realizing that his throne would descend to his only heir, a baby girl called Mary. As the hopelessly romantic Queen of Scots, Mary has generated more column inches than any other Stewart, but no amount of sympathetic guff can disguise the fact that she was actually just plain hopeless. Her reign saw the collapse of the Scottish Church and the temporary eclipse of the monarchy. For most of the remainder of the century, Scotland became a political football for England and France, with warring pro-English and pro-French factions struggling for control at the Scottish court.

It is hardly surprising that, during these dark days, very few new tower houses were built. As we have seen throughout this chapter, people rarely began major building projects during periods of civil unrest. It was not, in fact, until the last decades of the sixteenth century, when the political situation began to improve, that castle construction was resumed on any scale. The adult rule of James VI ushered in a new age of peace and prosperity. Even the ancient practice of feuding began to die out during his reign. One effect of the Scottish Reformation was a condemnation of the notion that peace could be restored by compensation. Murder was increasingly seen as a crime and a sin that should be punished by the state and the church; the individual offender found he could no longer make amends with an offer of money, goods, or marriage. Infused with a new sense of morality, Scottish nobles stopped reaching for their swords and guns, and began instead to attack each other with lawyers. Under James VI, Scotland had never had it so good, and his reign saw a wide-scale resumption of the building of tower houses.

Craigievar Castle, near Aberdeen, is the finest of this last genera-tion of Scottish tower houses. Built toward the end of James VI's reign, between 1610 and 1625, it was the work of a man called William Forbes. As a younger son, William did not stand to inherit much from his father's estate, and therefore had to make his own way in the world. He set himself up in the pine tree business, and began trading with Germany and Scandinavia. This earned him a nickname—Danzig Willie, they started to call him—and ultimately a huge fortune. Like so many of the other self-made men in this book, he decided that he needed a grand new home to mark his newfound importance. In his day and age, there was still only one option for a man who wanted to announce to the world that he had arrived: he was going to build a castle.

The tower that Willie built at Craigievar, however, is a world away from its distant ancestor at Threave. Built from pretty pink granite, it is more Walt Disney than Archibald the Grim. The tower is all about ornamentation; just a quick glance is enough to tell you that defense was not very high on Willie's list of priorities. The castle is liberally studded with windows, more numerous at the top, but also noticeably vulnerable and accessible at lower levels. The doorway, although reinforced with the traditional iron yett, is at ground-floor level; even tiny Mervinslaw is stronger in this regard. The biggest difference, however, is at the top. When they came to construct the last generation of tower houses, builders dispensed with the battlements and machicolations of yesteryear. Instead they chose to crown their creations with gabled roofs and rounded turrets. Masons and patrons alike were evidently enamored of the effect produced by "corbelling"—building the rooms and turrets so that they stood proud of the main tower. It is easy to see why. The effect is strikingly beautiful—Craigievar bursts out at the top like a flower in bloom. From the point of view of defense, however, such architecture is useless, since it leaves the defender with no access to the wall-head. The only place to stand in the open at Craigievar is on a small balcony right at the very top. This, however, as its rather incongruous Renaissance balustrade suggests, is not a fighting platform, but a spot to take in the view: a place for Danzig Willie to stand, whisky in hand, gazing out over his estate.

The concern with display is carried over into the inside of the castle, where some aspects of the original interior decoration survive in perfect condition. Were he to view the hall today, Danzig Willie might be dazzled by the light pouring in through the big nineteenth-century windows, and puzzled by the riot of nineteenth-century tartan. He would, however, recognize many features in the room. The table that now stands in the center is thought to date from the early seventeenth century, and the carved wooden paneling is also part of the hall's original decor. But the most striking aspect of the castle's interior is its ceilings, which are decorated throughout with ornamental plasterwork. The effect is best appreciated in the hall, where the vaulted ceiling begins at eye level and invites you to follow its arches inward and upward. Roman emperors as well as heraldic beasts stare back down—like the balcony on the roof, they are a reminder that this is a post-Renaissance castle. Had he got the decorators in just a few years earlier, Willie would have had to make do with painted ceilings, like the wonderful examples that survive at nearby Crathes Castle. As luck would have it, however, good timing offered him a whole new way to show off his wealth. Plastered ceilings were the very latest thing when he had them installed in 1626 (the date appears in the design). Only a few examples pre-date Craigievar, beginning with those created for James VI at Edinburgh in 1617. Willie was rich enough to employ the king's plasterers, and to follow the fashions of royalty to the letter.

Stunning décor aside, the most impressive thing about Craigievar is not the plasterwork or the carved wood paneling, but the design of the building itself. The castle was built by a family of masons called Bell, who produced several similar towers in the Aberdeenshire region in the late sixteenth and early seventeenth century—Craigievar has close relations at Crathes, Midmar, and Castle Fraser. Danzig Willie's tower, however, is generally reckoned to be the best of the bunch.

Such was the ingenuity of the master mason that, without in any way compromising the slender and elegant shape of the tower, he nevertheless contrived to include all the domestic features that one could only reasonably expect in a horizontal layout. Take, for example, the service arrangements in the castle's hall. The designer has managed to include a screens passage and minstrels gallery (both of which survive, though the gallery has been chopped in half by the insertion of a large window). A door on the left leads to the tiniest of pantries, while a door on the right opens to reveal a spiral stair winding down to the buttery below. In other words, the conventional service arrangement that we saw at Bodiam has been achieved by an ingenious vertical deployment of the rooms. Moreover, having the buttery on the floor below naturally means it can be far bigger, which is never a bad thing for a wine cellar. No less cunning, the top floor at Craigievar boasts a long gallery (see Chapter Six for more on these). This really is the most ridiculous proposition in a tower house—from the outside, the tower had to look tall and slender, but contemporary fashion now demanded an interior room that was as long as possible. Somehow, however, the mason at Craigievar managed to reconcile these contradictory demands, and executed a quite remarkable architectural balancing act. Danzig Willie obviously wanted the best of both worlds—a castle built in the grand Scottish tower house tradition, but cleverly contrived so that he could live the life of an early-modern Scottish gentleman. He must have been very pleased with what he got.

Craigievar Castle marks the end of a three-hundred-year tradition that can be traced right back through Urquhart and Borthwick to

Threave. All four buildings, of course, are castles, built with defense in mind; sometimes, as with Threave, their defenses were tested to the limit. It would be wrong, however, to suppose that just because Scotland has a lot of castles, it was a place where violence was an everyday occurrence. A closer reading of these towers suggests otherwise, as do the lives of their owners. The Stewart kings may have led violent lives and come to sticky ends, but Archibald the Grim, William Borthwick, John Grant of Freuchie, and Danzig Willie all lived to be old men, and died peaceful deaths.

Tower houses flourished in Scotland because it was a different type of society, one where power was exercised locally rather than concentrated centrally with the king. Communities were regulated by feuds rather than royal edicts, but this did not mean that they were forever fighting; on the contrary, the feud could be a means of achieving peace. Of course, violence was always a possibility, and towers and tower houses therefore remained popular right down to the start of the seventeenth century; but by the middle of this century, the possibility was fast diminishing. James VI's reign had seen the widespread decline of feuding in the lowlands. The rule of law had been introduced to the Borders. The king's succession to the throne of England seemed to remove the ancient and abiding threat of war with "the Auld Enemy."

How terrible, then, that just as its age of castles was drawing to a close, Scotland was the flashpoint for the bloodiest war ever fought on British soil. The decades of peace that had graced the start of the seventeenth century were suddenly shattered, and the resultant conflagration engulfed the whole of Britain in a catastrophic civil war. Above the entrance hall at Craigievar Castle, Danzig Willie's grandson added his badge to the original plastered ceiling. "Doe not vaken sleiping dogs," his motto reads. In 1637, however, the dogs of war were woken.

CHAPTER SIX

# THE CASTLE'S LAST STAND

———✺———

W hen we visit a ruined castle, its former beauty is often difficult to picture. To see the whitewashed walls gleaming and the flags fluttering in the breeze, we have to screw up our eyes and work our imaginations hard. However noble and refined the interior may once have been, chances are it now seems crude and Spartan. We constantly have to remind ourselves that, despite the dripping rainwater, grassy floors, and mossy walls, castles were once sophisticated, sumptuous buildings, full of light, warmth, and good cheer.

Raglan Castle, however, is an exception. Hidden in the hills of south Wales, this magnificent building is one of the grandest ruins in Britain, where every inch of stonework speaks of past splendor. Heraldic devices and coats of arms still adorn the walls; gargoyles grimace at us over the gate. The stained glass is gone from the windows, but the fine stone tracery remains intact. Everything seeks to persuade us that this was once the most splendid place imaginable.

With a great tower and a moat, two courtyards and gatehouses, and built on the site of an earlier motte and bailey, Raglan is almost overqualified as a castle. Yet for all its bona fide credentials, it feels more like an Oxford college or an Inn of Court, suddenly abandoned after some unforeseen tragedy. The evidence of past luxury only reminds us of its present absence, and suffuses the castle with a terrible sense of loss. How did it happen, the curious visitor will want to ask, that this wonderful place, where the walls still whisper of former glories, became so desperately sad?

Travel back, for a moment, to the year 1640, and meet Raglan's owner: Henry Somerset, marquis of Worcester. At sixty-four years old, he is a man in the autumn of his life, and as such he has seen a lot of water flow under the bridge. Looking back to his boyhood, he can still remember the dark days when the Spanish Armada threatened England with invasion. He can also recollect happier times; his teenage years at Oxford, and his early twenties reading law at the Middle Temple. Most of all, he is able to reflect with some satisfaction on a long and successful career as a loyal servant of the Crown. Henry has been a courtier to no less than three successive monarchs: Elizabeth I, James I and Charles I.

Now, however, he has more or less withdrawn from public life, to spend more time with his family. His long marriage to Countess Anne, celebrated forty summers ago, came to an end with her death the previous year. All that remains to him now is the prospect of playing out his final years at Raglan, surrounded by his many children and grandchildren, safe in the knowledge that, in the fullness of time, they will inherit his castle and fortune. To him, these seem modest hopes and ambitions. After all, his ancestors built the castle some two hundred years ago, and his family have enjoyed its custody ever since—he can see no reason why they should not go on enjoying it for another two hundred. England is the most peaceful place in Europe. No one alive can remember having to defend a castle in war.

The marquis does not know it, but war is just around the corner—the bloodiest war ever fought on British soil. Castles everywhere are about to dragged back into military service. From Corfe to Conwy, from Pembroke to Pontefract, sieges are about to take place on a scale unseen for centuries. This time, however, castles will not be up against the trebuchets and crossbows of former times, but the latest and deadliest technologies of the age—the cannon and the mortar. And these killing machines will eventually come in record numbers to Raglan, to take part in one of the biggest, longest, and hardest-fought sieges of the entire conflict.*

This conflict was the English Civil War, as it is still generally known, despite its Scottish and Irish dimensions and the fact that the fighting also extended into Wales. Raglan Castle owes its present appearance to its experiences during the war, and the decisions taken by Henry Somerset in the summer of 1646.

The castle has an importance independent of its role during the 1640s, for it was one of the last great castles to be built in England (or Wales). Its massive scale and strength reflects the wealth and ambitions of its builders, a father and son team who, in classic late-medieval style, found fame and fortune on the battlefields of France. William ap Thomas (Henry Somerset's great-great-great-great-great grandfather) was a man very much in the mold of Sir Edward Dallingridge. Despite his fairly humble gentry background, he distinguished himself in the Hundred Years' War (fighting alongside Henry V at Agincourt), prospered in the service of a great magnate (in this case, the duke of York), and married a rich lady called Elizabeth. Because she was a widow, with sons by a previous marriage, William only acquired a life interest in her estate. In 1432, however, he purchased the manor of Raglan from his stepson for £666, and began to build the castle.

---

* Both Henry Somerset and Raglan have complicated identities. Somerset was earl of Worcester until March 2, 1643, at which point he was promoted to the rank of marquis. For simplicity's sake I have called him "the marquis" throughout. Monmouthshire was considered part of Wales when Raglan was built in the fifteenth century, but its status became ambiguous after 1536, and it was often treated as an English county. The ambiguity persisted until 1974, when the county was absorbed into the Welsh administrative region of Gwent.

In 1445, William ap Thomas died, and his son, also William, picked up the building program where his father had left off. Also a veteran of the French wars, William junior further increased his family's fortunes by investing heavily in the wine trade and supporting the duke of York in his bid for the English throne. In 1468, the duke, now king, rewarded William's loyalty by making him earl of Pembroke. The speed of the earl's rise was outstripped only by the rapidity of his fall. Within a year both he and his career had been abruptly cut short—when the Yorkists lost the battle of Edgecote, he was beheaded.

By this stage, however, Raglan Castle was almost finished, and was more or less the same size and shape that it is today. Most of the castle is the work of the younger William, whose investment was longer and heavier than that of his father. The contribution of William senior, however, was by no means negligible. In particular, he was responsible for Raglan's most prominent and distinctive feature—its huge, isolated great tower. Even today, though sadly much reduced, this part of the castle dwarfs the other buildings; when it was first built it stood five stories and over a hundred feet high.

Between them, the two Williams had built a castle in the very latest French fashion. With its hexagonal towers, prominent machicolations (currently only visible over the gatehouse and the closet tower, but probably once crowning the top of the great tower, too) and "bascule" drawbridges, Raglan has close affinities with contemporary castles in Brittany and along the River Loire. As with other late medieval castles, such flamboyant design features raise the question of style over substance. Evidently there was a desire on the part of the builders to create a castle that was pleasing to the eye; if you look carefully at the machicolations on the top of the gatehouse, you will see gargoyles grinning back down at you. Such decorative features are more common on churches and colleges than castles. In addition, some of the military hardware seems either spurious or, at best, ill-conceived. For example, the gun-loops in the gatehouse, like those at Bodiam, have been judged ineffective by some modern commentators, since they do not offer a comprehensive field of fire.

But the defensibility of Raglan is not really in doubt. The drawbridges, now replaced by spans of stone, were once fully operational. The portcullises, now also vanished, patently worked. Although the castle is not concerned with protecting itself to the same degree as, say, Caernarfon, it nevertheless has a passive strength that puts it on a par with castles of an earlier age. The great tower, in particular, has walls that are ten feet thick.

The big question that hangs over Raglan Castle is not whether its defenses "work" (to the extent that it had them, they worked just fine), but why its owners bothered to build them in the first place. By the time of the younger William's death in 1469, few people in England were building castles any more. The country had been mostly peaceful for well over a century, largely as a result of sending its warlike young men to fight in France. True, when the Hundred Years' War finally clattered to a halt in 1453, there was trouble at home. For the next thirty years, England witnessed a series of domestic conflicts known as the Wars of the Roses. These, however, far from being the bloody nightmare depicted by Shakespeare, were intermittent, small-scale dynastic affairs. While they could have dire consequences for the individual aristocrats involved (William, earl of Pembroke, was not the only man to lose his head), they had no effect whatsoever on architectural fashions. Nobody felt the need to invest in elaborate defenses because of such minor civil disturbances. Equally, with the end of the war in France, no one was making a fortune from soldiery any more either. By the century's end, the people who were really prospering were not soldiers but courtiers—men who worked in the service of the Crown. When they built new homes, they forsook all the cunning and elaborate forms of defense that their forebears had devised, and lavished their money on courtyard houses. A well-known example is Hampton Court, built in the early part of the sixteenth century by Henry VIII's one-time first minister, Cardinal Wolsey.

While Henry VIII's nobility set about building non-defensible residences like Hampton Court, the king himself constructed a chain of tiny coastal forts, stretching from Pendennis in Cornwall to Deal in Kent. Throughout the Middle Ages, the English Crown had been growing steadily stronger, increasingly able to raise large national taxes and fund a bureaucracy on an ever greater scale. By Henry's day the Crown was also willing to take on the burden of defending its subjects from foreign attack. When they first appeared, Henry's new defenses were christened "castles," and surviving examples (like Camber, Sandown, and Walmer) still go by the name of castle today. Without being too judgmental about what is and what is not a castle, however, I think they are rightly excluded from the castle club. Their function is purely military—they have no residential dimension at all.

By the start of the sixteenth century, therefore, castles (according to my definition, at any rate) were already a thing of the past. Everywhere you traveled, the great fortresses of earlier centuries stood empty, their owners having moved out into comfy courtyard houses. Very quickly, these abandoned buildings fell into disrepair. Castles might look tough, but at the end of the day they require a lot of care and affection. You have to clean out their drains and their gutters, and repair holes in the roofs. Surveys of royal castles, which survive from the middle of the thirteenth century, make it perfectly clear that the king and his custodians fought a constant battle against the elements just to keep them in working order. A few years of neglect or one big storm was enough to wreak considerable havoc with the fabric of a building. Traveling writers and official surveyors in the sixteenth century noted that most castles were in a very bad way.

Only a minority of aristocrats stuck it out in castles, either because abandoning the ancestral pile was unconscionable, or because the castle was sufficiently well-appointed to meet their more refined requirements. In the case of Raglan, it was probably a mixture of both reasons. The castle had been in the same family for generations, and as a fifteenth-century building it was also extremely well provided and handsomely fitted out. Nevertheless, the sixteenth-century owners of Raglan, like other die-hard castle-owners with less up-to-date models, still felt compelled to upgrade the medieval buildings to bring them into line with the latest architectural fashions. It was essential to keep up with the owners of courtyard houses in terms of luxury and refinement. If you were a castle-owner in the sixteenth century, you had to make home improvements.

The man who undertook these improvements at Raglan was the grandfather of the marquis of Worcester, William Somerset (d. 1589). Most of his alterations were concentrated on the castle's eastern courtyard, which he enlarged by destroying an earlier range of buildings and constructing a new office wing. He also substantially altered the castle's hall, rebuilding its eastern wall (again, part of the eastern courtyard) and fitting a handsome new hammer-beam roof of Irish oak. At the same time, Somerset improved the hall's service arrangements, in particular by extending the size of the buttery. The castle was brought up to speed to cater for the more demanding tastes and larger household of an Elizabethan courtier. The commodity that Somerset really craved in abundance, however, was light. Like other Tudor castle-owners, he wanted to make his dingy medieval castle as bright and sunny as a courtyard house. This meant, of course, big new windows.

In the second half of the sixteenth century, the replacement window trade in England was booming, thanks to a minor revolution in the glazing industry. Glazed windows had been the norm for aristocratic dwellings since the thirteenth century, but glass could only be produced in small sheets, and was expensive to manufacture. Curiously, the sudden improvement in the later sixteenth century cannot be linked to any dramatic technological change (that came slightly later, in the early seventeenth century, when glaziers began to use coal-fire furnaces). The advances made in William Somerset's day were due solely to the arrival of Continental artisans, equipped (it seems) with nothing more than greater savoir-faire than their English counterparts. Coming from Normandy and Lorraine, attracted no doubt by the prospect of untapped markets, these glaziers set up shop in Sussex and Staffordshire and promptly made a fortune. Windows were suddenly cheaper and bigger. For the less well off, this meant that they could enjoy the benefits of a product that had hitherto been restricted to only the very wealthy. For the very wealthy, it meant they could indulge themselves with fantastical amounts of glass. Elizabethan courtiers began to build great "prodigy" houses, with hundreds of giant windows. At Hardwick Hall in Derbyshire, such was the scale of the glazing job that locals coined the rhyme "more glass than wall at Hardwick Hall." For castle-owners, the new market in glass meant that the small narrow windows of yesteryear could be ripped out and replaced with grand new ones. At Kenilworth Castle, the twelfth-century keep had large windows inserted on the first floor. At Carew, a late thirteenth-century castle in Pembrokeshire, enormous ranges of glass were added to the original buildings. The great thirteenth-century tower at Chepstow (Marten's tower) was flooded with light in a similar fashion.

*Raglan's fifteenth-century hall, with its sixteenth-century windows.*

At Raglan, William Somerset's principal concern was his rather dingy great hall—one of the oldest parts of the castle. When he rebuilt its eastern wall, he provided the main body of the room with three large windows, while at the far end he treated himself to a grand oriel window (a window which projects from a building), better to illuminate his guests at dinnertime.

Tudor aristocrats were not simply content, however, with replacement windows. The courtyard style that was gaining popularity in the sixteenth century had led to the creation of a new species of room, and the availability of better, cheaper glass only encouraged the fashion. At aristocratic residences all over the country, masons and glaziers set to work to construct long narrow corridors, typically over a hundred feet from end to end. Such rooms were called (appropriately enough) long galleries, and every self-respecting homeowner had to have one.

Castle-owners looked on enviously. The architecture of a castle could occasionally extend to indulge the private whims of its noblest inhabitants; some castles, especially later ones, were provided with private chambers, parlors, and gardens. On the whole, however, castle architecture was predominantly functional. Halls were for dining and entertaining, kitchens for cooking, bedrooms for sleeping. The invention of long galleries suddenly raised the stakes in terms of frivolous opulence.

There was no fundamental need for a long gallery—it was not a covered walkway to link two other rooms; no one would sleep or dine in one; it did not, like the chapel, bring you closer to God; and it was certainly not provided with toilets. A long gallery, in the words of Roger North, a seventeenth-century authority on the subject, was "for no other use but pastime and leisure." Its point was recreation. In North's opinion, the idea had originated in Italy, where sophisticated members of society would pass their time in conversation while wandering along outdoor colonnades (columned walkways). Such architecture was fine for the villa-owning elite of southern Europe, but England was far too chilly for such al fresco chats. The obvious solution was to bring an equivalent amount of space indoors, and the long gallery was the result. It provided an interior area where genteel ladies could take a stroll without fear of catching cold. Gentlemen who needed to brush up on their fencing could repair to the gallery if rain stopped play outside. Both groups could convene in the gallery in order to rehearse their dance moves. But one did not need a specific reason; it was simply the nicest possible room for enjoyment and relaxation—a place to sit and while away the time, to make pleasant conversation, and to exhibit the trappings of wealth and taste. By the end of the sixteenth century, such was the popularity of galleries that people had even started to hang pictures in them.

Fitting a gallery inside a castle was no mean feat, but that of course did not stop fashion-conscious castle-owners from trying. We have already seen how Danzig Willie's designer struggled to squeeze one inside Craigievar, in spite of the overriding importance of making the castle tall and slender. The result just about works, but its position high up on the castle's fifth floor would not have impressed gallery connoisseur Roger North. For him a gallery had to be down low, ideally on the first floor—off the ground, but easy to access. "Higher than the next floor it must not be, for such as are in garrets, as I have often seen, are useless, because none will purchase the use of them with paines of mounting." When you climb the stairs to the gallery at Craigievar, you can see what he means—the ascent in itself is exercise enough. Willie's descendants evidently agreed with North's estimation that it was "irksome to think of climbing so high"; the gallery was later converted to servants' quarters.

William Somerset, faced with the challenge of adding a gallery to Raglan, managed to pull it off with considerably more panache, though the position of his gallery on the second floor would still have irked Roger North. He might, however, have been tempted up the stairs by the sheer scale of Somerset's gallery. It stretched over the roof of the existing chapel, screens passage, and buttery, and a brand new section of castle allowed it to extend further still; from end to end it measured 126 feet. North might also have been placated by the quality, both of the interior fittings and the spectacular views from the far end, where the gallery concluded with a grand set of windows looking out across the hills to the north. This magnificent room, however, did not even survive until North's day; it is one of the most comprehensively ruined places in the castle. A few broken pieces of the great north window, and one half of a fine Renaissance fireplace, are all that remain of what was once Raglan's most glorious room. However, some idea of its vanished splendor can be gained from contemporary equivalents. The gallery at Haddon Hall in Derbyshire, for example, if hung with paintings, would look very similar to the one that graced Raglan.

William Somerset's additions to Raglan were not confined to the infrastructure of the castle. He also began a redevelopment of the grounds and gardens that was continued by his son and grandson, transforming his home from a castle into a pleasure palace. By the time we finally catch up with Henry Somerset, marquis of Worcester, who inherited his father's estate in 1628, the castle was, in the words of a contemporary, "accounted one of the fairest buildings in England." The moat around the great tower had been ringed with a walkway, complete with niches containing the busts of Roman emperors. From the water rose a great fountain, its plume leaping to the same height as the castle walls. To the west lay a bowling green, admired for its situation and fine views. Beyond lay gardens and meadows, "fair built with summer houses, delightful walks, and ponds." Into the distance stretched "orchards planted with fruit trees, parks thick planted with oaks and richly stocked with deer."

No one arriving at Raglan in 1640 would have been in any doubt that they were in for a good time. The marquis of Worcester, with an income of £24,000, was accounted one of the richest individuals in the kingdom. His household extended to some five hundred persons; besides him and his large family, there were the steward, the comptroller, and the cook; the master of arms and the master of hounds; the wardrober and the secretary; brewers, bakers, and bailiffs; footmen, grooms, ushers, and doormen; chaplains, foresters, and falconers; waiters, parkers, and pages.

We also have some sense of what the marquis of Worcester was like at this time, thanks to one of his chaplains, Dr. Thomas Bailey. Later in life, Bailey collected a number of his former master's favorite stories and reminiscences, and published them under the somewhat misleading title *Wittie Apophthegmes*. Few are genuinely clever or funny—for the most part they are the self-indulgent tales of an old man, doubtless much improved by constant retelling. Nevertheless, Bailey claimed to have compiled them with "exactness and choice," and they provide us with a portrait of a kindly, good-natured man, with a nice line in self-deprecating humor, and much liked by his family and household.

For over two hundred years, the marquis and his family had lived at Raglan castle, making it bigger and better with each year that passed—more opulent, more brilliant, more lavish. They could afford to do so because England was a peaceful place. The biggest danger to the marquis was gout; according to Dr. Bailey, he was more than partial to a drop of claret. ("Give it to me, in spite of all physicians and their books," he once quipped. "It never shall be said I forsook my friend to pleasure my enemy.")

But the days of small talk in long galleries were drawing to a close. For the first time in its history, Raglan was going to experience war. It only remained to be seen whether the marquis and his ancestors, by customizing their castle, had compromised its defenses.

The war was the English Civil War, or as some historians more appropriately call it, "The Wars of the Three Kingdoms." To say what sparked the conflagration is difficult. A complicated mixture of causes combined to bring society to its knees in the 1640s. Some were longterm, deep-rooted problems that had existed for many decades; others were catastrophes brought about by particular individuals and specific events at the time.

Certainly one of the major causes was religion. The three king-doms had been moving in different directions for a hundred years since the Reformation. Ireland, although it had been settled by a powerful minority of Protestants, remained a Catholic country. Scot-land, by contrast, had become fiercely Protestant, having adopted an uncompromising form of worship known as Presbyterianism. It was England, however, that had ended up with the strangest arrangement of all. The Anglican Church was a curious blend of contradictory positions: a lot of the doctrine was Protestant, but the Church itself was still governed along traditional Catholic lines. Most of the popu-lation in England were regular attendees of Anglican services, some of them zealously so. There remained, however, a small but powerful Catholic minority who were not. They tended to be aristocrats, who had both the chapels in which to practice their religion privately, and the money to pay the fines that the government imposed for non-attendance at Protestant services.

The marquis of Worcester was one such Catholic aristocrat. In his chapel at Raglan (of which very little remains) he would have continued to listen to mass surrounded by gold and silver plate, and the icons and crucifixes that many of his fellow countrymen would have considered idolatrous. But despite being a member of a small religious minority, penalized if not persecuted, the marquis himself does not appear to have been a zealot. He was a godly man, certainly; Dr. Bailey recalled that in all the years he spent in the marquis's household, he "never saw a man drunk, nor heard an oath amongst any of the servants . . . very rare it was to see a better ordered family."

But the marquis could not see much point in arguing about religion.

"Men are often carried by the force of their words further asunder than their question was at first," he once said. "Like two ships going out of the same haven, their journeys' end is many times whole countries distant."

This tolerant attitude was no mere pose; the marquis applied his philosophy when recruiting his domestic staff.

"What was most wonderful," Bailey recalled, was "half of them being Protestants and half Papists, yet never were at variance in point of religion."

Under the marquis's roof at Raglan, Protestant and Catholic worked side by side, with the marquis—genial, tolerant, and wise—presiding over all like a good father.

If only as much could have been said for his king. Charles I, son of James I (James VI of Scotland) had come to the throne after his father's death in 1628. A silly and stubborn man by nature, Charles contrived to make himself even more unpopular by his stance on matters of religion. The king and his court hankered after bells and smells in their church services, despite the fact that many Protestants saw this as Catholicism creeping in by the back door. Charles had also further compounded his error in the opinion of his subjects by choosing to take a Catholic as his queen.

None of this would have mattered quite as much had the king not also had a very inflated sense of his own importance and rectitude. Whereas the marquis of Worcester appears to have been tolerant and wise, Charles was dogmatic, headstrong, and foolish. In 1637, in a misguided attempt to bring unity to his three kingdoms, the king tried to force his Scottish subjects to use the new English Prayer Book. The staunchly Presbyterian Scots, as the more prescient of the Charles' advisers had forecast, rose in rebellion.

Telling his Scottish subjects what to do would have been a lot easier for Charles had he been listening to his English ones; unfortunately he had not. By the time the king was ready to get to grips with the Scottish crisis in 1640 there had been no Parliament in England for eleven years. Charles had preferred to govern the country as he saw fit, raising money by arbitrary methods of dubious legality. Lack of funds to deal with Scotland, however, left him with no choice but to summon Parliament, and this unleashed a storm of complaints against his rule; MPs refused to cooperate over the Scottish business unless the king first addressed their long-nurtured grievances. Charles refused, jammed his fingers in his ears, and tried to sort out the mess himself; but things just got messier.

In October 1641, the king's Catholic subjects in Ireland rebelled, and many people in England regarded this new rising as a Popish plot engineered by Charles. Events finally came to a head at the end of the year when MPs in England presented their complaints to the king in a document they called the Grand Remonstrance. Charles, however, was not about to start listening at this late stage. He tried instead to arrest his leading parliamentary critics—but failed dismally. By the time the blundering monarch and his troops arrived in Westminster, the individuals in question were long gone. But the cat was now out of the bag. Charles stood exposed as a king who had no respect for law or Parliament; a tyrant who would use force against his own subjects. As the king hurriedly gathered up his family and left London under cover of darkness, Royalists were already rallying to his aid. Parliament, meanwhile, began to organize itself to fight for its privileges. The slide toward war had begun.

For the next three years, Parliamentarians (or, disparagingly, "Roundheads"), slugged it out with Royalists ("Cavaliers"), but neither side managed to achieve a decisive victory. Broadly, London and the southeast fought for Parliament, while the north and west of England backed the king; but this simple analysis disguises the complexity of the conflict. The reality was a patchwork of allegiances, shaped and distorted by religious beliefs, regional rivalries, and, ultimately, whether individuals put loyalty to the Crown above liberty and consent.

Commanders on both sides struggled to transcend these difficulties as well as their own personal antagonisms. At the start of 1645, Parliament responded by creating a new national army—the so-called "New Model Army." The Royalists, in an ebullient mood, misinterpreted their enemies' decision to reorganize as a sign of weakness. By the middle of the year, each side was confident that it could beat the other in battle. When they met at Naseby

(Northamptonshire) on June 14, it proved to be the most decisive battle of the war—the turning point after three long years of fighting. Outnumbered and outgeneraled by the Roundheads, the Royalist divisions surrendered. As the king and the remnant of his army beat a retreat, they were left reflecting on the loss of four and a half thousand men, eight thousand weapons and all their great guns. From Naseby they headed west, deep into the Royalist heartlands of south Wales. Late in the day on July 3, King Charles arrived at Raglan Castle.

At Raglan, Charles knew he was guaranteed a warm welcome. The marquis of Worcester might not have been an arch-Catholic, but he was definitely an arch-Royalist. In the three years since the outbreak of hostilities he had poured nearly a million pounds into Charles' war effort—more money than any other individual. Immediately after his arrival, in his hour of greatest need, the king appealed for more cash, and rather brazenly at that. Dr. Bailey relates how the king demanded access to the castle's great tower, believing that his principal backer was still keeping some gold in reserve in the basement (he wasn't). It didn't matter, however, how rude or foolish Charles appeared to be (from Bailey's reports of the king's behavior, the marquis had ample justification for being offended on several scores). For men like Henry Somerset, supporting the king was a matter of principle. Kings were appointed by God, and loyalty to them was absolutely non-negotiable. The marquis therefore bailed the king out again with such money as he had remaining, and permitted Charles and his army to reside at Raglan for three weeks. The only thing the marquis had not done up to this point was fight for the king in person; as a man in his mid-sixties, plagued by gout, he was unlikely to be found charging into battle. His opportunity to prove himself, however, was about to arrive: the battle was now coming to the marquis.

The history of the Civil War is normally recounted as a series of battles: the quiet fields of Edgehill, Marston Moor, and Naseby are all familiar to us because of the bloody mayhem of three and half centuries ago. As in the Middle Ages, however, so too in the seventeenth century: battles were actually the exception. Throughout the Civil War, the most common form of military encounter was the siege. Before the battle of Naseby, and apart from the major engagements mentioned above, the war had been conducted as a series of sieges by small local armies. After Naseby, the fighting once again took this form. The New Model Army split into smaller contingents and set about flushing out Royalist resistance, especially in the west of England.

This was bad news for Royalists who had invested their money in luxurious but undefended mansions. In a sad echo of the Hardwick Hall rhyme, one Irish homeowner expressed the general feeling of aristocrats everywhere. "My house I built for peace," he wrote, "having more windows than walls." In such circumstances, castle-owners did rather better. At Sherborne in Dorset, the local Royalist garrison put up a spirited defense, but even so the castle surrendered after only two weeks, battered into submission by Parliamentarian cannon.

Successful defense, however, required not just strong walls but strong wills. The castle at Bristol, where the walls once stood seventeen feet thick, was expected to hold out no matter what. In addition to its mighty defenses and lofty position, the castle was under the command of Prince Rupert, the king's nephew. But when the New Model Army attacked Bristol on the night of September 10, the expensive new defenses that ringed the city proved worthless. With the town itself overwhelmed and the castle surrounded, Rupert decided that further resistance was pointless. By the end of the day he had surrendered.

Charles, who was at Raglan organizing troops in order to relieve Bristol, received the news of his nephew's capitulation with utter disbelief. The town was his last toehold in western England; with it went any hope of landing extra troops from overseas. The odds were becoming impossible, as many of the king's supporters began to realize. As Charles slipped away from Raglan back to his temporary capital in Oxford, other Royalists started to surrender, sensing that all was lost. In October, the garrisons in the castles of Chepstow and Monmouth (both of which belonged to the marquis of Worcester) submitted to their enemies.

This was a war, however, where the fighting was motivated not by *realpolitik* but by real conviction. There were some who, in spite of the odds, would rather fight on than surrender. The marquis of Worcester was one such man. His other castles may have fallen; the king might have left him to his fate; the chances of success might be minuscule; but the marquis prepared to make his last stand.

This was not just a matter of steeling himself and his family for the inevitable. Preparation for war in Britain at this time had became an arduous and time-consuming affair. Since the outbreak of the Civil War, both Roundheads and Cavaliers had been trying desperately to catch up with the military advances that had been taking place in Europe for the past hundred years. While England had enjoyed domestic peace during the sixteenth century, in Europe religious wars raged. Across the Continent soldiers and civilians, men and women, young and old, had died in their tens of thousands. City authorities and rich individuals in France, Germany, Italy, and elsewhere had invested heavily in their own protection, in some cases spending up to half their annual budgets on the upkeep of their defenses. These new fortifications were very different to the tall, crenellated walls that had been built in the Middle Ages. The advent of cannon had led to a radical rethink. Walls were no longer built tall, but massively thick and squat. For the most part they were built of earth, and only revetted (reinforced) with stone, which enabled them to absorb cannon shot without cracking. Battlements had become useless (a single shot from even a small bombard could blow them away), and so they disappeared. Instead, defenders protected their walls by building bastions—diamond-shaped platforms of earth designed to carry cannon. They were thrust forward from the walls, in order to give covering fire along the length of the defenses, as well as outward in the direction of an approaching enemy.

Defenses like this were unknown in Britain (only the border town of Berwick-upon-Tweed had anything even remotely comparable). At the outbreak of war, the country's defenses were hopelessly outdated. Across all three kingdoms, and especially in England, towns and castles had to be brought up to speed rapidly. The only solace for defenders was that artillery in Britain also lagged behind that of Europe, and nobody was experienced in the arts of siege warfare. Both Royalists and Parliamentarians recruited experts from the Continent to advise on both the conduct of sieges and the construction of defenses. Huge new earthworks went up around cities like London, Colchester, Oxford, and Exeter.

Having decided to stick it out and fight, the marquis of Worcester was faced with exactly this task—converting his stately castle at Raglan into a military stronghold. Exact details as to how and when he carried out this process are lacking. We know that he had maintained a Royalist garrison in the castle since the start of the war. One contemporary put the number of infantry at three hundred men; another suggested that the total number of people inside the castle was eight hundred, but indicated that this figure included members of the marquis's own household. The garrison was certainly large, and the precautions they took were correspondingly extensive. Inside, the castle was knocked around and modified. With nowhere to grind gunpowder for their twenty cannon, the Royalist soldiers converted the basement of the closet tower into a powder mill: the doorway has apparently been widened to enable barrels of gunpowder to be carried in and out. More importantly, the soldiers began to construct a ring of earthen defenses around the castle. They may have started at an early date, but the context of certain comments made by Dr. Bailey suggests that work was still being carried out at the time of the king's visit in 1645. One of the bastion towers they built to the south of the castle has survived, though its contours have been much reduced by erosion (its shape can be best appreciated from the top of the great tower). From what survives, the completed defenses are reckoned to have been vast, extending outward from the walls by several hundred feet. Describing the stables and barns constructed for the garrison, an eyewitness thought them "built like a small town."

The marquis, therefore, had taken every possible precaution: the castle had been customized, the earthworks constructed; the cannon had been rolled into place on top of the new bastion towers, the smaller artillery pieces mounted on top of the castle walls. All he and his household could do was sit and wait for the inevitable. An anxious Christmas came and went, with no sign of trouble. In the New Year, however, they sensed the net about them drawing tighter. In February, Cardiff fell to the Roundheads. By the spring, Parliamentary forces were beginning to mass in Monmouthshire. Finally, at the start of the summer, the inevitable arrived in the shape of Parliament's Colonel Thomas Morgan, who drew up one and a half thousand troops to the east of Raglan. On June 3 he sent a letter to the marquis, written in the typically deferential tone of the times. Slightly abridged and simplified, it read:

> *Sir, I am commanded to summon you to surrender unto me . . . the castle of Raglan, with all the arms, artillery, ammunition and . . . military provisions therein. You have no reason to hold [it], being out of all hopes of relief—all or most of the king's garrisons are surrendered, and Raglan is one of the last. If you refuse to surrender it upon these summons, the country will consider you a disturber of the peace of this kingdom, and deprive yourself and those with you from the honorable conditions which you may now receive.*

The marquis responded with a refusal—equally polite but equally uncompromising.

"We must here," he concluded his letter, "to the last man, sell our lives as dear as we can; and this not out of obstinacy or any ill affection, but merely to preserve that honor that I desire should attend me with death. And God assist them that are in the right."

The siege of Raglan had begun. The first task facing Morgan's troops was to look to their own protection. To this end, they began building earthworks and digging trenches just as their Royalist opponents had done. Like trenches in the First World War, the two lines ended up very close to each other; Morgan described how he had brought his approaches to within pistol shot of the enemy lines. The Colonel had with him a skilled engineer, one Captain John Hooper, who had recently scored a great success in defeating the Royalist castle at Banbury. Hooper set about building platforms on which to mount the Parliamentary cannon; their faint outline can still be seen in the fields to the east of the castle. Soon the Roundhead gunners were in position and ready to begin their bombardment.

The barrage, when it began, was relentless. The Roundheads pounded the castle with up to sixty shot a day. The noise was deafening, the stench from the guns sickening. Once they had found their range, Morgan's gunners were easily able to destroy the tops of the castle towers, and with them the lighter Royalist guns that had been placed there. The battlements at Raglan were only eight inches thick, and quickly crumbled under the assault. The Parliamentarians began to concentrate their fire on the larger guns around the perimeter, and also on their main objective: blowing a breach in the castle walls.

The walls, however, held out. According to a contemporary witness, "the [great] tower itself repulsed bullets of 18 to 20lb weight, hardly receiving the least impression." The walls of the rest of the castle proved equally defiant. Along the eastern face of the castle, the damage caused by the Parliamentary artillery is still very evident—the walls are chipped and battered, and a number of cannon balls have been found embedded in them. But the medieval masonry neither cracked nor collapsed under the barrage. To judge from the above comments on the size of the shot, it would seem that Morgan's guns were simply not big enough. A gun firing shots of eighteen to twenty pounds would have been a culverin. This was a fairly impressive piece of equipment, weighing in at around five thousand pounds and measuring thirteen feet from breach to barrel. It could not, however, smash through stonework. For that, Morgan would have needed larger guns—demi-cannon, or whole-cannon. Capable of firing balls of up to eighty pounds in weight, these were a convincing answer to even the stoutest stone walls. Morgan appears not to have had them—at least, not at the outset. The problem with cannon was getting them where you wanted them in the first place. Whereas a culverin could be shifted by a team of twenty horses, a single cannon would have required two or three times as many beasts to get it moving. Even with such large trains, the biggest siege guns could only be moved a few miles a day. Trundling them along muddy tracks took weeks on end and, as such, was prohibitively expensive. Both sides were reluctant to commit cannon to the fray unless there seemed to be absolutely no alternative.

Morgan did, in fact, have other options open to him, but they were extremely tedious. While his gunners could continue to try and destroy their enemy's artillery, his troops could hope to pick off individual defenders by using muskets. Muskets had been around for some time (about a hundred years) and had proved effective in battle, where they could be massed together and fired in volleys. In a siege situation, however, they were less useful, not having the accuracy required for long-distance sniping. Although you would be extremely lucky if you survived a shot from a musket, you would have to be exceedingly unlucky to get hit by one in the first place.

On one occasion during the siege of Raglan, the marquis of Worcester enjoyed just such mixed fortunes. One evening after dinner, he and his dining companions had withdrawn into his private parlor beyond the great hall—a handsome room, "noted for its inlaid wainscoting and curious carved figures, as well as for . . . a large and fair compass window on the south side." The redoubtable Dr. Bailey, who (as ever) was there to witness events, described what happened next. As the marquis was about to entertain the assembled company with one of his pleasant after-dinner discourses, there was a distant crack, a whizz, and a sudden shattering of glass.

A musket ball came crashing through the ornamental window, glanced off a little marble pillar, and struck the marquis on the side of the head. As the flattened bullet dropped to the table with a gentle thud, some of the ladies present fainted from the shock. The marquis, however, saw a golden opportunity for the kind of witty apophthegm that later enabled Bailey to dine out for decades.

"Gentlemen," he said, turning the musket ball in his fingers, "those who had a mind to flatter me were wont to tell me that I had a good head-piece in my younger days; but if I do not flatter myself, I think I have a good head-piece in my old age—or else it would not have been musket-proof."

Joking aside, the marquis must have realized he had had a lucky escape. By this stage, moreover, he can have had little else to joke about. The loss of his great ornamental window was just the latest in a long line of disasters to befall his beautiful castle. If he had dared to peek over the parapets, he would have hardly recognized the scene before him. Where there had once been ornamental gardens, orchards, and ponds, there was now a war zone—a no-man's-land where every tree had been torn down and every building destroyed. The Royalist situation was becoming desperate, and five weeks into the siege, on July 12, the garrison attempted to break out; four hundred infantry and eighty cavalrymen poured over the defenses to engage Morgan's troops. Within half an hour, however, it was all over: the Royalists were beaten back, having sustained heavy losses.

But if the Royalists could not break out, the Roundheads could not break in. Despite the successful defeat of the sortie and the destruction his guns had wreaked on the castle, Colonel Morgan was still no closer to ending the siege. All he could do was keep tightening his grip, and order Captain Hooper to keep driving forward his trenches.

Meanwhile, events elsewhere were shaping Raglan's fate. In May 1646, even before the siege had begun, Charles I had slipped out of his headquarters at Oxford and traveled in secret to Newark, where he handed himself over to a waiting Scottish Army. It was a desperate move, choosing what he considered to be the lesser of two evils and hoping to divide his enemies. For the Royalist troops who remained in Oxford, however, it was the beginning of the end. Negotiations began almost immediately, and within a few weeks it was all over. Having been besieged and blockaded for years, the exhausted city finally surrendered on June 25.

The consequences of Oxford's fall were first felt at Raglan two weeks later, when Parliament's Major-General Skippon and Colonel Herbert arrived outside the castle with two thousand extra men. They arrived the day after the garrison had attempted to break out of the castle, and their presence put paid to any further thoughts of flight on the part of the Royalists. Joshua Sprigge, a chaplain who had arrived with the new troops, noted the scales were beginning to tip against the defenders.

"The enemy," he wrote, "was reduced to more caution, and taught to lie closer."

It was not Skippon or Herbert, however, who ended the siege, but two new characters who arrived at the start of August. The first was Sir Thomas Fairfax. A man of thirty-four years, Fairfax had cut his teeth fighting in the Netherlands, and made his reputation in the north of England during the early stages of the war. Although by no means a striking figure—he suffered from poor general health, and his physical sufferings had been compounded by two separate musket wounds—Fairfax demonstrated both skill as a military commander and a refreshing lack of egotism. At the start of 1645 he had been the natural choice as leader of the New Model Army. At Oxford, he had managed to persuade the Royalists to submit without a fight, and had avoided having to fire his great guns into the city. The ancient colleges had been saved, and Fairfax had taken the trouble to post a guard around the Bodleian Library in order to stop it from being sacked. He now hoped to bring the siege of Raglan to a similarly bloodless conclusion.

By the time Fairfax arrived at Raglan on August 7, it was all but the last garrison in England still holding out for the king.

The fall of Oxford had been the signal for those few remaining Royalist strongholds to surrender. Only the tiny Henrician fort at Pendennis in Cornwall, strengthened by massive Civil War earthworks, was putting up a resistance comparable with Raglan's. As Joshua Sprigge poetically put it, "many other garrisons that attended [Oxford's] fate fell with it, even like ripe fruit, with an easy touch; but the two garrisons of Raglan and Pendennis, like winter fruit, hung long on."

The garrison at Raglan, however, knew nothing of distant Pendennis. When Fairfax wrote to the marquis shortly after his arrival, he stretched the truth in order to emphasize the hopelessness of the old man's situation.

"Raglan only obstructs the kingdom's universal peace," he told him, before proceeding to pile on further pressure. He had come into Monmouthshire "with such a strength as I may not doubt," and was now offering the marquis a last chance to surrender on favorable terms. If, however, the marquis delayed or refused, "such terms . . . cannot be hereafter expected."

But the marquis continued to play the same game as before. In his letter back to Fairfax, he referred to the castle as his "house," and added that (having lost both Chepstow and Monmouth) Raglan was "the only house now in my possession to cover my head in." This was not a mere word game, or the sentimental blubbering of a foolish old man. The marquis was choosing to make a point about personal property and his inalienable rights as a landowner that had been a familiar theme of Royalist propaganda throughout the war. Concluding his letter, he referred to his "house" for a final time, and wondered aloud how, "by law or conscience I should be forced out of it."

Fairfax, exasperated, sent back a testy reply. "For that distinction which your lordship is pleased to make [i.e., between castle and house]; it *is* your house. If it had not been formed into a *garrison*, I should have not have troubled your lordship with a summons; and were it dis-garrisoned, neither you, nor your *house* should receive any disquiet from me!"

*Roaring Meg.*

But Fairfax knew that he did not have to waste time with the marquis debating the legal merits of their respective positions. Even as he had drawn up his forces at Raglan, another character had appeared, and one with a far bloodier reputation than the general. This was a lady, no less, but one whose name struck fear into the hearts of grizzled soldiers. Roaring Meg had come to Raglan.

Meg was a mortar piece—a squat metal tub measuring just four feet from end to end, but nonetheless the most terrifying weapon imaginable in the seventeenth century. She was a gun, but not intended, like a conventional cannon, to smash through walls. Mortars like Meg were designed to lob their missiles clean over the defenses of a town or castle, right into the heart of the enemy camp. These missiles, furthermore, were not the solid iron balls fired by cannon, but large hollow grenades, twelve inches across and two hundred pounds in weight. Typically made of copper (or a similarly brittle metal), the grenade was packed with gunpowder, and lit by a fuse before being launched toward its target. When the powder ignited, the grenade exploded, sending shrapnel flying in all directions, killing or maiming everything within a wide radius.

The mortar was, in short, an anti-personnel weapon, intended to destroy human life rather than wear down defenses. Of course, a well-aimed shot weighing two hundred pounds could rip right through the roof of a building, and the explosive force of a grenade could easily start a fire. But they were not always successful, or even reliable weapons. A grenade was, in essence, a very crude type of shell—one without a detonator. It therefore required great skill on the part of the gunner to judge not only how far to fire it, but also how long to make the fuse. Too short and it would explode in mid-flight; too late and it might give the defenders the chance to render it harmless. There is a famous example of how, during the siege of Gloucester, a quick-thinking woman extinguished the fuse of a mortar grenade by throwing a bucket of water over it.

Above all, however, mortars could be relied upon to produce fear and panic among your opponents. During the siege of Lathom House in Lancashire in 1644, one of the defenders indicated the terror that a falling grenade could provoke.

"Little ladies had stomach to digest cannon," he wrote, "but the stoutest soldiers had no heart for this . . . the mortar piece had frightened 'em from meat and sleep."

From an attacker's point of view, mortars were satisfyingly effective. Parliamentarian troops trying to break Banbury Castle in 1646 reported screams every time the mortar was fired.

When Roaring Meg arrived at Raglan in August 1646, she was still only a few months old, having been specially cast earlier in the year for the purpose of defeating the Royalist garrison at Goodrich Castle. The young lady came with powerful friends. Escorted by Colonel John Birch, Meg rolled up with five of her sister-pieces, as well as all the conventional cannon that Parliament was able to spare. In terms of the mortars, at least, this was the greatest concentration of firepower so far deployed in the Civil War. Captain Hooper, who was still busy digging his way toward the Royalist lines, now began to construct platforms for the new weapons sixty yards from the castle's defenses.

As the marquis of Worcester watched Roaring Meg and the other mortars being rolled into position, he knew he was caught between a rock and a hard place. The level of danger had suddenly become far, far greater. No longer could he hide behind his ancestral walls; if the mortars were fired, there was a good chance that he or a member of his family would be killed. By the same token, surrender was not a tempting prospect. Who knows what a vindictive Parliament might do to him? As he confessed in a letter to Fairfax, the prospect of surrender "doth a little affright me."

Fairfax, sensing the old man's desperate dilemma, hammered his advantage home. Come to terms, he urged.

"If you stand it out to the last extremity," he wrote to the marquis, "[you risk] your person, those of your family (which I presume are dear to you), and the spoil of the castle."

Fairfax also chose to invoke the memory of another marquis who had defied Parliament to the bitter end.

"Your Lordship has no reason to expect any better than the marquis of Winchester received. He made good Basing House to the last, narrowly escaped with his own life, lost his friends, subjected those that escaped to great frights, and hazarded his house and estate to utter ruin, and himself to the extremity of justice."

At the same time, Fairfax reassured the marquis that he would receive fair treatment at Parliament's hands. "That what I grant," he promised, "shall be made good."

And so, after more than two months besieged in his castle, the marquis decided that it was time to surrender. Over the weekend of August 15–16, negotiators thrashed out the terms of the cease-fire, and on Monday a deal was struck. In two days' time, it was agreed, the Royalist troops would march out of Raglan castle, unmolested by their opponents, and disband. Certain individuals, including the marquis himself, were exempted from this pardon; and when, on the eve of the surrender, the marquis presented the terms to his men, they pledged to keep on fighting. Their master's mind, however, was made up. Like Jonah, he said, he would be cast overboard rather than see them all perish. Accordingly, the next morning, the Royalist garrison marched out of Raglan, with "colors flying, drums beating, [and] trumpets sounding," just as the negotiators had agreed.

Both the marquis and Fairfax had good reason to be happy with the conclusion. For Fairfax, it was the bloodless outcome he had hoped for—once again, he had achieved victory without needless expenditure, either of men or of money. The marquis also had reason to be grateful. His castle and his household had got off lightly, even if he himself now faced an uncertain future. When the two men met that day, the marquis, true to form, was in good spirits. As the general was taking his leave, the old man made what Dr. Bailey called "a merry petition" on behalf of a couple of pigeons, which he had been feeding throughout the siege. Would the great general take the two young birds, as it were, under his wing? With so many hungry soldiers about, the marquis was concerned for their safety.

The only individual who was apparently less than pleased by the bloodless conclusion was Colonel Morgan. He was, after all, the one who had started the siege back in June, and since then he had endured the hardship of living under canvas and fighting in trenches for the best part of two months. Now, thanks to Fairfax's negotiated surrender, his opportunity to heroically storm the breach had vanished. Worse still, he hadn't even got to fire a mortar—Roaring Meg had on this occasion stayed silent. Writing to the Speaker in the House of Commons on the day the cease-fire was agreed, Morgan began, "After long and hard duty performed, it hath pleased God that commissioners on both sides have agreed upon articles for the surrender of the castle and garrison."

You can hear the disappointment and the petulance in his voice when he finally adds that, "truly, had not this happy conclusion been made, our mortar pieces would have played very suddenly, and we were come very near with our approaches."

With the siege and the war now over, Fairfax was treated to a cele-
bratory dinner at Chepstow in the evening, before returning home
to Bath the next day. In the meantime, the marquis of Worcester
was being transported to London, where he would shortly learn
whether the general's promises would be honored now he was at
the mercy of Parliament. In both houses, there was much debate
over what should be done with the defeated Royalists and their
castles. On the one hand, these were dangerous fortifications
that had cost hundreds of thousands of pounds and the lives of
many men to capture. Their continued existence was a temptation,
an invitation even, for the king's supporters and sympathizers
to attempt to retake them. If, heaven forbid, they succeeded in
doing so, then the same battles would have to be fought all over
again. Even simply guarding them against attack would entail a
huge commitment of manpower at a time when Parliament was
trying to demobilize its armed forces. In such circumstances, the
best way to prevent future trouble seemed to be to destroy castles
completely. Colonel Birch certainly thought this would be the
best way to deal with Goodrich Castle when he and Roaring Meg
had finished battering it into submission. Writing to Parliament
in order to ascertain "the pleasure of the house concerning the
demolition or keeping of the castle," he could not resist venturing
his own opinion. "I humbly conceive [it] is useless, and a great
burden to the country."

On the other hand, Parliament had to consider its own security.
After four years of punishing civil war, the country at large was
restless, and Parliament, although victorious, was far from being
universally popular. Perhaps, some MPs argued, it would be better
to hang on to a few castles for safety's sake, and keep them garrisoned, regardless of the cost. There were also Members of Parliament, especially the great landowners in the House of Lords, who
sympathized with the plight of men like the marquis. Castles were,
after all, homes, and the right of an individual to enjoy his property
without interference from government had been one of the things
that they had supposedly been fighting to protect.

In the specific case of the marquis of Worcester, however, Parliament had already made up its mind long before the old man himself finally arrived in London. Just one week after Raglan's fall, MPs had voted to demolish the castle and imprison its owner. The marquis was to be sent to the Tower (he was later committed to Black Rod in Covent Garden), and the remains of the castle were to be sold off "for the best advantage of the state."

Destroying a castle, however, especially one as large as Raglan, was easier said than done. When demolition of the castle began in August 1646, it was carried out by teams of men with pickaxes. They began on the top of the great tower and, after a great deal of what one eye-witness called "tedious battering," they managed to remove just one of the five stories. Sending the old man himself to prison was no problem, but his castle, even in defeat, was proving to be a tough nut to crack.

They could have speeded things up by using explosives, a technique that had been tried earlier in the year at Corfe Castle in Dorset. A mighty twelfth-century keep perched high on a hill, girded by huge circuits of thirteenth-century curtain walls, Corfe had been unsuccessfully besieged several times during the course of the war. When it finally fell to the Roundheads through treachery in February 1646, Parliament wasted no time in ordering its destruction. Sappers set to work undermining some of the walls, and large quantities of gunpowder were used to break the keep and the gatehouses. But as well as being extremely dangerous, this was prohibitively expensive; and for all its advantages of speed, gunpowder left untidy results. The ragged lumps of stone that resulted could not be sold for profit, which was Parliament's express intention at Raglan.

When, therefore, in the summer of 1647, Parliament finally came to a decision about what to do with castles in general, those who urged moderation and financial prudence won the day. A general cull was resisted, and only those fortifications that had been constructed since the outbreak of hostilities were ordered to be demolished.

———

By this date, members had an even greater dilemma on their hands. In order to defeat Charles I, his opponents had buried their widely differing opinions on politics and religion. Having beaten the king, these deep-seated divisions now resurfaced. Parliamentary leaders saw the opportunity to foist their religious views on the kingdom. The Army, politicized by years of continuous campaigning and smarting at attempts to disband it, rebelled against Parliament, before turning in on itself. Charles I, who had been purchased from the Scots at the start of the year, looked on with ill-concealed amusement. He was ferried around the country from place to place, a willing pawn in the game his enemies were playing against each other.

In 1648, the dispute between the different factions broke down irrevocably, and a second Civil War broke out. In a series of risings across the country, both discontented New Model Army veterans and die-hard Royalists once again seized castles and garrisoned them against Parliament. The hard-liners, it was now clear, had been right all along: they should have pulled down the castles while they had had the chance. With that chance now gone, and another major struggle ahead, those who advocated more ruthless policies gained the upper hand.

The hard-line attitude, both toward the king and the castles, was ultimately epitomized by one man: Oliver Cromwell. Although Cromwell and the Civil War are frequently referred to in the same breath, it was only at this stage in the conflict that the former East Anglian farmer began to come into his own. Driven by his views on religious liberty, Cromwell had fought in the first war with an uncompromising passion and, through his intuitive military genius, had risen to become one of the leading voices in government by the time the war was over. When trouble erupted in 1648, it was to Cromwell as much as to Fairfax that Parliament now looked for its deliverance. The fighting that year was localized but extremely fierce. Fairfax dealt with revolts in the southeast of England, at Maidstone in Kent and Colchester in Essex. Cromwell, in the meantime, had been sent into south Wales to break the rebels in

Pembrokeshire, a job that took him most of the summer. In August, Cromwell marched to engage a Scottish army that had crossed the border into Lancashire, and won a resounding victory at Preston. By the start of September, the only thing that stood between Parliament and total victory was the castle of Pontefract in Yorkshire.

Pontefract was a truly impregnable fortress where, as at Raglan, the medieval defenses had been massively strengthened by the addition of new earthworks. During the first Civil War it had been besieged for months on end by Parliamentarian troops who, despite being armed with cannon and mortars, were unable to take the castle by storm. When it finally fell in July 1645, it was starvation rather than bombardment that had persuaded the Royalists inside to surrender.

In May 1648, however, the king's supporters had recovered Pontefract without a fight. It was taken by an ingenious ruse, described over half a century later by the last surviving participant, Captain Thomas Paulden, in a letter to a friend. Paulden explains how he and his fellow-conspirators first attempted to sneak into the castle under cover of darkness one night in the middle of May. They had persuaded one of the corporals in the Parliamentary garrison of the justness of their cause, and he in turn had arranged to be on guard that night.

The simple plan backfired when the Royalists approached the castle walls. "The corporal happened to be drunk at the appointed hour," said Paulden, "and another sentinel was placed where we intended to set our ladder." Inside the castle the alarm was raised, and the Royalists beat a hasty retreat.

When the Parliamentary governor heard the news, he strengthened the garrison with hundreds of extra troops, and it now seemed that taking the castle would be impossible. Then, very shortly afterward, the Royalists received a piece of news that gave them a brilliant idea. With all the extra soldiers now in the castle, the Parliamentarians had run out of sleeping space, and had therefore sent out orders into the town for extra beds. Paulden and company therefore decided to pose as bed-delivery men. "Dressed like plain countrymen and constables . . . but armed privately with pocket pistols and daggers," they escorted the furniture right into the heart of the castle. Once inside, they threw off their disguises, whipped out their pistols, and imprisoned the Roundheads in the castle's dungeon.

Like Greeks at Troy, the daring band of Royalists had pulled off the most audacious coup. They must have been overjoyed; astounded at their good fortune and delighted with their own cunning. "Pontefract was thought the greatest and the strongest castle in England," said Paulden, and yet he and a handful of friends had snatched it from right under Parliament's nose.

The Cavaliers, however, were not laughing for very long. In August, the news came that their Scottish allies had been beaten. By September, the castle was surrounded by five thousand Parliamentarian troops. Finally, in November, Cromwell himself arrived at Pontefract, determined to take the castle at any cost.

Before his arrival, the siege had been under the direction, loosely speaking, of the splendidly named Sir Henry Cholmondley, a Blimpish figure who for months had been furnishing his superiors in London with rosy reports of his progress. In actual fact, Cholmondley had been so busy quarreling with other Parliamentarian officers on how best to prosecute the siege that he had not even managed to mount an effective blockade; supplies were still finding their way to the Royalists inside the castle.

Cromwell, when he arrived at the start of November, therefore found he faced a near-impossible task. Regarding the castle itself, he echoed Paulden's estimation of its defensive advantages.

"The place is very well known to be one of the strongest inland garrisons in the kingdom," he wrote to Parliament, "well-watered, situated upon a rock in every part, and therefore difficult to mine. The walls are very thick and high, with strong towers, and . . . very difficult to access, by reason of the steepness of the graft."

Disabusing MPs of the notion that victory was close to hand, he wrote, "My Lords, the castle has been victualed with 240 cattle within these three weeks, and they also gotten in salt enough for them, so that I apprehend they are victualed for a twelvemonth. The men inside are resolved to endure to the utmost extremity, expecting no mercy—as indeed they deserve none."

Having made his assessment and stated his case, Cromwell proceeded to list the tools necessary for the job. To break Pontefract would require at least three regiments of foot, two regiments of horse, five hundred barrels of gunpowder, six good battering guns, and eighteen hundred cannonballs. A couple of mortars would also be nice, he added, if Parliament could spare them.

As at Raglan, it was going to be weeks before any of these items arrived at Pontefract. In the meantime, Cromwell wrote to the Royalists and demanded their surrender. In response, their captain sent only a teasing letter—was Cromwell quite sure that he had full authority in this matter? Perhaps he ought to check with Sir Henry Cholmondley, and see what he thought? When they had sorted it out between them, could they get back in touch? Cromwell's answer, written or otherwise, is sadly not recorded. But after two more weeks of waiting, he turned from Pontefract, and headed toward London. He had not, however, given up on his Royalist enemies: on the contrary, he was about to play his trump card.

Cromwell arrived in London on December 6, and that evening sent Colonel Pride to purge the House of Commons of his political opponents. Now that the fighting was all but over, the Army had grown tired of Parliament's dithering about what to do with the king. As far as Cromwell and his comrades were concerned, Charles I was a tyrant and a traitor, a king who had made war on his own people, "a man of blood." Like the criminal that he clearly was, Charles was going to be tried, convicted, and punished. For a man guilty of such crimes, there was only one possible punishment. On January 30, 1649, the king was led to the scaffold in Whitehall, and publicly beheaded.

By this shocking, unprecedented act, the siege of Pontefract was brought to an end. For the Royalist garrison, who by now were being pounded by cannon and mortars, the king's death was a crushing blow to their cause. After they heard the news, they made a show of pledging their support to Charles's son, but a few weeks later their resistance crumbled. At the start of March, negotiations for a surrender began, and by March 22 the Royalists had capitulated. Pontefract was retaken, and the second Civil War was over.

Having killed the king, Cromwell and his supporters now set out to kill the castle. No way was there going to be the kind of general reprieve that had followed the last war. Pontefract, recently the biggest thorn in the government's side, was one of the first candidates for the chop. This was far from being an unpopular decision. As early as March 24—just two days after the siege had ended—the cry had gone up for the castle to come down.

"The chief news now," wrote one local correspondent, "is that the grand jury of York, the judge . . . and almost all this county are petitioning to get this castle pulled down."

Parliament concurred in this opinion—with the Commons shorn of its more hesitant members in December, and the House of Lords recently abolished as "useless," power was in the hands of uncompromising men. When the order was given that Pontefract "be forthwith totally demolished and leveled to the ground," this time they meant it. When you visit the castle site today, you can see how literally the commissioners and the people of south Yorkshire took the decision: hardly one stone was left standing on top of another. Pontefract, one of the mightiest royal castles in England, was reduced to a pile of rubble.

Similar severe punishments were dealt out to other castles in the wake of the king's execution. At Belvoir, Montgomery, and Nottingham, destruction took place on a scale comparable to Pontefract. Significantly, both Belvoir and Montgomery had escaped destruction in 1647, when only the new works that had been added to them were destroyed.

Parliament soon found, however, that the cost of such wholesale demolition was unbearable. At Pontefract, even though the sale of the lead, stone, and timber from the demolished castle had raised £1,779, the townspeople still found that the job saddled them with a debt of £145. At Belvoir and Montgomery, the government hit upon the idea of paying the owners to pull down their own castles. Since both were the property of former Royalists, who were heavily fined for supporting the king, "payment" was simply a matter of reducing their fines rather than actually shelling out hard cash.

But where demolition was not self-financing, it became much harder to enforce. Local government was soon complaining about the cost of carrying out orders for total destruction, and in many places those orders were not carried out for lack of money. In other instances, a lack of expertise also created problems on the ground. There were laughable scenes at Belvoir when the earl of Rutland had finished pulling down his castle. Parliament naturally wanted the work inspected to make sure that the job had been done properly. Unfortunately, however, the men they appointed to view the work were local gents rather than military engineers, who were forced to confess they did not know whether the castle was now indefensible or not. Faced with such difficulties, central and local government arrived at a compromise. Castles in future would not be demolished but "slighted." Rather than outright demolition, the authorities would be content with limited destruction that made castles untenable—left standing in places, but incapable of being defended in battle.

Slighting was the solution that was finally adopted at Raglan, and the castle as it stands today bears testimony to the terrible effectiveness of the procedure. Having tried and failed to bring down the great tower stone by stone with pickaxes, engineers opted instead for the quick fix of undermining its walls: the same technique that King John had used to devastating effect at Rochester four centuries beforehand. "The weight of [the tower was] propped with timber," said an eye-witness, "while two of the sides were cut through; the timber being burned, it fell down in a lump." There was more to slighting, however, than simply making a castle indefensible. By throwing down the walls of the homes of the nobility, walls that for centuries had symbolized the power of an aristocratic elite, the revolutionary government was making a striking visual point about its own power. No longer, it said, would individuals be allowed to defy the state (the Commonwealth, as it would soon be called) in the name of privilege. The broken towers at Kenilworth and Scarborough, Helmsley and Corfe, were witness to their owners' impotence in the face of Parliament's might. At Raglan, the deliberate and systematic spoliation of what had been one of the greatest, fairest, and noblest buildings in the country was carried through with savage thoroughness. Every window was smashed, every fireplace ripped out, every valuable removed. The banks of the ponds and the moat, both still teeming with carp, were broken. The chapel, filled as it was with images of Popish idolatry, was singled out for special attention. Most callously, and in direct contrast to the way in which the Bodleian in Oxford had been spared, the huge library of rare books and manuscripts at Raglan, reckoned one of the most important collections in Europe, was deliberately put to the torch. What took place at Raglan was not just an act of essential demolition—it was an act of vengeance.

While the heart was being ripped out of his castle at Raglan, Henry Somerset, the marquis of Worcester, lay dying in London. His ancestral home, he now knew, would not be passing to his heirs, as he had always imagined it must. The assurances of fair treatment made by General Fairfax had, in the end, counted for nothing. Having fought what he considered an honorable fight in defense of his faith and his king, the marquis had good cause to reflect on his shabby treatment at Parliament's hands. By his bedside stood Dr. Bailey, his chaplain, remembering the old man's last words even as he administered the last rites.

"Ah, Doctor," said the marquis, "I forsook life, liberty and estate . . . and threw myself upon their mercy; [but] if to seize all my goods, to pull down my house, and sell my estate . . . be merciful, what are they whose mercies are so cruel?"

Nevertheless, in spite of his appalling experience that summer, the plethoric constitution that had preserved him for seventy years still refused to desert him. Even as he stared into the abyss, the marquis of Worcester managed one last witticism. He asked where he was to be buried, and was told that his final resting place would be the great chapel at Windsor Castle.

"Why then," he quipped, "I shall have a better castle when I am dead than the one they took from me when alive."

# EPILOGUE

—⁓—

Henry Somerset, marquis of Worcester, died on December 18, 1646. He was aged about seventy. One week later, on Christmas Day, his body was laid to rest in the great chapel of St. George in Windsor Castle. A marble tablet on the chapel wall still commemorates his passing.

A little over two years later, the marquis was joined by his king. After his execution, Charles I's head was sewn back on to his body, and his corpse was brought to Windsor in the midst of a blizzard. Attended by only a handful of mourners, and without any form of ceremony, the dead king was interred in the same royal chapel, alongside the marquis, and amid the bones of his ancestors.

The Royalist cause, it seemed, was similarly dead and buried. Defeated in two separate conflicts by their Parliamentary opponents, the late king's supporters were either imprisoned or had escaped into exile. Their estates were seized and their property impounded. In September 1651, the die-hard among them made a last-ditch attempt to reverse matters, only to be smashed with ease by Oliver Cromwell at Worcester. The figure they now championed,

Charles I's namesake and eldest son, fled the field of battle, and was last seen hiding in an oak tree.

The Commonwealth regime, however, survived its royal victim for barely a decade. With so many competing voices and ideas in government, and so few genuine supporters in the country at large, the administration was held together only by the magnetic personality and iron will of Cromwell. When he died in September 1658, the revolution was undone. Quicker than anybody could have imagined, the monarchy was restored. On May 29, 1660, amid scenes of great rejoicing, Charles II was crowned king at Westminster.

Yet while the monarchy could be resurrected, the same was not true of the castle. The Civil War and the Commonwealth had dealt the ancient homes of the aristocracy a fatal blow. The destruction that had taken place at Raglan and Pontefract was repeated all over the country. Splintered and broken, undermined and collapsed, shelled, torched, and smashed, castles everywhere were effectively written off. By the time the cull had finished, it was cheaper for the nobility to build from new than to restore the shattered homes of their ancestors. It was the dramatic end to a long-drawn-out process of abandonment. The aristocracy, who had been quitting their castles by stages and degrees for centuries, now deserted them en masse. After the Restoration, they invested in fashionable new stately homes, where the architecture spoke with a new vocabulary. Portcullises, drawbridges, and battlements were consigned to the past. In came columns, porticoes, and cupolas—neo-Classical elements for a new age.

When the grandson of the marquis of Worcester decided to invest in a new home after 1660, he built just such a house: a grand new building in the fashionable Palladian style. But it was not at Raglan, nor even in Monmouthshire, that he made his new home. Like scores of other nobles, the new marquis moved on, leaving the old neighborhood as well as the castle behind him. The future home of the Somersets would be on the opposite side of the Severn, in the Gloucestershire village of Badminton. The mansion he built is there to this day—as indeed are his descendants, who live in it.

At Raglan, time began to take its toll. Broken and exposed, the castle had to contend not only with the ravages of wind and rain, but also with the depredations of anyone seeking a convenient source of stone. The damage inflicted in the aftermath of the siege was compounded in the decades that followed by those in search of a nice fireplace or windowsill. In this respect the castle was no different to any other; almost every abandoned site suffered a similar fate. In some cases, destruction continued to be carried out for the sake of security—after the Restoration, Charles II countenanced the slighting of Caernarfon, Conwy, and Beaumaris. But in most cases, opportunistic pillage and plunder wreaked the most damage. The monarchy may have been welcomed back with open arms, but castles were still viewed with suspicion, hostility, and contempt. Thomas Paulden, for example, escaped from Pontefract and lived to a ripe old age, but in the course of the siege he lost two of his brothers. Countless thousands of others like him had seen loved ones die in defense of castles, or fighting to reach their walls. While the memory of the war remained, castles could count on little sympathy.

There were, however, exceptions to this pattern—survivors among the general carnage. In the period between the end of the first Civil War and the restoration of Charles II, when the worst cases of destruction occurred, a distinction was observed between coastal castles and those in land-locked counties. The fear of invasion persuaded even the most extreme hard-liners to preserve those buildings that might prove useful in the defense of the nation. In the southeast, castles were left intact at Dover and Rochester, Bodiam and Arundel, Hedingham and Orford. Elsewhere, castles survived because they were simply too strong. The efforts made to pull down Edward I's great Welsh castles fortunately came to very little, because demolishing their stone fabric was uneconomical.

In Scotland, castles fared far better than elsewhere during and immediately after the Civil War. Several tower houses suffered during Cromwell's invasion of Scotland in 1650, including Borthwick, where the effects of the Parliamentary barrage can still be seen on the rear of the tower. Others, like Castle Urquhart, suffered as a result of later wars. Overall, however, Scottish castles were left far less scarred by the experiences of the seventeenth century than their counterparts in England and Wales. Yet while this may have protected them from total extermination, continuous occupation into the modern age has wrought its own change on these buildings. Very often they have had to endure radical customization and reconstruction by later owners, whose desire to modernize and improve their homes has altered many tower houses beyond all recognition.

Throughout the eighteenth century, castles continued to be dismantled, sold for scrap, and plundered for stone. Where preservation occurred, it was down to individual eccentricities. In 1766, a noble twelfth-century tower at Bungay in Suffolk was destroyed in order to provide rubble for new roads. What remained of the gatehouse, however, was acquired by the wife of a local solicitor, and converted into a home. But even the best intentions could have regrettable side effects. In Colchester, the great keep of William the Conqueror had been reduced to half its height thanks to the assiduousness of a local ironmonger. The surviving portion was purchased in the early eighteenth century and "restored," but unfortunately the new owner believed he had acquired a Roman ruin rather than a Norman one. His new terracotta tiled roof, cupola, and weathervane complete the catalog of indignities inflicted on an already much-maligned building.

It was only really at the end of the eighteenth century, and into the nineteenth, that indifference to castles started to give way to genuine affection. The thirst for a forgotten, Romantic British past, encouraged by writers like Sir Walter Scott, made castles desirable places to visit. Picturesque painters like Turner made them identifiable. Railways made them accessible. Once again they became treasured possessions, not just for the handful of people who had once owned them, but for everybody in the country. Men, women, and children of all degrees could now visit the great homes of the Middle Ages and contemplate a vanished world.

And now, almost a thousand years after their introduction to Britain, castles continue to exert a powerful hold on the public's affection. We, however, can get nearer to them than our Victorian forebears. They preferred them as nature had left them, all ivy-covered archways and crumbling walls. But in the course of the last century, the majority of ruined castles have been taken into the care of the state. Their walls have been shored up, their moats repaired and refilled, the trees and the bracken that had enveloped them have been cut back. Today castles stand closer in appearance to their original selves than they have done for centuries. It only requires us to visit them and use our imaginations, and their restoration is complete.

# FURTHER READING

## INTRODUCTION

The standard introduction to the subject of castles in England and Wales remains R. A. Brown, *English Castles* (3rd edn, London, 1976). Also useful are M. W. Thompson, *The Rise of the Castle* (Cambridge, 1991) and *The Decline of the Castle* (Cambridge, 1987). For a fresh perspective, see M. Johnson, *Behind the Castle Gate: From Medieval to Renaissance* (London, 2002). For Scotland, see the section on Chapter Five below.

## CHAPTER ONE: HUMBLE ORIGINS

Justice has finally been done to early castles in R. Higham and P. Barker, *Timber Castles* (London, 1992). For Hen Domen, see *Hen Domen: A Timber Castle on the English-Welsh Border* (Exeter, 2000) by the same authors. See the early sections of *The History of the King's Works*, ed. R. A. Brown, H. M. Colvin, and A. J. Taylor (6 vols, London, 1963) for the castle-building of William the Conqueror. R. Eales, "Royal Power and Castles in Norman England," *Ideals and Practice of Medieval Knighthood III* (Woodbridge, 1990) is a very important and useful essay. For fortified homes in England before 1066, see A. Williams, "A Bell-house and a Burh-geat: Lordly Residences in England before the Norman Conquest," *Medieval Knighthood IV* (Woodbridge, 1992). For the politics of the period before 1066 in England and Normandy, see F. Barlow, *Edward the Confessor* (3rd edn, London, 1997) and D. Bates, *Normandy before 1066* (London, 1982). The career of an early castle-builder in England is dealt with in A. Williams; "The King's Nephew: The Family and Career of Ralph, Earl of Hereford," *Studies in Medieval*

*History Presented to R. Allen Brown*, eds. C. Harper-Bill, C. J. Holdsworth, and J. L. Nelson (Woodbridge, 1989). For a biographical treatment of the Norman ducal dynasty before and after 1066, see D. Crouch, *The Normans* (London, 2002). Politics in England after the Conquest are explored in R. Bartlett, *England under the Norman and Angevin Kings* (Oxford, 2000) and M. T. Clanchy, *England and its Rulers* (2nd edn, Oxford, 1998). Compare the vehemently pro-Norman account in R. A. Brown, *The Normans and the Norman Conquest* (2nd edn, Woodbridge, 1985) with the version of events in A. Williams, *The English and the Norman Conquest* (Woodbridge, 1995). The most accessible biography of William the Conqueror is D. Bates, *William the Conqueror* (London, 1989), although D. C. Douglas, *William the Conqueror* (London, 1964) contains much useful information. The purpose of Domesday Book continues to be debated, but I still adhere to the view set out in J. C. Holt, "1086," *Domesday Studies*, ed. Holt (Woodbridge, 1987). For the difference in military tactics between the English and the Normans, see M. Bennett, "The Medieval Warhorse Reconsidered," *Medieval Knighthood V*, ed. S. Church and R. Harvey (Woodbridge, 1995) and "The Myth of the Military Supremacy of Knightly Cavalry," in *Armies, Chivalry and Warfare in Medieval France and Britain*, ed. M. Strickland (Stamford, 1995), as well as M. Strickland, "Military Technology and Conquest: the Anomaly of Anglo-Saxon England," *Anglo-Norman Studies XIX* (Woodbridge, 1997). The principal primary sources for the history of this period are *The Ecclesiastical History of Orderic Vitalis*, ed. and trans. M. Chibnall (6 vols, Oxford, 1969–80) and *The Anglo-Saxon Chronicle*, ed. and trans. G. N. Garmonsway (2nd edn, London, 1972).

### CHAPTER TWO: TOWERS OF STONE

An excellent up-to-date introduction to stone castles in the century after the Conquest is given in E. Fernie, *The Architecture of Norman England* (Oxford, 2000). For a more detailed view, *The History of the King's Works*, ed. R. A. Brown, H. M. Colvin, and A. J. Taylor (6 vols, London, 1963) is still in most respects unsurpassed. A revisionist perspective can be found in C. Coulson, "Peaceable Power in English Castles," *Anglo-Norman Studies XXIII* (Woodbridge, 2001). P. Dixon, "Design in Castle-Building: the Controlling of Access to the Lord," *Château Gaillard*, 18 (1998) explores a similar theme. For the two main castles discussed in this chapter, see R. A. Brown, *Rochester Castle* (2nd edn, London, 1986) and P. Dixon and P. Marshall, "Hedingham Castle: A Reassessment," *Fortress*, 18 (1993). The politics of the twelfth century are covered by Clanchy, Bartlett, and Crouch (see above), but see also C. Warren Hollister, *Henry I* (London, 2001) and W. L. Warren, *Henry II* (London, 1973). For John's reign, W. L. Warren, *King John* (3rd edn, London, 1997) is still a rip-roaring read, but should be tempered with the views expressed in *King John: New Interpretations*, ed. S. D. Church (Woodbridge, 1999). S. Painter, *The Reign of King John* (Baltimore, 1949) and K. Norgate, *John Lackland* (London, 1902) can still be read with profit. For early thirteenth-century politics, see D. A. Carpenter, *The Minority of Henry III* (London, 1990) and J. Gillingham, "Magna Carta and Royal Government," *Richard Coeur de Lion* (London, 1994). I also referred to I. W. Rowlands, "King John, Stephen Langton and Rochester Castle, 1213–1215," *Studies in Medieval History Presented to R. Allen Brown*, eds. C. Harper-Bill, C. J. Holdsworth, and J. L. Nelson (Woodbridge, 1989) and R. Eales, "Castles and Politics in England, 1215–1224," *Thirteenth Century England II* (Woodbridge, 1988). For siege warfare, see *Medieval Warfare: A History*, ed. M. Keen (Oxford, 1999), J. Bradbury, *The Medieval Siege* (Woodbri. dge, 1992) and M. Prestwich, *Armies and Warfare in the Middle Ages: The English Experience* (Yale, 1996).

### CHAPTER THREE: BUILDING AN EMPIRE

Arnold Taylor made Edward I's Welsh castles his own. Above anything else, see his guidebooks for Rhuddlan, Harlech, Conwy, Caernarfon, and Beaumaris, all published by CADW: Welsh Historic Monuments. For more detailed expositions, his sections of *The History of the King's Works*, ed. R. A. Brown, H. M. Colvin, and A. J. Taylor (6 vols, London, 1963), and his own *Studies in Castles and Castle-Building* (London, 1985) are the places to look. For Caerphilly, see D. Renn, *Caerphilly Castle* (CADW, 1997).

M. T. Clanchy, *England and its Rulers* (2nd edn, Oxford, 1998) is excellent for thirteenth-century politics, all the more so now it includes an epilogue on Edward I. The king has been given an expansive biography by M. Prestwich, *Edward I* (London, 1988). For a less sympathetic portrait, and an exploration of English imperialism in this period, see R. R. Davies, *Domination and Conquest* (Cambridge, 1990) and more recently *The First English Empire* (Oxford, 2000). The same author has written the definitive history of medieval Wales in *Conquest, Coexistence and Change: Wales 1063–1415* (Oxford, 1987), reprinted as *The Age of Conquest* (Oxford, 1991), superseding the previous standard work, J. E. Lloyd, *A History of Wales, from the earliest times to the Edwardian Conquest*, (2 vols, London, 1911). For a blow-by-blow account of the conquest, see J. E. Morris, *The Welsh Wars of Edward I* (Oxford, 1901). Edward's interest in the legendary British past is examined in R. Morris, "The Architecture of Edwardian Enthusiasm: Castle Symbolism in the Reigns of Edward I and his Successors," *Armies, Chivalry and Warfare in Medieval France and Britain*, ed. M. Strickland (Stamford, 1995), building on the earlier work of R. S. Loomis, "Edward I, Arthurian Enthusiast," *Speculum*, 28 (1953). For an introduction to medieval building practices, look no further than N. Coldstream, *Masons and Sculptors* (London, 1991).

### CHAPTER FOUR: AN ENGLISHMAN'S HOME

For later medieval English castles, see in general M. Johnson, *Behind the Castle Gate: From Medieval to Renaissance* (London, 2002) and M. W. Thompson, *The Decline of the Castle* (Cambridge, 1987). M. C. Prestwich, "English Castles in the Reign of Edward II," *Journal of Medieval History*, 8 (1982) is important for the early fourteenth century. For Bodiam in particular, there are dozens of articles debating the question posed by D. J. Turner, "Bodiam, Sussex: True Castle or Old Soldier's Dream House," *England in the Fourteenth Century* (1986). The castle's military reputation, however, has been blown clean out of the water by C. Coulson, "Some Analysis of the Castle of Bodiam, East Sussex," *Medieval Knighthood IV*, eds. C. Harper-Bill and R. Harvey (Woodbridge, 1992). See also his "Structural Symbolism in Medieval Castle Architecture," *Journal of the British Archaeological Association*, 132 (1979). The castle's environs are examined in P. Everson, "Bodiam Castle, East Sussex: castle and its designed landscape," *Château Gaillard*, 17 (1996). The early Dallingridges have been exhaustively studied by N. Saul, "The Rise of the Dallingridge Family," *Sussex Archaeological Collections*, 136 (1998), while there is biographical material on Sir Edward himself in *The History of Parliament: The House of Commons 1386–1421*, ed. J.S. Roskell, L. Clark, and C. Rawcliffe (4 vols, Stroud, 1992). For Edward's run-in with John of Gaunt, see S. Walker, "Lancaster Dallingridge: A Franchisal Dispute in Fourteenth-Century Sussex," *Sussex Archaeological Collections*, 121 (1983). For the Hundred Years' War, see C. Allmand, *The Hundred Years' War: England and France at War, c. 1300–c.1450* (Cambridge, 1988) and D. Seward, *The Hundred Years' War: The English in France* (London, 1978). J. Sumption, *Trial by Fire: The Hundred Years' War II* (London, 1999) covers the campaigns in which Dallingridge participated early in his career. Richard II's reign is dealt with comprehensively in N. Saul, *Richard II* (London, 1997). For Arundel's rebellion, see A. Goodman, *The Loyal Conspiracy: The Lords Appellant under Richard II* (London, 1971). For English knighthood in general, see P. Coss, *The Knight in Medieval England, 1100–1400* (Stroud, 1993) and M. Keen, *Chivalry* (Yale, 1984). As to what people thought about knights in Dallingridge's day, compare the contrary views of T. Jones, *Chaucer's Knight: The Portrait of a Medieval Mercenary* (3rd edn, London, 1994) and M. Keen, "Chaucer's Knight, the English Aristocracy and the Crusade," *Nobles, Knights and Men-at-Arms in the Middle Ages* (London, 1996). For the lifestyle of people like Edward and Elizabeth, see C. Dyer, *Standards of Living in the Later Middle Ages: Social Change in England, 1200–1520* (Cambridge, 1989), J. Catto, "Religion and the English Nobility in the Later Fourteenth Century," *History and Imagination* (London, 1981), and P. Coss, *The Lady in Medieval England, 1000–1500* (Stroud, 1998). N. Saul, *Scenes from Provincial Life: Knightly Families in Sussex, 1280–1400* (Oxford, 1986) provides some charming tableaux, but the comments on the Dallingridges have been superseded.

### CHAPTER FIVE: SAFE AS HOUSES

First mention must still go to the encyclopedic work of D. MacGibbon and T. Ross, *The Castellated and Domestic Architecture of Scotland from the Twelfth to the Eighteenth Century* (5 vols, Edinburgh, 1887–92). S. Cruden, *The Scottish Castle* (London, 1960) shares the same status as R. A. Brown on *English Castles*—somewhat superannuated, but nevertheless invaluable as an introduction to the subject. For an accessible but authoritative modern introduction, see C. Tabraham, *Scottish*

*Castles* (London, 1997). R. Fawcett, *Scottish Architecture: From the Accession of the Stewarts to the Reformation, 1371–1560* (Edinburgh, 1994) covers similar ground with equal panache. A comprehensive modern gazetteer has been compiled by M. Coventry, *The Castles of Scotland* (3rd edn, Musselburgh, 2001).

For more detailed explorations of certain topics, see J. Zeune, *The Last Scottish Castles* (Buch am Erlbach, 1992) on masons' marks at Borthwick, and C. J. Tabraham, "The Scottish Medieval Towerhouse as Lordly Residence in Light of Recent Excavation," *Proceedings of the Society of Antiquaries of Scotland*, 118 (1988) for the findings at Threave. The revisionist approach to Scottish castle studies was pioneered by Geoffrey Stell. See his "Architecture: the changing needs of society," *Scottish Society in the Fifteenth Century* (London, 1977), "Kings, Nobles and Buildings of the Later Middle Ages: Scotland," *Scotland and Scandinavia, 800–1800*, ed. G. G. Simpson (University of Aberdeen, 1990), "Late Medieval Defences in Scotland," *Scottish Weapons and Fortifications, 1100–1800*, ed. D. H. Caldwell (Edinburgh, 1981), and "The Scottish Medieval Castle: Form, Function and Evolution," *Essays on the Nobility of Medieval Scotland* (Edinburgh, 1985).

For the three centuries of Scottish politics covered in the chapter, it is only possible to give an overview here. A good general history is M. Lynch, *Scotland: A New History* (London, 1991). For the revisionist view of late medieval Scotland, see the groundbreaking volume *Scotland in the Fifteenth Century*, ed. J. M. Brown (London, 1977). Also try J. Wormald, *Court, Kirk and Community* (Edward Arnold, 1981) and I. D. Whyte, *Scotland before the Industrial Revolution: An Economic and Social History, c. 1050–c. 1750* (Longman, 1995).

The Stewart kings have all found new biographers in recent years. See M. Brown, *James I* (Edinburgh, 1994), C. McGladdery, *James II* (Edinburgh, 1990), N. Macdougall, *James III* (Edinburgh, 1982), N. Macdougall, *James IV* (Edinburgh, 1989), and J. Cameron, *James V: The Personal Rule, 1528–1542* (East Linton, 1998).

For Archibald the Grim and his successors, see M. Brown, *The Black Douglases* (East Linton, 1998).

On the subject of blood feud, read J. Wormald, "Bloodfeud, Kindred and Government in Early Modern Scotland," *Past and Present*, 87 (1980) and K. M. Brown, *Bloodfeud in Scotland, 1573–1625: Violence, Justice anti Politics in an Early Modern Society* (Edinburgh, 1986). See also R. R. Davies, "The Survival of the Bloodfeud in Medieval Wales," *History*, 54 (1969) for comparative purposes.

The problems created for historians by Walter Scott and his contemporaries are addressed in *The Manufacture of Scottish History*, eds. I. Donnachie and C. Whatley (Polygon, 1992).

For more on the medieval Highlands, see *Acts of the Lords of the Isles, 1336–1493*, ed. J. Munro and R. W. Munro (Scottish History Society, 4th series, 22, 1986) and J. L. Roberts, *Lost Kingdoms: Celtic Scotland and the Middle Ages* (Edinburgh, 1997).

John Grant of Freuchie, his ancestors and descendants are honored in lavish style in W. Fraser, *Chiefs of Grant* (3 vols, Edinburgh, 1883).

Buildings in the Borders are the subject of P. Dixon, "From Hall to Tower: The Change in Seigneurial Houses on the Anglo-Scottish Border after c. 1250," *Thirteenth Century England IV*, ed. P. R. Coss and S. D. Lloyd (Woodbridge, 1992) and "Towerhouses, Pelehouses and Border Society," *Archaeological Journal*, 136 (1979). Bastles are dealt with briefly in I. Whyte and K. Whyte, *The Changing Scottish Landscape, 1500–1800* (Routledge, 1991).

The best account of Craigievar's history is to be found in the current guide-book, I. Gow, *Craigievar Castle* (Edinburgh, 1999).

### CHAPTER SIX: THE CASTLE'S LAST STAND

For the later castles in general, see Thompson and Johnson (Chapter Four, above). Thompson is particularly good on destruction and slighting, and Johnson has some new ideas on Raglan. For Raglan and Pontefract, see above all the excellent guidebooks by J. Kenyon, *Raglan Castle* (2nd edn, Cardiff, 1994) and I. Roberts, *Pontefract Castle* (West Yorkshire Archaeological Service, 1990).

The conversion of castles is discussed in C. Platt, *The Great Rebuildings of Tudor and Stewart England* (London, 1994).

For an overview of the seventeenth century, try M. Kishlansky, *A Monarchy Transformed: Britain 1603–1714* (London, 1996). For a military account of the Civil War, J. Kenyon, *The Civil Wars of England* (London, 1988) cannot be bettered. Up-to-date information on all aspects of the fighting can be found in *The Civil Wars: A Military History of England, Scotland and Ireland, 1638–1660*, eds. J. Kenyon and J. Ohlmeyer (Oxford, 1998), and the effect of the conflict on castles and towns is measured in S. Porter, *Destruction in the English Civil Wars* (Stroud, 1994).

For more information on Henry Somerset, marquis of Worcester, his ancestors and descendants, see the family entries under Worcester and Beaufort in the G. E. Cokayne, *The Complete Peerage of England, Scotland, Ireland, Great Britain and the United Kingdom*, ed. V. Gibbs and others (12 vols, 1912–59). To hear the man in his own words, seek out T. Bayly, *Wittie Apophthegmes of James I, Charles I, the Earl of Worcester, Lord Bacon, and Sir Thomas More* (London, 1658). The other contemporary voices I relied upon were J. Sprigge, *Anglia Rediviva (England's Recovery)*, facsimile with an intro by H. T. Moore (Florida, 1960), and T. Paulden, *An Account of the Taking and Surrender of Pontefract Castle* (Oxford, 1747). Despite the misleading title, there is much useful material on the third siege of Pontefract in W. D. Longstaffe, *Nathaniel Drake: A Journal of the First and Second Sieges at Pontefract Castle* (Surtees Society, 37, 1861). Easier to locate should be *The Fairfax Correspondence: memoirs of the Reign of Charles the First*, ed. G.W. Johnson (2 vols, London, 1848) and *The Letters and Speeches of Oliver Cromwell*, ed. S.C. Lomas (3 vols, London, 1904).

# PICTURE CREDITS

—∿∿—

# INDEX